Ka

Harmonizing Heavens and Earth

MASTERS OF PEACE

edited by the

UNESCO Chair for Peace Studies
of the University of Innsbruck / Austria

UNESCO Chairholder:
Wolfgang Dietrich

Board of Editors:
Josefina Echavarría, Belachew Gebrewold,
Daniela Ingruber, Franz Jenewein,
Norbert Koppensteiner,
Andreas Oberprantacher, Alan Scott,
Wolfgang Sützl, Johney Xavier

Redaction of current volume: Norbert Koppensteiner

Volume 9

LIT

Kathleen McGoey

Harmonizing Heavens and Earth

A Daoist Shamanic Approach to Peacework

23 Nov. 2014

Dear Anne Marie,

I am enchanted by your clarity, curiosity, and perception. Thank you for appearing here and discovering the way of Dao with me.

With love,
Kathleen

LIT

Bibliographic information published by the Deutsche Nationalbibliothek
The Deutsche Nationalbibliothek lists this publication in the Deutsche
Nationalbibliografie; detailed bibliographic data are available in the Internet at
http://dnb.d-nb.de.

ISBN 978-3-643-90455-3

A catalogue record for this book is available from the British Library

©LIT VERLAG GmbH & Co. KG Wien,
Zweigniederlassung Zürich 2013
Klosbachstr. 107
CH-8032 Zürich
Tel. +41 (0) 44-251 75 05
Fax +41 (0) 44-251 75 06
E-Mail: zuerich@lit-verlag.ch
http://www.lit-verlag.ch

LIT VERLAG Dr. W. Hopf
Berlin 2013
Fresnostr. 2
D-48159 Münster
Tel. +49 (0) 2 51-62 03 20
Fax +49 (0) 2 51-23 19 72
E-Mail: lit@lit-verlag.de
http://www.lit-verlag.de

Distribution:
In Germany: LIT Verlag Fresnostr. 2, D-48159 Münster
Tel. +49 (0) 2 51-620 32 22, Fax +49 (0) 2 51-922 60 99, E-mail: vertrieb@lit-verlag.de

In Austria: Medienlogistik Pichler-ÖBZ, e-mail: mlo@medien-logistik.at
In the UK: Global Book Marketing, e-mail: mo@centralbooks.com
In North America: International Specialized Book Services, e-mail: orders@isbs.com
e-books are available at www.litwebshop.de

On the evening of summer solstice, I danced and sang with the rattle and drum under a nearly full moon. I was filled with happiness, a bubbling spring of delight, and a sense that all was well and everything was possible. In my mind's eye I could see myself made of many cells, each one containing the imprint of countless ancestors. The cells were radiant with the white light of infinite joy.

I would like to dedicate this book to my ancestors, and in particular to my grandparents, Fred & Brownie Morse and Bill & Anne McGoey. Thank you for your compassion, will, integrity, and love.

TABLE OF CONTENTS

PREFACE 9
FOREWORD BY IMANERA 12
CLARIFICATION OF TERMS 16
CHAPTER 1: PERSONAL PERSPECTIVE AS AUTHOR 17
    1.1 Personal Relevance: Developing this Research Project 19
    1.2 Early Steps in My Journey: Family, Spirituality & Art 20
    1.3 Experiencing the World, Discovering Shamanism 21
    1.4 Facilitating Los Embajadores, Making Connections 26
    1.5 Studying Peace and Integrating Shamanism 26
CHAPTER 2: RESEARCH INTEREST & RESEARCH QUESTION 29
    2.1 Why Shamanic Practices for Peace and Why Now? 30
    2.2 Peace Students' Needs: Observations from a Shaman 31
    2.3 Why Write? 32
CHAPTER 3: METHOD 34
    3.1 Context and Audience 34
    3.2 Conceptual Frame 35
    3.3 Definitions of Relevant Concepts 37
        3.3.1 Peace(s) 37
        3.3.2 Energy 38
        3.3.3 Transformation 39
        3.3.4 The Shaman and Shamanism 40
    3.4 Courses of Action 44
        3.4.1 Survey of Relevant Literature 44
        3.4.2 Transpersonal Methods: Embodied Writing 44
        3.4.3 Lectures and Interviews 46
CHAPTER 4: LITERATURE REVIEW 48
    4.1 Philosophy of Peaces and Elicitive Peacework 48
    4.2 Daoism 49
    4.3 Intuition, Transpersonal Experience & Meditation 50
    4.4 Shamanism 52
CHAPTER 5: MEETING IMANERA... (OR NOT) 53
    5.1 Meeting Imanera 53
    5.2 Lineage and Teachers 55
    5.3 The Daoist-Shamanic Path 56

CHAPTER 6: DAOISM AS AN ENERGETIC APPROACH TO PEACE 60
   6.1 What is Daoism?.. 61
   6.2 History of Daoism: Philosophy, Religion, Way of Life................... 64
      6.2.1 Shamanic Roots of Daoism.. 64
      6.2.2 Upheavals and Flourishing of Daoism................................... 68
   6.3 Daoism as Energetic Peace: The Great Triad 73
   6.4 Birth, Death, and the Dao 78

CHAPTER 7: *YI JING,* THE BOOK OF CHANGES 79
   7.1 History of the *Yi Jing*... 80
   7.2 Daoism and the *Yi Jing* 82
      7.2.1 Time, Change, & Transformation 82
      7.2.2 *Yin-yang*: an Overview 85
      7.2.3 *Yin-yang* in the *Yi Jing*.. 86
   7.3 The Map of the *Yi Jing* 87
   7.4 Embodied *Yi Jing:* the *Bagua* 88
      7.4.1 Soul Retrieval with the *Bagua* 88
      7.4.2 Embodying the Eight Energies: A Shamanic Practice 89

CHAPTER 8: INTUITIVE WISDOM: UNDERSTANDING THE DAO 91
   8.1 Interpreting Intuition: Enlightenment and the Still Small Voice Within 92
   8.2 Awakening Intuition 95
   8.3 Transpersonal Experiences 97
   8.4 Non-Peakers and Cognicentrism 103
   8.5 Spiritual Intuition: A Shamanic Perspective 106
      8.5.1 Shamanic Painting: Knowing and Unknowing 107
   8.6 The Wisdom of the Dao and *Wu Wei*.. 112
   8.7 The Aim of Daoist Practice 115
   8.8 Addressing the Challenges of Living in the 'Western' World......... 117

CHAPTER 9: MEDITATION AND THE MIND 120
   9.1 Meditation's Many Forms 121
   9.2 Common Features of Different Meditative Practices..................... 123
   9.3 Suspension of Ego and Shamanic Trance 127
   9.4 Understanding the Mind and Ego 128
   9.5 The Brain and Meditation: A Western-Science Perspective 132
   9.6 Meditation: An Energetic Perspective 134
   9.7 Meditation as a Transformative Process 137
   9.8 My Research Journal: Quieting the Monkey Mind........................ 140

CHAPTER 10: DAOIST PRACTICES.. 143
   10.1 Breath, *Qi,* and the *Dan tians* 144
   10.2 Mudras.. 148

- 10.3 My Meditation Challenges 151
- 10.4 Transforming Emotions into Virtues 153
- 10.5 *Qigong* – Body Awareness 156
  - 10.5.1 *Qigong*: Variety in styles and approaches 157
  - 10.5.2 Peace *Qigong*: Effects 160
  - 10.5.3 Confidence in Creative Expression 167
  - 10.5.4 *Qigong* in Support of Others 168
  - 10.5.5 *Taiji* 169
- 10.6 Visualization and 'Fusion of the Five' 170
- 10.7 My Meditation Enstasy 173
- 10.8 Daoist Internal Alchemy and Transforming Energy 175

CHAPTER 11: ELICITIVE PEACEWORK AND DAOISM 177
- 11.1 An Elicitive Approach to Peacework 178
- 11.2 Transcending Violence: the Moral Imagination 179
- 11.3 Elicitive Peacework and Daoist Practices: Making the Connection 181
  - 11.3.1 Seeing the Unseen: Transcendence in the Creative Act 181
  - 11.3.2 Deep Listening 182
  - 11.3.3 Letting Go 183
  - 11.3.4 Non-Duality and the Web of Interconnectivity 184
  - 11.3.5 Utilizing Intuition and Embodied Energetics 186
  - 11.3.6 Serendipity and the Dao 187
- 11.4 Growing our Planetary Consciousness 187

CHAPTER 12: CONCLUSIONS 191

LIST OF REFERENCES 196

APPENDIX A 203

FURTHER READING 205

THANK YOU 206

Preface

Experiential learning has always been the most effective way for me to comprehend the world. In writing this book, I set out to have a direct experience in Daoist shamanism and peacework, to allow that experience to unfold over time, and to be carried along in its current, both personally and transpersonally. By transpersonal I mean an occurrence or sensation that proves almost indescribable when approached via logic or reason. You might think of it as a mystical or spiritual moment, a contact with bliss or ecstasy. These moments often transform the way we perceive and interact with life, such is their power and immediacy.

I have attempted to capture these transcendent experiences in words, to share them with you through a transpersonal diary, and to combine that diary with my own personal (rational) interpretations, which are guided by other authors' perspectives. With this approach, I found myself in a new quandary: I would need to create a unique structure to make possible this dialogue between my transpersonal and personal voices. My challenge was to remain receptive to journeying into a deep, vast transpersonal space, while frequently returning to shore to ground and integrate. I would leap back and forth, with one foot leading into an energetic realm, the expansive no-place, while the other foot remembered where to land firmly on earth, to engage all aspects of my being in concentration of immediacy: to communicate. The structure of this text reflects that juggling act of the self.

My transpersonal diary accounts root within academic discussions of consciousness and peace. Of *peaces*, to be more precise. Their eventual branches and flowers – the ideas of this book – serve as explorations that revolve around the core of my experiences; they are by no means exhaustive investigations of these themes. This content is meant to be practical, to inspire conversation between people who wish to devote their lives to creating peace. At the very least, I ask you to reflect on how we humans conceive of peace and conflict, individually and as communities, locally and globally.

I underwent an unsettling sequence of events since writing the first draft of this book, which was originally submitted as a Master's thesis for my degree in Peace and Conflict Studies from the University of Innsbruck, Austria. As I completed the thesis, I was unemployed, I moved out of my home, and important personal relationships were changing. It may not have been obvious to those around me, but my inner world was thrown into chaos, overwhelmed by a repeated sensation of inward collapse. After months of delving so deeply into peace research through such profoundly nurturing practices, I found my own self in the throes of inner conflict, and some of the darkest moments of my life. I was operating from a place of scarcity and depletion, a place where any small addition of stress pushed me closer to emotional collapse. What happens when you begin to lose your center, when you are no longer the rooted willow tree that bends gracefully with the breeze?

I continued my practice daily. For several months, I refined my *qi* with a *qigong* form called Eight Piece Brocade. I then moved into 100 days of practice of The Daoist Five *qigong*, cultivating the health of my five major organs. Even on the hardest days, I returned to my meditative practice. And no matter how close to collapse I came, there I found respite – even if only a momentary pause of centered stillness, a rest from strain and sadness. The Daoist Five was a small dose of daily medicine that went a long way. It was calming, relieving, like pressing a reset button for my entire system. When my energy felt dispersed and weak, I was recharged. When I felt frantic or nervous, I became grounded and calmed. Practicing *qigong* daily was the path to restoring a sense of embodied knowing. My feet still connected with the earth. My crown was still kissed by the heavens. I would be ok.

An inner voice told me I needed to be alone. At my teacher Imanera's suggestion, I went on a personal retreat, during which I spent most days in silence, meditating, painting, and walking through the snowy mountains with my dog. Several decisions and opportunities aligned, and suddenly I was crawling out of the cave. During this transition, I found myself wanting to lie belly-down on the earth, to feel embraced, to sink fully into my root chakra as it grew warm and strong. Having restored my roots, my heart could open again without fear of collapse. With an open heart, I could interact joyously with life and find harmony in the rhythms around me. My practice continued, and of course my experiences changed. I began to distill the *qi*, create a protective white mist, and fill my center with golden light.

Now, I work in the field of Restorative Justice in Longmont, Colorado.[1] My colleagues and I direct community and school programs that ask people to take responsibility for their parts in crime and conflict, and assist them in finding

---

[1] www.lcjp.org

ways to actively repair relationships with themselves and others. We seek to create a space for respectful dialogue where all members have the opportunity to gain new perspectives and reach new understandings. The restorative circle is a place where creativity is key in drawing out unexpected possibilities, where deep listening and reflection accompany gentle transformation. The insights I gained in writing this book lend depth and meaning to each restorative process we facilitate. I am keenly aware of energetic presence, and harmonizing or moving energy through embodiment. I am fortunate that my job offers an exceptional platform for applying the techniques and concepts explored in this book, an avenue for continued research via direct experience, and an environment for creating harmony in the ongoing balancing act of life.

As I finalize this book – which for me is also a journey in process – I walk the four paths of the Daoist shaman that you will read about in Chapter 5. As a martial artist and healer, I work in conflict and crime to offer alternatives to a punitive system. I bridge intercultural worlds, speaking Spanish and building relationships across borders. As a priestess, I meditate with the living and the dead. After the recent sudden death of a beloved family friend, I began to journey with his spirit, accompanying him in the transition from this world. My altar is dedicated to my grandparents so that I may nurture relationships with my ancestors and invite their guidance into my life. As a scholar, I write of evolving consciousness by first growing my own spirit – in part through shamanic painting, which appears in Chapter 8. Every morning, I travel down the canyon to the narrow riverbed of Left Hand Creek and listen to the water as I practice *qigong*. As a Daoist shaman, I harmonize heavens and earth within me, and strive to bring that balance to the surrounding world.

I am honored to be publishing Volume 9 of this unprecedented Peace Studies series. I am inspired by the diversity of the volumes that precede this one, and intrigued by their allusions to transpersonal experience. I can only hope that my addition to the series contributes to increased awareness of and research into a transrational interpretation of peaces, and that it will help advance new ideas and approaches in the field of peace and conflict.

Kathleen McGoey
October 13, 2013

Foreword by Imanera

"Daoism is the concentrated record of ancient people". – Shifu –

Look at the *sri yantra* on the cover of this book. It can be traced back to 1200 BCE. Draw the image. As you draw, you feel the duality of triangles pointing up and down. Yet they intertwine, creating a third principle of unity which subsumes the two. Don't take my word for it; just draw the picture on the cover. Feel the flow, a holistic sensation that results from acting with total involvement. This can become your portal (or way) into becoming a Master of Peace. Now draw the point at the center, and you will see what is known in the shamanic world as 'Guarding the One.' Dot the eye, awaken the spirit. Shamanism is the science of experience.

Daoism evolved from shamanic practices of China. Today, we see them in the Daoist Priests' Liturgy (public services to the deities) – the practice of star stepping, talismans drawn in the air with a sword. We hear the music and smell the smoke from the burning of messages. Daoist practice is rooted in the dialectical philosophies. Traditional Chinese views see the entire universe as composed of spirit, and the Chinese Empire as a replica of the heavens. "The way" is the moral principle governing the worlds of beings. Follow the natural way and you will find harmony – or not. The key is to say and not say. Daoism is paradoxical.

A shaman sees the world as emerging patterns, where *yin* becomes *yang* and *yang* erupts into *yin*. She practices the art of divination as a method to resolve human problems through the meeting of humanity with the spirits. By seeing from multiple perspectives – being pantoscopic, truly open-minded – she becomes a peacemaker. Daoism is a way of thinking, a way of life, a way of self-cultivation. As practicing Daoists, we begin to embody mystical spirits. This book is a candid journey into the methods of an American Daoist Shamaness learning to see with *yin* eyes into the invisible realms. Her invisible technique is in cultivating *qi*. By holding her thoughts and emotions still she embodies a mystic trance. Her hand mudra becomes the *bagua* of lake, and she becomes the lake that heals. She was trained by me, Imanera, a spirit medium.

When I first met Kathleen (Kati) McGoey she was a wandering Daoist who didn't realize it. She was dedicated to self-exploration on her path to becoming a peacemaker. Kati is now like a wild bird obtaining the wind. From a very brave and personal perspective, she has bridged many worlds with this landmark book. We have worked side by side next to the koi ponds at the Daoist Dipper Arts School in Colorado for over a year. Appropriately, koi fish are symbols of the love and friendship that has manifested in our relationship. Together we have practiced methods of replenishing, cultivating and growing our *jing*, *qi* and *shen* (essence, vitality, and spirit) that have led to changes in our states of consciousness. Her sense of self has undergone a transformation. Her body is not only a combination of natural patterns and energies but also an inner sphere containing supernatural landscapes and divine beings. She has gathered the heart-mind and can connect the Heavens and Earth to establish harmony. She has learned to open the doors of her intuitive perception and value this information through an embodied divination technique to cast the *Yi Jing* with the bones of her hands.

Kati is an artist who is curious about people who connect with the mysterious. There were times in her journey when stress shook her very foundation. Unwanted energetic parasites got under her skin, and she went through a difficult process of extraction. She experienced total collapse – and then shamanic soul retrieval. Kati now exists on the other side. Her yellow dragon, the symbol of her center, is now nurtured. Her heart has grown and it distills down to her yellow court and opens her will power. Kati's commitment to daily practice for over a year allowed the voice in her head to calm, her emotions of anxiety to transform into order and peace. In this stress-ridden, technology-driven world, she has become calmer and more inwardly focused – and simultaneously more community-oriented. She has awakened her energetic transfiguration. Her right eye is the moon and her left eye is the sun. Her resolve blossomed and this book was born.

And so this text embodies *"inwardly still outwardly reverent"*, an energetic approach to peace. Its purpose is to raise your consciousness and connect to your subconscious. By reading about personal insights obtained on a wày, you will also increase your relationships to authentic voices and spirits. Kati has evolved through quietistic, ritualistic, cosmological, exorcistic, literary/artistic, and meditative areas of practice. She consistently reaches the *qi* and this nurtures her spirit. Next she will explore alchemical and syncretistic methods to learn about ascension in broad daylight.

Daily life has many challenges. How do we maintain our inner power/spirits when faced with existential anxiety or even bigger stressors like war, imprisonment, torture or genocide while working for peace? A shaman is medicine and helps you learn to communicate and influence the spirit worlds. In community ritual space, we use a wooden-fish drum to calm the *p'o* souls. In self-cultivation, a secret drum is used: the base of the skull and the clacking of the shaman's teeth to summon the spirits. We merge the sacred and the human interactions in what can be called trans-rational responses. When facing difficulties it is imperative to have a practice of meditation that allows the dirt to settle so we can see clearly, within and all around us.

When we become conscious of what is actually going on in our global communities, we see the many forms of false imprisonment worldwide. In China, for instance, the cultural fiasco of 1966-76 continues. The Chinese government has never acknowledged the Tiananmen Square massacre of June 4th, 1989. (See the film *Never Sorry,* about Ai Weiwei,[2] a political and cultural art activist.) Religion in China is marginalized, an oligopoly with some sects having special privileges under strict government control (Yang, 2012). It requires allegiance to the state before the ancestors. But spirit cannot be killed, so perhaps the Daoist immortals are popping up in a global movement. The 2010 Nobel Peace Prize was awarded to imprisoned Chinese human rights activist Liu Xiabo for his long and non-violent struggle for fundamental human rights.[3]

Imagine now a pantheon so vast it is impossible to know all the names, especially as a Daoist deity may have different names at different stages of development. The Green Dragon of Spring, the Red Bird of Summer, the Golden Dragon of the Center, the White Tiger of the Fall, the Black Turtle and Snake of Winter – a few of my favorites. The pantheon would also include the Pole Star Deities that open portals to other realms, as well as billions of nature spirits, pools of water, caves, rocks, and trees.

The harsh reality of our epoch indicates that economics trump environmental worth. With the commodification of human beings, it seems the market determines our value. How much do we value life, truly? Recall past genocides. From 1958 to 1961, an estimated 18 to 45 million Chinese people starved to death through coercion, terror and systematic violence by the country's Communist party. It was called "The Great Leap Forward", a catastrophe that created many hungry ghosts. Approximately 11 million people were killed

---

[2] http://aiweiweineversorry.com/
[3] http://www.nobelprize.org/nobel_prizes/peace/laureates/2010/xiaobo-facts.html

by the Nazi Holocaust. The U.S. military killed some 50 million Indigenous people of America, some by smallpox, some by slaughter. In the Congo, deaths have occurred in excess of 10 million. Even one death by misguided maniacs is too much. But how many will be killed more subtly by Monsanto, the corporation that controls the production and degradation of our food? In the United States, corporations have legal human rights, and humans have fewer rights. Where do we turn for answers? Witnessing our political, environmental, and social collapse, how can we regain our power?

Perhaps an answer resides in the slogan, "the personal is political". Boycott the soybeans of Monsanto and demand labeling of all genetically modified food. For sublimating anger, nothing is better than poetry. Participate in a ritual of cosmic renewal, the *jiao*, to feel the flow of life. Act naturally. When life becomes unglued and uncertain, consult the *Yi Jing* (Book of Change), translated into English in 1965 by John Blofeld. He explains there how he used this divination book with reverence to gain insight into the hostilities between India and China in 1962. He noticed that the newspapers could predict only one outcome: that the Chinese armies would advance. He had lived in both China and India and felt great affection for both peoples, so he was looking for other points of view. With an open heart, he consulted the Book of Change. His answer predicted withdrawal, and two weeks later the prediction came true.

With an equally open heart, enjoy the journey *this* book will now take you on: a way beyond war and peace.

Dao An ("Peace in Dao"),
Imanera
July 14, 2013

Clarification of Terms[4]

Pinyin	Wade-Giles and other translations
dan tian	tan t'ien, dan t'ian, dan tien
Dao / Daoism	Tao / Taoism
dao-yin	Tao yin
jing	ching
Guanzi	Kuan-tzu
qi	ch'i, chi
qigong	ch'i-kung, chi gung
taiji / taijiquan	t'ai chi / t'ai chi ch'uan
Dao De Jing	Tao Te Ching, Daodejing
Yi Jing	Yiching, I Ching, Book of Changes

---

[4] Scholars have devised various systems for representing Chinese pictures and ideograms with Roman letters. For many years, the Wade-Giles system was used, but did not establish an international standard. In 1958, Chinese linguists developed the Pinyin system as a means of representing Mandarin phonetically (Cohen, 1997: xvii-xviii). I have chosen to use Pinyin translations in my writing, but other versions appear in some citations.

Chapter 1: Personal Perspective as Author

> There are millions of years of evolution in our cells. A deep store of wisdom lies within and we must look within to access it. We can use our discomfort and dissatisfaction with life to investigate other possibilities or ways of living. We can invite our intuition, our wise knowing, to govern or lead our choices toward a full embrace of life (Palmer, 1990: 11).

At the age of 9, I wrote an autobiography for school where I stated that when I grew up, I wanted to be "someone who helps other people with their problems". Twenty-two years and various pursuits and inspirations later, I seem to have ended up with the same vision for my 'grown up' life, but with a broadened perspective about how to fulfill this goal. This book tells the story of the most recent phase of my journey in rediscovering the meaning of helping others.

I am a woman who happened to be born in the United States, who regularly negotiates complex feelings towards my country of origin: from appreciation of its vast expanses of untouched wilderness and supportive networks for human ingenuity, to disgust over its massive consumption and self-promotion on a global scale. I am a little sister, a daughter, and an aunt who is delighted and challenged by the constant stream of new lessons learned through changing family dynamics. I am adventurous and live like a turtle, with my home on my back; I have not resided in any one country for more than a year since I was 18. Spanish is my second language and my heart continues to gravitate towards Latin America and its cultures more than any other place I know on the planet.

I have always been something of a perfectionist, confronting the self-judging voice that likes to remind me I could do better. For some time, that voice insisted that to best help others, I should not reveal any problems of my own. Rather, I should assume an upbeat attitude in order to 'be there' for people who needed me. I was eventually able to break the rules of my own inner critic with the right combination of a few humbling mistakes, some wise advice from friends, and many new opportunities to wear masks other than that of control and constant cheer. I continue to discover other ways of being that keep that voice at a reasonable volume. They allow me to reach into the depth of my own human needs and emotions, to choose how to address and express them with conscious awareness. Slowly but surely, I have begun accepting my imperfect nature and knowing my full range of humanness: light and shadows, gifts and sacrifices. From there I seek ways to change and heal, free from judgment and expectation. I gain deeper, wider perspective that aids me in fulfilling my childhood vision of helping others. In short, helping others entails an ongoing commitment to helping myself.

The experiences and research that inform this book emerged from the complex task of helping myself to help others. In pursuing my Master's degree in Peace Studies, I became more aware of the sources of my own self-critic, the inner judge that so often determines reactions, choices, and priorities based on its clinging to past patterns and habits. I explored techniques for observing those patterns and creating more avenues for spontaneous guidance through a different source of inner truth. This exploration was fueled by a sincere desire to be a peacemaker. It reinforced the fundamental lesson that I am not well prepared to work for peace in the world if I have not first established peace within myself – and that the two are not actually separate processes.

Inevitably, this undertaking entails much reading, writing, and analyzing – activities governed by the brain. And yet, I present direct experiences explicitly requiring me to *get out* of my rational mind, to speak from another source, from something more holistic, more transpersonal, more cosmic. My own relationship with spirituality has been ambiguous for most of my life. I have always been curious about my place in the 'bigger picture' and eager to orient myself. But until recently, I was mostly aware of my own spirituality through random divine moments of connection with people and nature that hinted at revealing some great magic of the universe. Yet I struggled to decipher these moments, perhaps because I lacked a suitable lens or vocabulary.

So my articulation here may hold more value if heard by your heart, digested by your breath, and moved through your limbs, than if only analyzed by your mind. I ask you, as I have asked myself, to proceed with reading, absorbing, and questioning in an active, rhythmic way. Pause, and let the words move through your cells. Be aware of your breath and your posture. Let go, as much as possible, your predominantly rational state of mind. Instead, seek resonance – consonant or dissonant, harmonious or not – with this journey in words. From there, I invite you to continue the conversation, the exchange, the embodied experience of how we will *be* peace ourselves.

1.1 Personal Relevance: Developing this Research Project

Of utmost importance to me is learning how humans perceive themselves and their roles in social environments, from the nuclear family to a global family. I am interested in the transformative processes of opening hearts and minds to become more in tune with an intuitive wisdom that I believe is universal and simultaneously held within each one of us. How is transformation elicited? How may it lead to new perspectives and holistic healing? How can the effects of such processes be sustained and integrated into daily life? Taking a wider perspective, I pose these queries because I am curious about what motivates people, individually and collectively, to act with or without a sense of responsibility and compassion for the well-being of themselves, others, and the earth.

These are rich and relevant topics for me because they derive from my own journey. Through transformative experiences – exploring new places, encountering new people and ideas, expanding my perspective, and growing spiritually – my understanding of self and how I relate to others and my environment(s) changes. As I previously mentioned, I have only recently begun to embrace my own shadows and address my own thought and behavior patterns rigorously. I was fortunate to have this opportunity within the context of an innovative Peace Studies program, which, after shaking my foundation, helped me to restore cohesiveness and live in a more connected way with my spiritual self. I have been similarly blessed with a loving, supportive family, a life that has gifted me so generously with so much joy, and a series of adventures that have inspired me to wonder how I can be of service to the earth and humanity.

These life experiences have motivated me to try on various roles and develop a variety of skills that have led me on an unpredictable journey towards creating and sharing peace. That journey is fluid and ongoing; there is no definitive point of peace from which I write, nor do I envision a particular destination of 'ultimate harmony' in the future. Even this text itself represents a challenge, an experiment, and another opportunity for stimulating transformation, the outcome of which is unknown and full of potential. I am ever changing, and it is my hope to elicit from the reader some resonance or curiosity about processes of transformation, both yours and mine.

1.2 Early Steps in My Journey: Family, Spirituality & Art

From early childhood, the diverse models of my parents and my two older brothers impacted me greatly. Our parents raised us within a Catholic belief system, asking us to attend weekly mass and encouraging us to accept the sacraments that are part of growing up in the Catholic Church. From my parents, I learned to use my mind to understand emotions, feel compassion for others by seeing the world through their eyes, and integrate volunteer service as an important part of life. My mother and father are impressive examples of commitment and hard work, and they always assured me that I could set my mind on, and accomplish, any goal. So it was natural that, as Catholic ritual was introduced as a routine in my life, I *wanted* to embrace this spiritual framework. I tried to believe what I heard in mass and in weekly classes, searching for the profound resonance the church teachings had for the believers around me.

But my two older brothers tempted me to question our religion. They held strong aversion to any participation in the church, and expressed their views openly. My brothers were active, constantly taking risks and pushing physical limits on their own and emotional limits with my parents. Fueled by a boundless creative drive, they led themselves and each other to new adventures and discoveries, especially outdoors. I adored them and held them up as the epitome of 'cool', longing for their attention and approval despite their apparent lack of interest in me. Since they appeared to have figured something out about Catholicism that I had not, I was torn between rejecting the religion versus following it for the guidance and answers it seemed to offer.

As a teenager, with my brothers out of the house, I was attracted to some of the teachings that comprised my Confirmation, the point at which I would become a recognized adult member of the Catholic Church. Messages about the irrelevance of material possession and serving God by serving others were comforting and appealing. At the same time, I had been inadvertently exploring other forms of spirituality, occasionally practicing meditation and visualization without actually knowing or labeling them as such. I created small rituals: I would light a beautiful candle, take some slow breaths, and allow troubling thoughts to surface – then envision them slowly disappearing, like the smoke from the candle. I would lie by the creek in our backyard and let the sound of the water soothe my nerves. To this day, I viscerally recall peacefulness that filled the space created by these meditative practices.

Socially, my behavior was influenced by witnessing the distress of conflict between my well-intentioned parents and rebellious brothers. In the overall family dynamic, I assumed the role of overachiever and pleaser, trying my best to keep everyone around me happy. For many years, this role would re-surface in how I related to others. I reached out to help people around me and maintained positive relationships, wanting to be well-liked and seen as someone in whom friends could confide. I learned to avoid confrontation, opting to sacrifice my own needs and soften personal boundaries to – as I perceived it – make things better for everyone.

Making art was one of my favorite pastimes and an important catalyst in developing confidence in my own creativity. In my artwork, I felt free to explore options, always daring to try a new idea. Drawing and painting also became unintentional forms of meditation early in my life. I could completely lose myself in the artistic process and follow inner vision instead of a directed, logical plan. I trained my vision to be more precise, and observed the effects of how my breathing affected me when deep in the creative act. Throughout high school and university, I devoted significant time and energy to intensive art training, eventually graduating with a Bachelor of the Arts in Studio Art (as well as a Minor in Latin American Studies). But in this training, I gradually became more detached from my own intuitive direction, and concentrated on developing proper techniques, fulfilling the requirements of assigned projects, and gaining approval for my work. While I continued to enjoy making art, the process shifted from being limitless to constrained by a framework of expectations and perfectionism.

1.3 EXPERIENCING THE WORLD, DISCOVERING SHAMANISM

In all of these experiences, I developed confidence and a penchant for independence. These enabled me to take risks and stretch outside my comfort zones to pursue what *felt* right instead of what I may have *thought* was right – particularly in seeking out opportunities to live, study and work internationally. This combination of pushing my own limits and trusting my intuition led me to leap out into the world, keeping my path open and somewhat unconstrained, motivated by a desire for change and new perspectives.

At the same time, during my undergraduate studies at the University of Notre Dame, one of the most Catholic universities in the United States, my Catholic devotion began to fade. At Notre Dame I found the apparent commitment and practice of Catholicism by most students simply did not inspire me. For many of my peers, going to mass was mostly motivated by social expectations, and I sensed hypocrisy in the lack of application of Catholic teachings to everyday life. As in childhood, I felt caught between the desire to believe and the intuition to reject. By the end of my first year of college, I stopped attending Catholic services.

My spirituality and worldview would take new shape with my first experiences living abroad. During the next four years, I followed an impulse – which turned into a trend – of leaving the United States. Participating in a cultural seminar in central Mexico, something 'clicked' for me as I was exposed to different lifestyles and values. Speaking Spanish and witnessing the daily rhythms in central Mexico resonated with some aspect of my soul, and led me to question – even criticize – my own background. From that point on, I looked for opportunities to return to Latin America as often as possible. I traveled to Santiago, Chile, and Oaxaca, Mexico for two semesters of immersion, study, and travel. I spent a summer volunteering in Tijuana, Mexico, and after graduation, I worked in the Netherlands. With each departure and return to the United States, I could sense a distancing from my own formerly held truths and identity. My expanding perspective affected my understanding of self and how I related to my communities both at home and abroad.

Despite the challenges involved, I thrived on change, struggling through feelings of insecurity, fear, and uncertainty provoked by moving and reorienting so often. My self-awareness grew as these unpredictable circumstances stretched and tested the limits of my comfort zones. I learned that, beyond just my own perceptions, I myself would be perceived very differently across various environments. Living abroad was an opportunity to shed old skin, to push limits, and to discover a new 'me'. Old frameworks for measuring my success were no longer relevant when I had the chance to re-create myself again and again. While this was unsettling at times, it also became an experiment in evaluating who I was and who I wanted to be, what role(s) I wanted to play, which mask(s) I wanted to wear, and which I should leave behind.

A major turning point in my spiritual awareness occurred in Oaxaca, Mexico, in an independent field study with a *curandera*,[5] Angela Mendez Hernandez. Angela introduced me to shamanism and presented me with a cosmo-

---

[5] In Latin America, a *curandero*(a) is a traditional healer or shaman using natural/alternative-healing methods, versus allopathic methods, for procuring good physical, mental, and spiritual health.

vision, or way of seeing the universe. She demonstrated our interrelation with the natural world: the vegetables we ate, the cold river we bathed in, the mountains we crossed, the sky and space above us. In her hometown of Benito Juarez, Angela walked me through her family's garden, taught me extensively about healing properties of plants and herbs, and trained me to conduct the healing ritual of the *temezcal*.[6] She went beyond the treatment of physical ailments to provide holistic healing, inspiring me with her interconnected vision, her respect for the power of plant medicine, and her attunement to reading messages from the natural world. I would have many more adventures – intellectual, cultural, and geographic – before returning to nurture the seeds planted during that enlightening month with Angela. Unbeknownst to me, her lessons would later help form the foundation of my own worldview, which was to emerge more clearly through studying peace.

This first exposure to shamanism would provide the inspiring guidance that I had wondered about as a child during Catholic mass. It relocated me as a tiny piece of the natural world, a vessel of cosmic divinity, and asked me to contemplate the ripple effects of my thoughts and actions, and to adjust them to be more in harmony with nature. Such perspective presented sharp contrast to the guilt and threats I associated with the Catholic concept of sin, and the notion that the priest would act as a medium between me and God. I had also been uncomfortable with the Catholic lesson that all my actions would eventually be judged to determine if I would be 'accepted' into eternal life – that spiritual rewards would be enjoyed then, not now. I was discovering a resonance with the shamanic worldview that I had never fully found in Catholicism – one which encouraged me to embrace and delight in life, in each and every moment.

Immersion in other countries and cultures taught me an appreciation for spontaneity and impermanence, two qualities that had not been adequately reckoned with in my Catholic upbringing (and will be discussed later as attributes of Daoist shamanism). In line with my own expanding appreciation of the world's tendency towards transformation, James Miller (2008) offers this insightful commentary comparing aspects of Daoism to other belief systems:

---

[6] The *temezcal* is a healing practice used by the pre-Hispanic indigenous peoples of Mesoamerica, using a sweat lodge. My training also involved elements of aromatherapy, circulation massage, and steps to promote the exit of toxins and energies from the body.

> In fact the human experience of change or transformation in our bodies and in the world around us lies at the heart of the Daoist experience in much the same way that faith in an eternal, unchanging deity lies at the heart of the Jewish-Christian-Islamic religious system. Whereas Western religionists seek to place their trust in an unchanging and invisible stability that somehow transcends the fleeting experience of time, Daoists recognize and celebrate the profound and mysterious creativity within the very fabric of time and space itself (Miller, 2008).

Pursuing adventures around the world had provided me opportunities for breaking away from the status quo of self-perception. Feeling displaced and confused in foreign cultures, struggling to communicate well, and making mistakes were all humbling experiences that created doubt about the person I had always thought myself to be. I developed a pointed bitterness with my country of birth for its greed-driven globalization. I realized painfully that my lifestyle, and the cultural ideals and norms I had grown up with, did not always respect the values I observed and admired in other cultures. This dissolution of such a fundamental part of my identity was at times isolating, distancing me from old friends and creating dissatisfaction when any given international journey ended and I had to return home. And yet, on the other side of that difficulty was a necessary shedding of expectations and assumptions about my life and the wider world. One thing was clear: I had to continue to venture into the world, cross borders, and stay unsettled.

Looking back at those transformative years of testing my limits and exploring my identity, I see the early stages of my deepening relationship with my heart and intuition. I began to discover the gifts of immediacy, delighting in unplanned and unexpected experiences that had arisen when I allowed myself to be spontaneous. In detaching from my strategic mind, I was allowing my intuition to flourish and my heart to thrive. Through all my displacement and disorientation, I was also learning to slow down, to let go of expectations for a certain path, to 'go with the flow' and to appreciate the subtle manifestations of joy and beauty of the present moment.

I began connecting with people on a deeper, more sincere level, and this connection brought the realization that building relationships holds enormous importance for me. It allowed me to learn about and celebrate the shared human experience. I was delighted to eat, drink, and dance until sunrise in small villages in Oaxaca, noticing that my story, background, and cluelessness about the dance steps were irrelevant in the rhythm of community ritual and celebration. Accepting the environment and circumstances, along with the occasional unfamiliar or uncomfortable conditions, meant easing into what clearly mattered: "Here we are, we have this moment to be thankful for, and we are in it together, alive". Hardships and struggles were not forgotten, but they were alleviated in that momentary pause to appreciate one another, the food, and the music. As I was exposed to the complex effects of globalization, migration, poverty and oppression, I began to see that art alone would not be a career for me, nor would 'changing the world' through policy. Rather, working with people at a grassroots level would inspire my passion for relationship and connection.

After university, I volunteered for and later became the Executive Director of a small non-governmental organization called *Los Embajadores* (The Ambassadors),where I facilitated a service-learning program for U.S. and Canadian students along the northern border of Mexico. I acted as liaison between these students and members of the Mexican communities, coordinating activities aimed at breaking down the barriers people tend to create between 'us' and 'them'. Students were asked to live simply, leaving behind as many unnecessary material possessions as possible, while they worked, played, shared, conversed, and lived with our Mexican hosts. The program stimulated reflection in its student participants as they were exposed firsthand to the contrast of life on the other side of *la línea* (the line).[7] Our partner communities and organizations in Mexico often changed their perceptions of their U.S. and Canadian neighbors, too. Stereotypes about their neighbors to the north being lazy, self-centered, materialistic, and generally uninterested in global events were altered when people from both sides of the line came together as neighbors. Relationship-building conquered these stereotypes as *Los Embajadores* participants inquired sincerely about divided families and smiled over shared mistakes. Preconceived fears of cultural differences dissolved in the first few passes of a soccer ball.

The unpredictable, often risky, environments of Tijuana and the northern state of Baja California provided me ample opportunity for creativity, teaching, and learning, often through trial and error. But the most fulfilling and motivating aspects of my job were found in the opportunities to accompany others along a path of reflection and transformation, and to witness growth of self-awareness and compassion for others. Suddenly I was facilitating for others the transformative experiences that had been so life-altering for me.

---

[7] In northern Mexico, *la línea* is the primary term used to refer to the U.S.-Mexican border, which highlights the fragile and ambiguous nature of this delineation.

1.4 Facilitating Los Embajadores, Making Connections

Los Embajadores introduced me to a new perspective on transformation; in this role, I could witness – sometimes even feel – change occurring in fellow human beings. Their 'ah-ha' moments were also shared energetic experiences that transcended the mind and senses. At the time, I may have described this sensation of cohesion as a leap of my heart, sheer joy, a sense of feeling completely alive in the present moment, with all as it is meant to be. It was also a phenomenon of unification, bridging communities and transcending barriers of language, culture and expectations. The boundaries of the individual experience often disappeared because the sensation of sharing something with others – a dance, a meal, laughter, music-making – was so extraordinary. For no more than a few moments at a time, I could feel the air charged with something captivating, reverberating amongst all. And I believed that experience was not confined to my particular body or that particular place.

I had no way of controlling moments like this or making them happen. But I began to notice how I might encourage their existence by striving to create a safe environment, by being present and patient. For all those transcendent moments, surely there were just as many I may have missed or obstructed with my impatience or distraction. Still, acting as a facilitator seemed to amplify my awareness and interpretation. Observing a situation *while* feeling its flowing, changing energy brought new depth and meaning to my past personal experiences. It also made me want to understand what was happening on that other level.

1.5 Studying Peace and Integrating Shamanism

After years of not knowing how to succinctly describe my passions or my fields of work, I had a revelation: the 'cause' uniting the roots of my motivation with the goal of my endeavors was *peace*. I enrolled in the International Master in Peace, Conflict, and Development Studies at the Universitat Jaume I in Castellón, Spain. There I found a diverse group of international students and a beautiful setting by the Mediterranean Sea. But the overall approach of the program itself felt stagnant, based in a modern[8] and post-modern understanding of peace(s).[9] I transferred to the University of Innsbruck's Master of Arts in Peace, Development, Security, and International Conflict Transformation, where I encountered a very different program. It validated my own perception of transformative experiences, and portrayed transformation of conflict, of self, of group energy as playing an integral role in understanding and creating peace.

At Innsbruck, I continued traveling the winding path of knowing and unknowing myself. In the midst of more change, I began to see and interpret my previous experiences with new perspectives. I realized I was most interested in holistic self-discovery processes – ones that engage people's spiritual and energetic aspects – that cannot be fully comprehended by reason alone. Addressing and activating this energetic aspect is a distinguishing feature of a transrational approach to Peace Studies.[10] Throughout our coursework at Innsbruck, my classmates and I not only studied this transrational approach, but also enacted it. We participated in humanistic and transpersonal methods that engaged the mind, body, and spirit, primarily through breath and bodywork. These techniques stimulate self-exploration to make us more conscious of known and unknown aspects of ourselves, including the shadows we may prefer not to see.

My coursework and practical training also brought shamanistic spirituality back into my life. Lectures by Wolfgang Dietrich and Norbert Koppensteiner about Elicitive Conflict Transformation (Dietrich, 2010a), "Why Peace Studies Go Native" (*Ibid.*, 2010b), and "Energetic Concepts of Peace" (Koppensteiner, 2011) explained the shamanic roots of humanistic and transpersonal modali-

---

[8] In a modern peace perspective, the world is understood as based on certain truths derived from scientific knowledge, logic, and reason. Thus peace is also approached with reason and rational discernment (Dietrich, 2012).

[9] The postmodern approach to understanding peace involves a condition of doubt and uncertainty that we can rely on the modern knowledge derived from reason, knowledge, and progress, once considered as basic truths, to create peace. It introduces the concept that differences in the human experience across history, culture, and individuals lead to a plurality of perceiving peace, thus the concept of 'many peaces' (Dietrich, 2006).

[10] From a transrational peace perspective, human beings are able to transgress the limits of rational perceiving. In other words, the human's energetic and spiritual faculties are valid forms for experiencing and interpreting, and thus play a significant role in transforming conflict. A transrational perspective sees the universe as a web of interconnectivity (Dietrich, 2012).

ties. As part of our studies, my classmates and I took weeklong courses with Peter Kirschner,[11] who led us in rituals of meditation, the sweat-lodge, and shamanic journeying. Kirschner also taught us to use the medicine wheel as a guide for creating balance and inner peace. This immersion enlivened memories of my previous experiences with shamanism, bringing them into the present and illuminating them with fresh appreciation and intrigue.[12] My vision for my own role in peacemaking was suddenly opened to exciting new possibilities.

Shamanic practices helped orient my changing sense of self, and I became more aware of the challenge and opportunity to integrate such transformative processes into my daily life. Through shamanism, I could bridge the worlds between the before, during, and after of a profound experience. Those 'ah-ha' moments of enlightened perspective did not have to appear, exist only in the moment they were elicited, and then end. Nor did they have to be stimulated by movement into a different physical or geographic space, as I had assumed because my own past growth seemed prompted by international travel. Rather, the lessons held in those magical moments are always available. They can be integrated and referred to for their lasting meaning, and in so doing, enrich life in an even more sustained, transformative way. Revisiting shamanism, I saw my energy and being as one small part of a much larger and longer lasting system. This would cause a drastic shift in how I perceived myself as a peaceworker.

---

[11] http://www.native-spirit.at/NATIVE%20SPIRIT_sf1+1+101431+++.html
[12] Throughout the weeklong experience during February 2011, I took flight on my first shamanic journey to nestle into the soft fur of a mama bear, released deeply repressed grief during a cleansing with birch branches which Peter calls *Raschelhütte* (literally, "rustling hut") and was reborn from the womb of the earth through the sweatlodge.

Chapter 2: Research Interest & Research Question

> True reality is without concept, beyond the duality of this and that. True *prajna*, true knowledge, is direct experience. It's knowing without the filter of self. Direct experience is wisdom itself – unborn, unceasing, neither still nor moving (Mipham, 2003: 190).

I am interested in holistic processes of transformation and their capacity to assist in working through conflict on intrapersonal and interpersonal levels. Drawing from my own experiences as a facilitator and student, I believe creating peace and living in harmony necessitates a process of searching deeply within ourselves. How can we bring about our own healing to find balance? How can we engage with intuitive wisdom to experience inner peace? How can increasing self-awareness help transform conflicts with others?

Shamanic practices stimulated a widening of perception that enabled me to reconnect with inner wisdom. This connection helped me integrate transformative experiences, which, in turn, affect how I relate to myself and others. My *original* research question was: *how can shamanic practices be understood as methods for peacework?* But as my research progressed and I became more involved with the direct, experiential nature of my work, I realized that 'shamanism' refers to a vast field with many different branches. Studying shamanic practices generally is a nearly impossible task; they vary so widely depending on particular ways of life, language, environment, and geographic location.

Reframing my query in a Daoist context would allow me to continue working in shamanism and gain focus by narrowing the scope of my research. Since my own direct experiences in Daoism with Imanera were increasing in frequency and depth, I would be following a natural flow by moving in this direction.[13] Writing about Daoism while developing my own Daoist shamanic practice supports the authentic approach to understanding what Michael Harner points out: "truly significant shamanic knowledge is *experienced*, and cannot be obtained from me or any other shaman" (Harner, 1990: xxiv). And so my question became: *how can <u>Daoist shamanic</u> practices be understood as methods for peacework?* In beginning to discuss this question, I include an overview of shamanism and a few common traits of shamans across cultures. But the majority of this text focuses on specifically *Daoist* shamanic practice, with emphasis on forms I have personally experienced and their relationship to peacework.

2.1 WHY SHAMANIC PRACTICES FOR PEACE AND WHY NOW?

In 1990, Michael Harner focused on the need to revive shamanism[14] in Western cultures, primarily as a means to heal and maintain well-being.[15] He and others witnessed the growing awareness that modern medicine, as powerful as it may be, is often not enough for these difficult tasks. The unique benefit of shamanic practices, he explained, is that they have been tested over centuries, far longer than more conventional methods and psychotherapeutic techniques. He invited us to explore the world of shamanism in an effort to supplement – not wholly replace – the ways of modern medicine.

My approach to peacework is similar to Harner's healthcare prescription. He does not propose renouncing conventional modern medicine, just as I do not suggest abandoning institutionalized peacemaking efforts. There is no single way of understanding peace, and there is no one all-encompassing tech-

---

[13] I discuss in section 10.5.1 how Daoist concepts and meditation actually helped me to accept this transition.

[14] It appears as though this popular revival is happening. An internet search for "schools shamanism" produced 13,000,000 results in .31 seconds.

[15] Other authors recognized for their contributions to introducing shamanism as a viable practice for Westerners, such as Carlos Castaneda, may portray the tasks of shamanism in a different light, i.e. warrior shamanism (Harner, 1990).

nique for peacebuilding. My research proposes that shamanic practices, and specifically Daoist shamanic practices, can offer a different vision and approach for how human beings realize peace in our world, our communities, and ourselves – here and now.

Timing is of the essence. As with medicine in Harner's day, there is currently an awakening of awareness that peace is not to be left to someone else. We cannot rely on distant treaties and accords to do the work for us. In the face of ongoing local and global conflicts, our commitment to realizing peace must begin with an openness to seeing life from new perspectives, and transforming accordingly. This means taking responsibility first and foremost for one's own actions and beliefs, and becoming aware of one's participation in perpetuating violent patterns and attitudes. From there, we must challenge ourselves to be held accountable, to seek options, change patterns, and pursue paths where self-awareness helps us live with more respect and understanding of others. I believe this work is realizable due to an inherent human desire to live in mutual harmony.

2.2 PEACE STUDENTS' NEEDS: OBSERVATIONS FROM A SHAMAN

I returned to Austria in the summer of 2012 and spoke with Peter Kirschner and Hanna Raab (2012), who lead experiences in shamanism for peace students at the Native Spirit camp in Innsbruck. Among the observations they shared was the following:

> What has been surprising about peace students is that I expected them to be 'advanced' beings. In reality, they are good people with big hearts and emotions, but they are not grounded enough. They need tools to get in touch with emotions and learn how to handle them. I realized students wanted more spiritual work versus team training. Team training leads to putting a new mask over an old mask, it does not always address root problems. Instead, the process should be first to work on one's self to get in balance, then work as a team. Individual processes are about learning how to handle oneself – to take care of one's own holy zone – where only

you decide who can enter. By working on oneself, the individual becomes more conscious and aware (Kirschner & Raab, 2012).[16]

Kirschner and Raab also pointed out that each student's process is different, and it is impossible to know exactly where each student is in that process, and where they will go. Kirschner sees it as his job to "awaken and provoke" students as individuals and as a group. He posed the quintessential peacework question: how can someone go out and help others in need, if she does not know how to take care of herself? His response revolves around learning how to come back to one's center.

2.3 Why Write?

I originally intended to avoid writing a Master's thesis, which would have prevented this book from coming to fruition. But with guiding insight from my supervisor, Norbert Koppensteiner, I began to see that an intensive, soul-searching project might offer a stimulus to bring clarity to my own next steps in life. This research endeavor has intimidated me for many reasons. One of the most significant derives from my own shadows: a fear of trying to write something beautiful, but not being able to express lucidly the wonder and joy I experience in the world. In that way, writing this book has given me the opportunity to address one of my biggest challenges, of not being so hard on myself, and accepting what I am able to be and create with love.

Adding to that challenge is the transparency I am asking of myself in trying to describe a very personal path. Delving into my own spirituality involves revealing much of my authentic and private self, removing masks, and telling a story as it happens. It embodies a process still in motion, and requires letting go of concerns about others' perceptions of what I believe. Inevitably, my own voice and perspective will change again and again. In that sense, the research and writing themselves contribute to my own transformation, and so I fall into the category of transpersonal researchers who, "analyze, interpret, and present

---

[16] Due to regular pauses and clarifications needed because of language obstacles, I have paraphrased Peter and Hanna's responses.

findings in ways that engage their own participation, attitudes, and life stories and prompt changes in the ways they feel and think about the topic, themselves, others, and the world" (Anderson and Braud, 2011: 1).

However demanding and confusing it often was, writing this book has proven to be a privilege and an opportunity to integrate and give fresh attention to the various transformative events of my life. Writing offers the possibility of articulating something that my spirit and soul know, but that words have, until now, not found a way to share. I have tried to honor those transcendent moments of my life, attempting to relate them candidly and to shed light on how I have arrived where I am now. The following passage about "Research with Soul in Mind" describes succinctly my wariness around writing and being able to fully depict the depth of respect and love I hold for the topic at hand.

> In the gap between the saying and what slips away there is a sense of sadness, a feeling of mourning… To write down the soul, then, is to attend to its 'greening,' to its motion and its movement, to its elusive quality, which resists our efforts to enunciate it. In the gap there is always a remainder that asks not to be forgotten. The shadow of the unsaid haunts our saying… This mourning resides in one's awareness of the gap between language and experience… For psychology the mood of mourning resides in one's awareness of the difference between the words one uses to speak of soul and the reality of soul… (Romanyshyn, 2007: 6).

Chapter 3: Method

"Everything touches everything". – Jorge Luis Borges –

3.1 Context and Audience

In his book *The Moral Imagination: The Art and Soul of Building Peace,* John Paul Lederach (2005) asks that his ideas be shared in a conversational style, instead of an authoritative one. Similarly, the aim of my writing is twofold. First, it reflects on my journey as a peaceworker, a student of Peace Studies, and a human being striving to experience and create peace. Second, like Lederach, it provides material for conversation, a proposal to be tested, debated, and discussed with others.

My knowledge of many topics covered in this book is budding; there will always be so much more to learn. Yet much that I write strikes a chord with people I greatly respect. Those with experience in shamanism react with relief and enthusiasm: "Finally someone is making this connection, and saying it out loud!". Peace students, too, grin at my research question, as if I am about to 'let the cat out of the bag' or reveal a secret that many of us sense but are hesitant to articulate. Friends and family who have seen me change over the years, even the most culturally conservative ones, are increasingly comfortable confiding in me. They share their stories, doubts and qualms, and inquire about my experience, as they seek to heal or expand their own perspectives.

As a result, I now see my audience as anyone seeking to know inner peace, not just academics or aspiring shamans. Their search is courageous, one in which the seeker must be prepared to undergo an authentic process of knowing and unknowing. It involves witnessing shadows buried deep inside, confronting sources of intrapersonal conflict, letting go of certain thought and behavior patterns, and pushing the limits of comfort zones to leap into the great unknown. This seeker is my intended audience, and I am a part of that audience.

I, too, still journey – reflecting, stretching, planting seeds, then moving onward, however imperfectly. I frame my ideas here within the field of peacework, and invite these partners in the journey to consider themselves peaceworkers, all of us working towards our own inner peace.

3.2 Conceptual Frame

To build the conceptual framework within which I discuss shamanism, Daoism, and peacework, I utilize Dietrich's (2012a) five peace families: the energetic, moral, modern, post-modern and transrational. I focus primarily on the energetic and transrational understandings of peace, and also refer to transpersonal psychology where it integrates current information on the human psyche with ancient knowledge of potential non-ordinary states of consciousness.[17]

From an energetic perspective, we recognize and create peace via harmonious relations between society, nature, and the cosmos, all things visible and invisible. We encounter this ancient concept of peace around the world, in the mystical traditions of Shamanism, Daoism, Buddhism, Hinduism, Judaism, Christianity and Islam (Dietrich, 2006, 1997).

> Energetic peace is thus never a state and it is not tied to objective conditions. This peace begins on the inside of the self and spreads from there as a harmonious vibration into society, nature, and the universe. The human being who does not first look for peace within herself will not find it on the outside, because there is no objectifiable peace there (*Ibid.*, 2012a: 56-57).

---

[17] Grof (n.d.) clarifies that "the term non-ordinary states of consciousness is being used mostly by researchers who study these states and recognize their value. Mainstream psychiatrists prefer the term altered states, which reflects their belief that only the everyday state of consciousness is normal and that all departures from it without exception represent pathological distortions of the correct perception of reality and have no positive potential" (Grof, n.d.:5). For more on non-ordinary states of consciousness and shamanic trance, see footnote 22.

A transrational understanding of peace takes the energetic and adds perspective gained through modern rationality. It sees humans as being both rational and *beyond* rational, holistic beings whose spiritual nature ultimately transcends rationality. This nature accounts for our energetic connectivity to the cosmos, our resulting perception of our place in the universe, and how we experience peace or a lack thereof. We exist within "an interwoven net of connectivity... there are no 'things' but only networks and interrelations" (*Ibid.*, 2010a).

> From the energetic approach, transrational peaces integrate the moment of transpersonality and spirituality, of intentionality as well as the connectedness between all things and thus the moment of peace out of harmony... they have passed through the modern rationality, and know and acknowledge it... In a simplified manner this means that transrational notions of peace do not decide between spirituality and rationality, but integrate both (*Ibid.*, 2012a: 266).

Transpersonal psychology provides the important link between the study of the human psyche and the transrational peace interpretation. It was created as, "... a new psychology that would honor the entire spectrum of human experience, including various non-ordinary states of consciousness" (Grof, n.d.: 3).

> Transpersonal psychology is interested in a significant subgroup of these (non-ordinary) states (of consciousness) that have heuristic, healing, transformative and even evolutionary potential. This includes experiences of shamans and their clients, those of initiates in native rites of passage and ancient mysteries of death and rebirth, of spiritual practitioners and mystics of all ages, and individuals in psychospiritual crisis ('spiritual emergencies') (*Ibid.*, n.d.: 5).

Transpersonal psychology validates the wisdom of pre-modern civilizations without romanticizing it. Researchers and practitioners utilize ancient local knowledge and traditions, making sense of them within a rational consciousness. They make this wisdom accessible for developing awareness in today's societies (Dietrich, 2006).

3.3 DEFINITIONS OF RELEVANT CONCEPTS

3.3.1 Peace(s)

> The world... needs more than one peace for concrete societies and communities to be able to organize themselves. *The peaces* do not become mutually compatible the moment everybody understands one another, but when all live in their own peace, that is, treat others like the members of their own kin, and so respect them even if they do not understand them (Dietrich and Sützl, 1997: 15-16).

This research springs from my own understanding of peaces and my role in realizing them. In my studies with Wolfgang Dietrich, founder and director of the Innsbruck program we shared the concept of *many peaces*. Students from around the world allowed for a variety of interpretations of the term, free from hierarchy, and thereby avoiding the often violent implications of the *one peace*.

> The search for the 'one peace' is identified as part of a larger universalist mode of thinking which in its totality rests upon disrespectful and therefore unpeaceful basic assumptions, so that the guidelines for action and the real politics that derive from it do at least have the potential for a continuous renewal of violence (*Ibid.*: 10).

In keeping with this notion, I invite the reader to consider his or her own understanding of peace. In order to ground my own perspective, though, I also offer my own reflection.

For me, peace resides in the ability to move from the changing energy of one moment to the next in a centered, calm and wholly present manner. I experience peace when I breathe deeply, when I dance lyrically out of chaos, or when I float in the vast potential of a quiet mind. Like many, I return to a state of inner peace in nature, stimulated by the senses: the sweet smell of mountain pines, the melodic sounds of water meeting land, the communal orchestra of crickets at dusk, or the golden embrace of late afternoon sun on my skin. I often look out to look in. Natural surroundings realign me with the quiet depths of the inner river that flows through my core, undisturbed by turbulence at the surface.

3.3.2 Energy

Throughout this book, I speak of *energy* in various contexts: flowing inside me, resonating with me, shifting around me. In everyday life, 'energy' is used colloquially to describe someone's sense of a place, a social atmosphere, an interaction with another being. Dietrich's (2012a) description of the human being's (microcosm's) relation to the universe (macrocosm) will help to ground the use of 'energy' in this text:

> ... the microcosm of the human body and mind is not only an inseparable part of the universe, but also corresponds to it in all its aspects... from the conception that this universe is cosmic breath or energy, derives the microcosm's desire to resonate in harmony with the macrocosm... That which we call existence at the same time is only perceptible if its "frequency" is distinct from that of the universe. The difference makes the being, and thus also the human being, whose simple *Dasein*[18] already implies deviation. Throughout her whole material existence she resonates around the basic tuning of the universe, until she again becomes reattuned and thus fades (Dietrich, 2012a: 56).

All matter vibrates at distinct frequencies within a universal spectrum, and during a human's worldly lifetime, she resonates at various frequencies. When her reattunement with her surroundings is reached, it marks the end of that physical life. Dietrich describes the interconnectedness of humans and the universe through "cosmic breath or energy", where they are distinct only in their unique energetic frequencies. I wish to explore practices that support humans in resonating harmoniously with this cosmic energy *within* this lifetime.

As Imanera (2012c) explains, "energy is the bridge between the physical body and spiritual body... between the physical mind and spiritual mind". In

---

[18] According to Dietrich, the simplest (though inexact) translation of the German *Dasein* is 'existence' (Dietrich, 2012: 16).

striving to create resonance,[19] the Daoist shamanic practices I write about tap into and alter this frequency via the body and breath. The frequency changes and the practitioner is able to align with her higher, spiritual self, experiencing a peaceful sensation. This peace originates within, but is 'conducted' outward, through thoughts, actions, words, and intentions, into the community and universe.

3.3.3 Transformation

Transformation is a holistic shift in this energy that affects the transformed person's relationship to her environment and perception of her role and greater potential. My use of the word aligns with Frances Vaughan's regarding exceptional experiences.

> Transformation really means a change in the way you see the world – and a shift in how you see yourself. It's not simply a change in your point of view, but rather a whole different perception of what's possible. It's the capacity to expand your worldview so that you can appreciate different perspectives, so that you can hold multiple perspectives simultaneously. You're not just moving around from one point of view to another, you're really expanding your awareness to encompass more possibilities (Vaughan, as cited in Schlitz, 2009: 168-169).

As with energy itself, this transformation is not confined to an internal experience. Transformation of the energetic frequency of one entity causes a shift in energy, however subtle, for all. So transformation is fundamental in processes that help someone attune with harmonious resonance, connect with intuitive wisdom, and experience peace. In Chapters 8 and 10 I elaborate on the concept of intuitive wisdom and the Daoist shamanic practices that stimulate transformation.

---

[19] "Resonance (*ganying*) refers to the ability of a stimulus to evoke a response through the vibrating medium of *qi*, even in the absence of a perceptible physical connection between the two" (Major, Meyer, Queen & Roth, 2012:8).

3.3.4 The Shaman and Shamanism

The word 'shaman' carries a wide range of interpretations and implications. Despite some culturally based variation in the qualities and expectations of a shaman, shamanism maintains many universal characteristics.

> Shamanic knowledge is remarkably consistent across the planet. In spite of cultural diversity and the migration and diffusion of peoples across the earth, the basic themes related to the art and practice of shamanism form a coherent complex. Cultural variations do exist – and yet, when examining the field, there are superficial features as well as deeper structures which appear to be constant (Halifax, 1982: 5).

Many contemporary healers, therapists, and facilitators describe their tools or methods as *shamanic*, but hesitate to refer to themselves as *shamans*.[20] The two spiritual guides who first introduced me to shamanism illustrate this. Peter Kirschner uses *'Erinnerer'* (The Rememberer), the name given him by a teacher. His website describes him as an "outdoor guide… taught the work of shamanism from various cultures".[21] Angela Mendez Hernandez is known as a *curandera* (female healer). Walsh comments on the evolution of the shaman's role and definition over time.

> As societies have become more complex and less nomadic, the presence of a shaman who 'did it all': healer, priest, medium, sorcerer/witch, has dwindled. Instead, people have begun to specialize in one of these roles, respectively in medical, ritual, spirit possession, and malevolent magic practices (Walsh, 2007: 18).

The majority of my acquaintances who work with shamanism exercise skills in several of these areas, though few would claim to practice them all.

In his seminal work *Shamanism: Archaic Techniques of Ecstasy*, Mircea Eliade writes "Shamanism in the strict sense is pre-eminently a religious phenomenon of Siberia and Central Asia. The word comes to us, through Russian, from the Tungusic *saman"* meaning "one who is excited, moved,

---

[20] This is true in my community in Boulder, Colorado, but most likely is not found consistently throughout other regions of the country.
[21] http://www.native-spirit.at/NATIVE%20SPIRIT_sf1+1+101431+++.html

raised"(Eliade, 1964: 4; Walsh, 2007: 13). Anthropologists agree that evidence of the role of shaman, mediator between heavens and earth, sacred and profane, seems to be as old as human society (Jakobsen, 1999). It has been identified as the mystical element of religions throughout the world, and applied to healers also dubbed medicine men, witch doctors, sorcerers, wizards, magicians, or seers. But not every medicine man or witch doctor is a shaman (Harner, 1990). Shamans are characterized by their unique interaction with spirits. While others in a tribe may see or be possessed by spirits, the shaman is distinguished by his or her ability to exercise some control over them, in order to "command, commune, and intercede with them for the benefit of the tribe" (Walsh, 2007: 13). This interaction takes place within the shaman's non-ordinary state of consciousness.

The shaman is also distinguished from her community by the intensity of her religious experience (Eliade, 1964). One common attribute globally is the initiatory experience, which sees the shaman-initiate endure some form of death, dismemberment, or sickness.

> Sometimes these singular experiences signify no more than a 'choice' from above and merely prepare the candidate for new revelations. But usually sicknesses, dreams, and ecstasies in themselves constitute an initiation; that is, they transform the profane, pre-'choice' individual into a technician of the sacred. Naturally, this ecstatic type of experience is always and everywhere followed by theoretical and practical instruction at the hands of the old masters; but that does not make it any the less determinative, for it is the ecstatic experience that radically changes the religious status of the 'chosen' person (*Ibid.*: 33).

An initiatory 'death' may be symbolic, occurring in a dream or ritual ceremony where the shaman experiences her own dismemberment. It may also occur during ecstatic experiences brought on by sickness or trance.

> The content of these first ecstatic experiences, although comparatively rich, almost always includes one or more of the following themes: dismemberment of the body, followed by a renewal of the internal organs and viscera; ascent to the sky and dialogue with the gods or spirits; descent to the underworld and conversations with spirits and the souls of dead shamans; various revelations and shamanic (secrets of the profession) (*Ibid.*: 34).

The initiatory theme correlates with the culture's particular religious orientation. After the initiation, the shaman will receive guidance in integrating her symbolic death from the shaman-elders of the community as she begins her own path.

Anthropologist Michael Harner – striving to create space for the role to be understood and practiced in modern societies – offers a particularly helpful definition:

> A shaman is a man or woman who enters an altered state of consciousness – at will – to contact and utilize an ordinarily hidden reality in order to acquire knowledge, power, and to help other persons. The shaman has at least one, and usually more, 'spirits' in his personal service (Harner, 1990: 20).

Roger Walsh (2007) shies away from two elements of Harner's definition: "contacting a hidden ordinary reality" and interaction with "spirits". This, Walsh asserts, describes what the shaman *believes* he or she is experiencing. (I will discuss concerns with linking phenomenology and ontology in the following pages.) Thus Walsh offers this simplified, more accessible definition:

> Shamanism can be defined as a family of traditions whose practitioners focus on voluntarily entering altered states of consciousness in which they experience themselves or their spirit(s) interacting with other entities, often by traveling to other realms, in order to serve their community (Walsh, 2007: 15-16).

There is serious concern over the cultural appropriation of shamanism in contemporary Western societies. In some cases, people assume the title without adequate preparation to manage the role responsibly. They may use their position as shaman merely in order to exercise power over others. In a modern context, those interested in exploring shamanism are advised to exercise caution and vet the shaman with whom they would like to practice or receive healing.

But not all contemporary shamans are to be distrusted. Malidoma Patrice Somé (1993), a medicine man and scholar from the Dagara tribe of Burkina Faso, sheds light on how one might exist outside a traditional indigenous environment.

> Modern cultures cannot, in their pursuit of the spirit, expect to reproduce the original indigenous way of existing. The modern world vibrates in such a way that it is impossible to translate or transplant. Anything aboriginal that enters the artificial space of Western culture is diminished, changed to fit into it. That which is indigenous can only live in a land that is indigenous. So in some ways, the shaman downtown is not the same as the *boburo* in the village because downtown does not emit the same energy as the village circle. But this does not mean that the modern-day healer is ineffective. It means that his status is commensurate with the situation in which he is supposed to work. And in this case everything he asks, as long as it is done with respect, honesty and integrity, cannot be looked at as a parody of spiritualism (Somé, 1993: 57-58).

From this perspective, what matters is not the particular roots and location of the shaman, but rather his capacity to act within the given energetic environment, and the intention with which he conducts his work.

For my purposes, the two most salient aspects of the role and practice are: 1) the shaman enters a non-ordinary state of consciousness, also known as soul flight, shamanic journeying, trance, or state of ecstasy.[22] 2) The shaman or her spirits interact with other entities to heal and gain knowledge that serves people and nature in the mundane realm.

As with Imanera's (2012f) Daoist approach, shamanic experiences are embodied, not taught; shamanic wisdom is derived from lived, direct experiences.

> ... Westerners can easily become initiated into the fundamentals of shamanic practice. The ancient way is so powerful, and taps so deeply into the human mind, that one's usual cultural belief systems and assumption about reality are essentially irrelevant... ultimately,

---

[22] In the past, interpretations of shamanism from a psychological perspective have been skeptical, mostly due to the influence of psychoanalysis and Freudian psychology. These schools tend to label the altered state of consciousness at the foundation of the shamanic experience as psychotic, often diagnosed as hysteria or schizoprenic behavior. Eliade's Shamanism goes into great detail to portray the shamanic trance and the shaman's capacities to work and heal in this ecstatic state not as mental disturbance or possession by spirits but as a mystical communing with spirits (Eliade, 1964; Walsh, 2007).

shamanic knowledge can only be acquired through individual experience (Harner, 1990: xviii).

Therefore I focus my research primarily on Daoist shamanic practices I have experienced personally – but which I also believe are accessible for others.

3.4 Courses of Action

3.4.1 Survey of Relevant Literature

A variety of sources guided this research. As a theoretical basis for shamanism, Daoism, and transpersonal psychology, I surveyed relevant literature, and will elaborate on specific authors in Chapter 4. This literature provided a foundation for interpreting my direct experiences.

3.4.2 Transpersonal Methods: Embodied Writing

Lederach (2005) refers to Carl Rogers' idea that the most personal is also the most universal. "When we attempt to eliminate the personal, we lose sight of ourselves, our deeper intuition, and the source of our understandings – who we are and how we are in the world" (Lederach, 2005: viii). My research attunes with this deep intuition, simultaneously personal and universal. My experiences as author and participant are a necessary aspect of the research and writing.

Over the course of this project, I have engaged in shamanic practices with teachers from several different cultural spheres. The majority of my direct experiences spring from my training in Daoism with Imanera. They constitute the most essential component of this book because they represent my own active immersion into the topic. In a sense, then, I serve as the 'guinea pig' of my own experiment, through which I gather data to answer my research question. This experiment aligns my work with a transrational approach to peace studies; it incorporates but transcends purely rational methods of reading, interpreting, and comparing others' ideas. Instead, I reflect on what I have experienced on myriad levels: physical, spiritual, energetic, emotional, and mental.

Writing transrationally about shamanic experience challenges me to put words to the energetic and ineffable. Walsh (2007) describes this task's most central difficulty: the leap between phenomenology (experience) and ontology (claims about reality). There is an academic risk in assuming that what I experience and believe I am doing is 'really' what is happening. But transpersonal psychology[23] helps to bridge everyday human perception of indescribable spiritual experiences.

> One of the distinguishing characteristics of the transpersonal movement has been the desire to integrate our understanding of human nature and behavior with the wisdom psychologies of the world's spiritual and religious traditions. From the beginning, Buddhism, Hinduism, and indigenous forms of shamanism were actively explored (Anderson and Braud, 2011: 11).

Within this field, three approaches – intuitive, integral, and organic – recognize "multiple intelligences", and value the use of personal, experiential research (*Ibid.*, 2011). Of the three, I rely primarily on intuitive inquiry:

> Epistemologically, intuitive inquiry is a search for new understandings through the focused attention of one researcher's passion and compassion for her- or himself, others and the world… intuitive inquiry affirms a world reality in flux and mutable and therefore, challenges conventional notions of a static worldview that is separate and distinguishable from the knower, the lover (*Ibid.*: 6, 17).

More specifically, throughout this paper I employ *embodied writing:*

> Embodied writing seeks to reveal the lived experience of the body by portraying in words the finely textured experience of the body and evoking *sympathetic resonance* in readers… embodied writing is itself an act of embodiment, entwining in words our senses with the senses of the world (Anderson, 2001: 1).

---

[23] In their book about transpersonal research methods, Anderson and Braud (2001) provide this definition: "Transpersonal psychology is the study and cultivation of the highest and most transformative human values and potentials – individual, communal, and global – that reflect the mystery and interconnectedness of life including our human journey within the cosmos" (Anderson & Braud, 2011:9).

Anderson describes sympathetic resonance as the reader feeling either *consensual validity* – when written material 'strikes a chord' – or *discriminative validity* – when the narrative evokes dissonance or neutrality. Like the musician creating soundwaves for the consideration of her audience, I use embodied writing to elicit consonance or dissonance with the reader and his experiences and perceptions.

Selections of my embodied writing are taken from the research journal I began in February 2012. Excerpts from this journal appear throughout the book in *italics*. In them, I reflect on a wide range of shamanic experiences, including journeying, painting, dance, and sacred community rituals honoring moon cycles and seasons. This immersion into a wide variety of practices has inspired me, enriched my work, and introduced me to new techniques that I will incorporate into a lifelong path of transformation.

However, most of the journal included in this text appears in Chapter 10 and pertains to my Daoist experiences, specifically meditation and *qigong*. I have also devoted one section of Chapter 8 to the shamanic painting I experienced in a class called "The Rattle and the Brush". Generally speaking, Daoist practices can be shamanic or not, depending on the context and intention of practice. I have had the opportunity to work with Daoist shaman Imanera, thus most of what I write pertains specifically to *Daoist shamanic* practices.

I have worked hard to engage with my topic on many levels. I meditate with my research questions. I request help and guidance from my spirit guides through shamanic journeying. When my creative energy seems blocked or I feel anxiety that my work is not satisfactory, I dance with my emotions and practice *qigong*. As I describe in Chapter 10, these methods have enabled me to interact with this endeavor through all aspects of my being, and alleviate the pressure and frustration that arose naturally throughout the process. As a result, I continue to have a positive, loving relationship with this project and am vastly appreciative for the insights and transformation it has inspired in me.

3.4.3 Lectures and Interviews

Several lectures and semi-structured interviews supplement my own research. These include my courses at the University of Innsbruck's Master of Arts in Peace, Development, Security, and International Conflict Transformation; my classes at Imanera's Dipper School of Daoist Arts; and the workshop "The Rattle and the Brush", taught by Ixeeya. In order to deepen my understanding of this coursework, I also conducted interviews with Peter

Kirschner and Hanna Raab (2012), Imanera (2012f), Ixeeya (2012c) and Wolfgang Dietrich (2012b).

Chapter 4: Literature Review

> As words give birth to words
> And thoughts arouse deeper thoughts,
> they smell like flowers giving off scent,
> spread like green leaves in spring;
> a long wind comes, whirls into a tornado of ideas,
> and clouds rise from the writing-brush forest.
>
> (Lu Ji, 1996: 10)

Conducting a survey of relevant literature, I have developed a foundational understanding of the primary themes of peace and peacework, Daoism, shamanism, intuitive wisdom and transpersonal experience. I use others' studies of these topics as lenses to see my own direct experiences and articulate my own narratives. This chapter presents the principal authors whose ideas I reference throughout the book.

4.1 Philosophy of Peaces and Elicitive Peacework

Wolfgang Dietrich's (2012a-b, 2011, 2010a-b, 2006) original contributions to Peace Studies are fundamental to my research. Dietrich is Austrian, the UNESCO Chair for Peace Studies, and the program director of the Master of Arts Program in Peace, Development, Security, and International Conflict

Transformation at the University of Innsbruck.[24] Dietrich's concept of the five peace families grounds my research, and his insights are the inspiration behind my transrational approach to studying the energetic tradition of Daoist shamanism.

My elicitive approach to conflict transformation comes from the works of peacebuilder John Paul Lederach (2011, 2005, 2003, 1995). Born in the United States, Lederach writes and teaches from extensive field experience in conflicts around the world, including Colombia, the Philippines, Nepal, Tajikistan and several countries in Africa. Lederach explains that his background as a Mennonite Christian influences his work and perspective. He is currently a professor of International Peacebuilding at the University of Notre Dame.

4.2 DAOISM

To explain the main principles of Daoism and Daoist shamanism, I focus on works by Livia Kohn (2011, 2010, 2009, 2008, 2006, 2000), Jean C. Cooper (1972), and Eva Wong (1997a-b). German-born Kohn is a member of the Daoist literati, an historian, demystifier, and long-time practitioner of *taijiquan,* yoga, and insight meditation. Cooper, born in China of English nobility, writes from the firsthand understanding of Daoism, Buddhism and Confucianism she acquired as a child raised by Chinese caregivers. In addition to writing, Cooper taught philosophy and religious studies in England. Eva Wong was born in Hong Kong and has translated multiple Daoist texts. She is an independent scholar and practitioner of the Daoist arts of the Pre-Celestial Way and Complete Reality lineages. Wong unites creativity and firsthand contact to transform myth into history, filling in the gaps where ancient Daoist texts have been lost.

For Daoist concepts in their original form, I cite translations of these ancient texts, including writings by Lao-tzu (1993), Chuang-tzu (1964), An Liu (2012), and Sun Tzu (1988). In addition to translations by Wong (1997b) and Kohn (2011, 2008), I reference excerpts of ancient texts translated by Wing-Tsit Chan (1963) and Burt Watson (1964). I also use Henri Maspero's *China in*

---

[24]http://www.uibk.ac.at/peacestudies/ma-program/

Antiquity (1978), one of the most lucid introductions to ancient China. Maspero taught Chinese at the Collège de France in Paris.

Complementing these more traditional sources are the introductions and translations of the *Yi Jing* by Thomas Cleary (1986) and Stephen Karcher (2009). Chapter 7 is dedicated to the *Yi Jing* – instead of other quintessential Daoist texts such as the *Dao DeJing* and *Chuang-tzu* – because the *Yi Jing* allows an embodied shamanic engagement. Cleary, born in the United States, is a prolific translator of Daoist, Buddhist, Confucian and Muslim texts, and in general works not previously available in English. I refer to his well-known edition of Sun Tzu's *The Art of War* in Chapter 11.

Karcher (2009), also from the United States, is one of the most creative and controversial scholars of *Yi Jing* studies, divination and myth. He describes himself as a "three legged man".[25] First, he is a scholar and intellectual interested in the wisdom of language and books. Next, he is a dancer and choreographer wishing to keep embodied meaning alive. Karcher resolves the tension between these first two roles with the third leg, the ritual space, which unifies dream image and 'imaginal body'. This is where he envisions the entrance of the *Yi Jing* in his life.

Lastly, I have referred to Ronnie Littlejohn (2009) for a contemporary perspective on Daoism. An American professor, Littlejohn is a scholar of Comparative philosophy whose work focuses on Confucianism and Daoism.

4.3 INTUITION, TRANSPERSONAL EXPERIENCE & MEDITATION

The ideas of Swiss psychoanalyst Carl Gustav Jung (1969) appear throughout this book. Beyond Jung's definition of intuition (1959), I incorporate his commentaries on consciousness and interpretation of the *Yi Jing* from his foreword to Richard Wilhelm's translation of that classic Daoist text (1949). Frances Vaughan (1979) and Roger Walsh (2007) are the guiding voices in my study of intuitive wisdom. Vaughan is a psychologist and leader in transpersonal and humanistic psychology from the United States. She has practiced Buddhist, Sufi and Hindu spiritual traditions, and in her counseling

---

[25]http://www.ichinglivingchange.org/stephen-karcher/

and writing focuses on nurturing inner wellness and healthy relationships with self, others and the world. Walsh and Vaughan have co-authored and co-edited various works, including *Paths Beyond Ego* (1993) and *Accept this Gift: Selections from A Course in Miracles* (1983).

I have drawn from Roger Walsh's work on both intuitive wisdom and shamanism (2007). Walsh, an Australian trained in medicine, psychiatry, and psychology, "was a confirmed skeptic of all things spiritual, until [he] tried the practices for [himself]" (Walsh, 2007: 9). Through practical and intellectual exploration of spiritual disciplines, he became deeply appreciative of their powers to heal and stimulate awakening. Walsh (2007) describes his research as "assumptive minimalism", making as few assumptions as possible when studying a topic. For example, he does not presuppose that shamans have the healing abilities they claim. Nor does he accept popular dismissals of these claims. Instead, Walsh formulates independent views via his own research and evaluation.

I utilize works by Abraham Maslow (1970, 1971) and Stanislav and Christina Grof (2009, 1993, 1990) to create a framework for interpreting transpersonal states of consciousness. Maslow was an American, one of the most influential psychologists of the 20th century, and a founder of both humanistic and transpersonal psychologies. Czechoslovakian Stanislav Grof is another founder of transpersonal psychology. He and his wife Christina have made rich contributions to the field through firsthand research and analysis. Grof and Frances Vaughan are considered pioneers in psychedelic studies.

In his writing about the 'Akashic field', Ervin Laszlo (2009, 2011) presents yet another perspective on transpersonal experiences and their sources. A Hungarian scientist, philosopher, pianist, and global visionary, Laszlo was nominated twice for the Nobel Peace Prize. His edited collection, *The Akashic Experience: Science and the Cosmic Memory Field* (2009), depicts various individuals' contacts with the field, as well as their suggestions for integrating wisdom gained through that contact. I drew in particular from the chapter by American anthropologist Marilyn Mandala Schlitz, who proposes a greater awareness and valuing of the Akashic experience via an innovative curriculum for "worldview literacy" (Schlitz, 2009).

In my discussion of meditation and the mind, I refer primarily to Kohn's (2008) comparative study of Buddhist, Hindu, and Daoist meditative traditions. To elaborate on certain aspects of these traditions, I reference works by Mipham (2003), Gawler and Bedson (2010). Born in India, Sakyong Mipham Rinpoche is a high lama of Tibetan Buddhism and the head of the Shambhala Buddhist lineage. Dr. Ian Gawler is Australian and Paul Bedson from the United States (2010); the former is a student of a Tibetan lineage, the latter practices *qigong* and Chinese medicine. Both are respected leaders in the field of mind-body medicine and meditation, applying ancient wisdom in a modern context.

4.4 SHAMANISM

To help understand my direct experiences in shamanism, I include several authors who approach it from different backgrounds. Romanian historian Mircea Eliade's (1964) book *Shamanism: Archaic Techniques of Ecstasy* is a standard-setting text examining the practice in a broad religious context. Michael Harner (1990) has been a key figure in re-introducing shamanic techniques as methods for healing in the modern Western world. Harner is an anthropologist and academic from the United States who has followed his own advice that shamanism must be learned through direct practice and training. Finally, as a medicine man from the Dagara tribe in Burkina Faso, Malidoma Somé (1993) provides firsthand perspective on shamanic experiences in a tribal community. Somé sheds light on how the shaman operates in modern society outside of indigenous cultures.

CHAPTER 5: MEETING IMANERA... (OR NOT)

"In Daoism there is no mind, no word for it.
There is a word for heart. Heart is consciousness".
(Imanera, 2012d)[26]

5.1 MEETING IMANERA

Early in the writing of this book, by a stroke of good fortune, I was invited to join a women's circle. This small group shares wisdom spanning generations and a wide range of experiences. As mothers, daughters, creative healers, curious seekers, and sisters, we gather in a community of mutual support and curiosity. In my first meeting with the group, I was partnered with a woman who welcomed me warmly with her bright smile. As we experimented with a technique called 'focusing',[27] I noticed what felt like a bubble of warmth forming between us. It was inviting, safe, and my mind could relax into this warm space. I felt immediate trust with the woman. At the same time, her mischievous grin hinted at a deeper understanding of what our exchange meant.

When my partner and I completed the exercise and I commented on the secure, loving 'bubble' she simply replied, "I've been cultivating that *qi* all day long". As we said our goodbyes and I briefly mentioned my research topic – at the time, "Shamanic practices as methods for peacework" – my

---

[26] The calligraphy on the right depicts the ancient Chinese character for *Wu*, meaning 'shaman'. Created by Kathleen McGoey.
[27] Developed by Eugene Gendin and used for tapping into the wisdom stored in the body. See http://www.focusing.org/

partner linked arms with me and, expressing great enthusiasm for the theme, laughed and declared: "Oh! I'm a scholar too"! This was the introduction to my adventures in Daoism with Imanera.

A week later, the two of us met to hike the breathtakingly beautiful wilderness and waterfalls of the Wild Basin area of Rocky Mountain National Park. We sat, perched over the rumbling falls, getting to know each other. I was enchanted by her bright blue eyes, and once again comforted by the ease with which she related to my background, my queries, and me. Imanera told me about the energetic healing effects of negative ions emitted by the waterfalls. We observed the water's swirling patterns, and she drew a life cycle picture of the five elements of Daoism: earth births metal, metal births water, water births wood, wood births fire, fire births earth. Repeat.[28] She interwove these illustrations with tales of her trials and triumphs as an occupational therapist, her discoveries and development of healing methods with high-gauss magnets, and the delights of wedding people as a priest. Imanera explained that she now blends all of these paths as a Daoist shaman.[29]

I felt an instant connection with this strange, wonderful woman. She invited me to be her student and begin practicing with her, suggesting that she might offer guidance and experiences to inform my research. This was the first of countless acts of generosity and immaculate timing extended by Imanera. I was uncertain what kind of commitment I would make in becoming her student. I was unfamiliar with Daoist shamanism; I had presumed that my research would focus on indigenous American shamanic practices. Yet Imanera was so grounded, so illuminating and encouraging, and asked only for my honesty and trust to start on this path. While the shift was unexpected, my intuition told me it could be another chance encounter that would reshape my perspective, and even my direction in life.

Before we left the forest, Imanera and I stood in a grove of pines, and she asked me to make a shape with my body that felt like a tree. I did this, and

---

[28] "The Five Phases (*wuxing*) represent the five paradigmatic manifestations of *qi*: Wood, Fire, Earth, Metal and Water. (The term *wuxing* is sometimes translated as 'five elements,' but this is misleading because the five are paradigms, not constituents, of physical phenomena.) The five are 'phases' of *qi* in the same sense that steam, liquid water, and ice are 'phases' of H2O" (Major, Meyer, Queen & Roth, 2012:7).

[29] I have consciously elected to use the female pronoun when talking about shamans throughout this paper, because three of the four shamans I have worked with personally are women. In terms of using 'shaman' and 'priest' versus 'shamaness' and 'priestess', I share Imanera's perspective that in her work, the shaman (or priest) transcends any gender-related confines of identity, thus attaching the suffix –ess is irrelevant.

she offered my first taste of *qigong*. She demonstrated adjustments in posture, breath, tongue position, and vision, and encouraged growing my roots deep. A buzz, something like a mild vibration that I had only experienced during Vipassana meditation, rolled through me in a wave. For just a moment, every cell attuned to this sensation – peaceful, stoic, ancient, reaching deep and rising tall. I was a tree.

'Imanera' means magnetic woman. The name suits her. A magnetic personality attracts people to her, an edgy charge in her teaching keeps students eager for more, a dynamic personality shifts back and forth easily between poles: reverence in her sacred practice balances ease in comic relief and contagious laughter. Yet, she is very free. Like the Dao, Imanera cannot be described in a dichotomy or followed in a straight line. She attempts to put words to her own life and experience – "a light that points to harmony... A mountain woman wrapped in outer and inner peace... A *shenren* (spirit-human)... I = we... Being spiritually pregnant, I really is we" (Imanera, 2012f).

Imanera believes a state of peace, contentment and happiness to be the fundamental matter of existence. Her response to why she is happy includes, "Working with people's expectations and shifting their perceptions allows them to practice what is in their heart... I can't know what makes you happy, but I can sit in reflective stillness and show light on harmony" (*Ibid.*). From my own perspective, she models the skills of an elicitive peaceworker.

5.2 Lineage and Teachers

In true Daoist shaman fashion, Imanera believes she was never born. Birthless means undifferentiated; all is interrelated (*Ibid.*). I have been to the land settled by her great-great grandparents.[30] Her great-great grandmother, an important figure in the family lineage, exemplified the virtue of helping the underdog. She felt great responsibility to "seek reconciliation with the masses of the unknown dead", the orphaned souls (*Ibid.*). Imanera has

---

[30] Imanera's great-great grandfather was a Colorado magnate of the steel industry.

carried on with her ancestor's tradition, attending to the spirits and hungry ghosts who linger among the living, not realizing they are dead.

Imanera's greatest teachers are nature and *Shifu*. She also names Tekakwitha, her patron saint, as an important guide since childhood. In her Daoist life, she has been trained in many lineages. Imanera was born (or not) in the year of the tiger; she is a white tigress, fearless, secure and radiating from her center. As a child mystic, she was aware of her own intuitive wisdom and cultivated relationships with nature, which kept her free from the psychic knots that typically develop in the solar plexus. As a result of a serious childhood surgery, she let go of her fear of death, and became an even freer soul (*Ibid.*).

5.3 THE DAOIST-SHAMANIC PATH

To reach Lazuli, Imanera's home, her other students and I earn merit by climbing a long, steep hill, panting. As we reach the top, Imanera appears on the deck smiling, her long wavy hair lifted wildly by the mountain winds. From there, we read the weather in the clouds, sensing when there are wildfires throughout the western United States. The land of Lazuli is vibrantly alive. Rabbits twitch tails, deer drink from lily ponds, chipmunks and songbirds vie for access to the birdfeeders and abundance of the grove. We find the remains of deer skeletons hidden in the brush, and Imanera points to where bears lie down for an afternoon nap.

Lazuli is nestled in the foothills of the Rocky Mountains, protected by a canyon wall to the North and facing a vast open expanse to the South. An auspicious location, the sleeping green dragons of surrounding mountain ridges protect it. Inside 'Bongo's Birdhouse', the shelter Imanera shares with her husband Bongo, I have rested under the canopy of jungle plants and listened as koi leap out of their indoor ponds. In the afternoons, Imanera usually remembers to rotate the solar panels. Her home functions completely off the grid. The evenings are magnificent, with wide skies for stargazing, a magnetic mattress for vivid dreams, and the howls of coyotes filling the night air.

Imanera is a Daoist shaman. When asked how Daoism is a form of shamanism, she offers, "Historically it is the other way around. First the foot then the shoe, or is it first the shaman then the -ism? A shaman is a mystic, a seeker of worlds and dimensions, stepping through the holographic universe

Daoist Paths of Divine Evolution
(Imanera, 2012c)

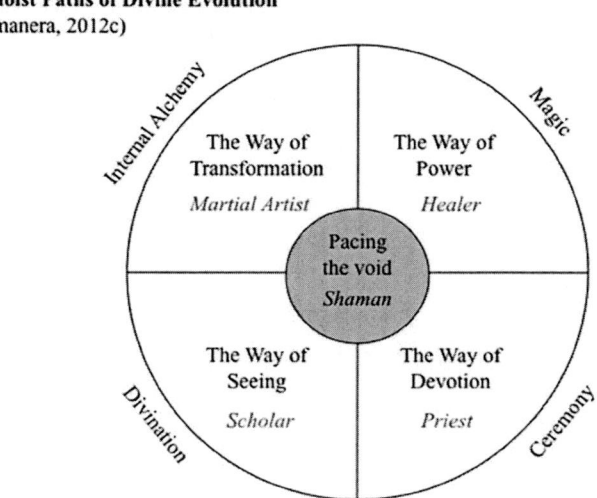

on a path" (*Ibid.*). Or as the chart above[31] illustrates, the path of the Daoist shaman is a blend of four other paths: the scholar, the martial artist, the healer and the priest.

These four paths can be ventured simultaneously; the skills developed along one complement the formation of skills on another. "The healing arts and the martial arts may be a world apart in ordinary usage, but they are parallel in several senses: in recognizing, as the story says, that the less needed the better; in the sense that both involve strategy in dealing with disharmony; and in the sense that in both[,] knowledge of the problem is key to the solution" (Cleary, 1988: 1).

Imanera presents martial arts as "a method of understanding the least effort for the greatest consequences... a method to stop fighting" (Imanera, 2012f). In this practice, she emphasizes prevention. She reads and uses energy, for example, extending her own deeply into the earth to stay rooted and prevent an attack (*Ibid.*). As a priestess, she leads sacred rituals and ceremonies, accompanying those at death's door. She describes this role as

---

[31] Reprinted with permission from Imanera (2012b).

bringing "a flood of joy and an afterglow of bliss in the face of death or challenges or changes" (*Ibid.*).

As a scholar, Imanera writes, publishes, and teaches. She has completed degrees in Social Philosophy and Occupational Therapy, and applies those branches of knowledge to enrich her wisdom and expertise along all four paths. She has founded her own publishing house and contributes as an author to an indispensable textbook for the American Occupational Therapy Association. She teaches multiple *qigong* visualization and meditation forms. Like many great teachers, she delights in her students' capacity to independently integrate her material into their own perspectives and lives.

Yet what makes Imanera's style so relevant is her adherence to the Daoist thought that direct experience is most important. When we shower her with rationally driven questions, wanting cerebral feedback, we are often met with indirect answers.[32] Take for example her response to the question, "How do you regulate the emotional mind?":

> Expectation is the worst emotional disturbance. Chasing the clouds. Cloud watching. No clouds. Methods of stopping thought: stop and look. Tie it up on your nose, restrain it, analyze it by: empty look (even the universe is ultimately empty), false look (remember the past and the future compared to now – emotional mind doesn't last long), centered look (only here and now). Behold the moon method. One-point focus on the *Ling,* the supernatural part of the *shen* in your third eye. The large hand stamp method (Imanera, *Ibid.*).

The reference to clouds is the part of this reply that makes most immediate sense to me, and that is because I have experienced it. As I have come to value learning and teaching through direct experience, I find this approach to be just as challenging as it is validating and inspiring.

As a healer, Imanera is a medical *qigong* practitioner and has directed a pain clinic, healing heart retreats, the Biomagnetic Therapy Association, and the Biomagnetic Institute and Research Center. She works with the "great toolbox" of five energy forms – light, heat, sound, electricity, and magnetism – using projected *qi* and high gauss magnets to unify, regulate, and direct these energies (*Ibid.*). There is no real distinction between one modality and

---

[32] For that reason, this chapter is titled "Introducing Imanera… (or Not)". The "or not" is often included in her advice and replies and has become one of my most beloved "Imanera-isms".

the next when Imanera treats a client; her approach is truly that of a Daoist shaman, drawing from all sources of wisdom, energetically shape-shifting, and calling on helping spirits while working in a trance. She accesses planetary gem elixirs, the embodiment of the Dao, to "bring in celestial influences that can transmute limited thoughts of the conscious, self-creating an energetic bridge to the spiritual realm of the divine self" (*Ibid.*). Imanera encourages the same independence in her clients as in her students. She provides a healing boost, indications and tools, to help clients progress on their own path of healing.

In addition to walking these four paths, Imanera is a peace activist, covertly and overtly. She has created a lifestyle in which she refuses to "work for the war machine", taking conscientious responsibility for her use of resources and energy sourcing. In the midst of conflict, she seeks to be "at ease with the natural ongoing processes of the natural flow both locally and non-locally. This is the flow of five phases: water, wood, fire, earth, metal: the cycles of creation and dissolution…" (*Ibid.*). Though she admits that "it usually takes me a few seconds to transform by letting go of my expectations, which conflict with what actually is" (*Ibid.*).

Imanera also sees herself as working for peace by teaching *qigong* forms that stimulate transformation and promote empowerment. They encourage people to open their hearts and let go of masks, to be coherent and clear in the present moment. In this sense, Imanera and I are working towards similar objectives and observing similar principles in the pursuit of conflict transformation.

Meeting Imanera, my teacher and friend, was quite serendipitous. I entered her world via the scholar's path, and she has supported me unceasingly in creating this book. At the same time, I have begun my journey as a shaman, and Imanera has introduced me gradually to practices from all four paths. It is with these experiences that I orient myself as an initiated Daoist-scholar-shaman-in-training. This book describes the practices and wisdom I have received from Imanera.

Chapter 6: Daoism as an Energetic Approach to Peace

In the great beginning, there was non-being. It had neither being nor name. The One originates from it; it has oneness but not yet physical form. When things obtain it and come into existence, that is called virtue (which gives them their individual character). That which is formless is divided [into yin and yang], and from the very beginning going on without interruption is called destiny (*ming*, fate). Through movement and rest it produces all things. When things are produced in accordance with the principle (*li*) of life, there is physical form. When the physical form embodies and preserves the spirit so that all activities follow their own specific principles, that is nature. By cultivating one's nature one will return to virtue. When virtue is perfect, one will be one with the beginning. Being one with the beginning, one becomes vacuous (*hsü*, receptive to all), and being vacuous, one becomes great. One will then be united with the sound and breath of things. When one is united with the sound and breath of things, one is then united with the universe. This unity is intimate and seems to be stupid and foolish. This is called profound and secret virtue, this is complete harmony (Chuang-tzu, as cited in Chan, 1963: 202).[33]

When I first met Imanera, I had no plan to pursue Daoism and little relationship to its philosophy or practices. Yet I seemed to embark immediately upon a

---

[33]This excerpt is taken from Chuang-tzu's text, "The Nature and Reality of Tao".

journey of *wu-wei,* letting happen. I was carried by a natural flow of opportunities that aligned organically with my research, my spiritual path, and my life in general. In this sense, my path of Daoist initiation was itself shamanic. My research since has explored Daoism via daily personal practice, sacred ceremony, initiation and magic ritual, self-healing, and assisting in healing Imanera's clients. In this chapter, I give a brief history of Daoism and explain how it exhibits an energetic understanding of peace.

6.1 WHAT IS DAOISM?

Scholars agree that defining Daoism is a challenging feat, an attempt to "express the inexpressible", since the Dao itself "surpasses all human definitions and contingencies and all finite thought" (Cooper, 1972: 9). This challenge reflects a fundamental characteristic of much of Chinese religion: the absence of concrete, conceptual, verbal definition (Schipper, 1993). Commonly translated as The Way, the Dao is "a reality experienced beyond words and concepts discovered through introspective meditation and silent observation of nature" (Cohen, 1998). Chinese philosopher Chuang-tzu wrote, "'The very name Tao is only adopted for convenience sake… It (Tao) exists prior to heaven and Earth, and, indeed, for all eternity… It is older than the most ancient, but it is not old'" (Cooper, 1972: 11).

Some Daoist philosophers of the Warring States Period saw the Dao as a neutral force. In the *Dao De Jing,* though, it is something more:"Hidden beneath transition and change, the Tao is the permanent underlying reality… this unnamed and unnameable power is not entirely neutral, it is benevolent" (Wong, 1997a: 23-24). Author Emile Hovelaque believes the Dao is not just energy. "'It is the principle of all energy, yet energy it is not, but merely one of its manifestations. It is the eternal principle of all life, but no life can express it, and all bodies, all material forms, are but its changing and momentary raiment'" (Hovelaque, as cited in Cooper, 1972: 11-12). Similarly, Littlejohn (2009: 1) portrays it as an energizing *process* that "permeates and animates all of reality to move in its ongoing process". Thus the Dao is everywhere, all encompassing, a universal integral truth.

> Tao is the potency of the universe. It includes all Gods, all deities, all divine beings, all spirits, and all souls. This means that all things have Tao as their deep root. Anyone who embraces Tao also embraces the

potency of the Universe. To embrace Tao is to become Tao, and nothing can be beyond you, nothing can occupy you… Tao does not change, because it *is* the change… to be not limited, defined or formed is Tao… Tao is integral truth. It is not a projection of a prejudice; it is not a partial truth that needs insistence; it is not a viewpoint or a philosophy. It is the universal integral truth, the truth of all lives, the truth that exists prior to any thought or statement" (Ni, 19987: 1, 11).

Poem 25 from the *Dao De Jing* illustrates this riddle:

> Something unformed and complete
> Before heaven and earth were born,
> Solitary and silent,
> Stands alone and unchanging,
> Pervading all things without limit.
> It is like the mother of all under heaven,
> But I don't know its name –
>   Better call it TAO.
>   Better call it great.
>
> Great means passing on.
> Passing on means going far.
> Going far means returning.
>
> Therefore,
>   TAO is great,
>   And heaven,
>   And earth,
>   And humans.
>
> Four great things in the world.
> Aren't humans one of them?
>
> Humans follow earth
> Earth follows heaven
> Heaven follows TAO.
>
> TAO follows its own nature.
> *Tao fa tzu jan*
>
> (Lao-tzu, 1993: 25).

Yet, forming an understanding of the Dao is essential for wrapping one's mind around Daoism. For the sake of this book, consider this concise description of Daoism offered by Cooper: "It is primarily a cosmic religion, the study of the universe and the place and function of man and all creatures and phenomena in it" (Cooper, 1972: 10). Littlejohn (2009: 1) establishes that, "Daoism is the spiritual tradition at the root of Chinese civilization". Living the Dao thus entails holistic engagement, embracing all of the human being's multi-faceted aspects. In the *Huainanzi*,[34] "the key to success in all human activities is that they be attuned to the Way" (Major, Meyer, Queen & Roth, 2012: 6). Daoism is not simply a theoretical approach that engages the intellect or emotions alone. Living the Dao – the real Daoism – is joyousness, an appreciation of the fullness of life. This joy, Cooper notes, is not the typical *emotion* of happiness versus sorrow. Rather, it attempts to encompass the play of Nature and the creative workings of spirit in the universe, in all their exuberance and generosity (Cooper, 1972).

The *Chuang-tzu*, an ancient Daoist text,[35] clarifies the distinction between emotional happiness and the virtue of joy. Kohn introduces her translation of the *Chuang-tzu* by saying it answers "the fundamental question of human existence: how to live in the world and attain a state of peace, contentment, and happiness" (Kohn, 2011: 2). People often think of happiness in terms of satisfying the five senses or seeking pleasure. Both the *Chuang-tzu* and *Dao De Jing* teach that these sources of happiness are fleeting. Instead, the *Chuang-tzu* teaches nonaction or inaction: "'Perfect happiness is being free from the need to be happy. Perfect accomplishment is being free from having to accomplish anything'" (Chuang-tzu, as cited in Kohn, 2011: 7). In her commentary, Kohn says the supreme state of happiness, "is just being in itself" (Kohn, 2011: 6). This state cannot be conceived of or described; that would require it to become separate from the subject experiencing the state.

---

[34] The *Huainanzi* is an important collection of knowledge dating from the Han dynasty (206 B.C.E. – 220 C.E.) arranged by Liu An, the king of Huainan. It offers a comprehensive compilation of contemporary knowledge, providing the reader with a detailed perspective on the intellectual and political life of China during this era (Major, Meyer, Queen & Roth, 2012).

[35] The sacred texts of the *Chuang-tzu* are attributed to Chuang-tzu, as well as additional authors. Chuang-tzu was a brilliant writer who presented and explained the Daoist teachings, adding figurative language and anecdotes to give them life and color (Maspero, 1978).

> I take inaction to be true happiness, but ordinary people think it is a bitter thing. I say: the highest happiness has no happiness, the highest praise has no praise. The world can't decide what is right and what is wrong. And yet inaction can decide this. The highest happiness, keeping live – only inaction gets you close to this! ... The inaction of Heaven is its purity, the inaction of earth is its peace. So the two inactions combine and all things are transformed and brought to birth (Chuang-tzu, 1964: 112).

Finally, the Dao cannot be thought of as a god. Daoism is non-theistic, and the Dao is impersonal and universal; "the strength that makes one a god lies within each being. Transcendence is not the result of a spirit separated from matter, an external divine force given to the world, but a spiritualization of *ch'i*, of energy-matter itself" (Schipper, 1993: 40-41). Indeed, there is no supreme being (Littlejohn, 2009). This aspect of Daoism aligns it with an energetic approach to peaces, in which the highest principle of the world and peace is a primal energy, not a single, personified Creator (Dietrich, 2012a). As a result, Daoism is not dogmatic. The absence of a single source of all life helps practitioners avoid the complacency of a clearly delineated path. Rather, they encounter the challenge and freedom found in pushing themselves to know through their own direct inquiries (Cooper, 1972).

6.2 History of Daoism: Philosophy, Religion, Way of Life

6.2.1 Shamanic Roots of Daoism

Just as shamanism had great impact on Western monotheisms such as Judaism, Christianity, and Islam, it also influenced Chinese Daoism. Ancient texts reveal that Chinese shamans were journeying with the cosmos before the dawn of organized religion. In particular, the *wu* class of ancient China demonstrated shamanic abilities (Eliade, 1964; Wong, 1997a). Noble families employed the *wu* to accompany the souls of the deceased – the *hun* – as they traveled to the heavens. "The ancient Chinese believed that man had several souls which came together in the living individuals but separated again after death to follow different destinies" (Maspero, 1978: 103-104). While the *hun* soul separated from the body upon death, the *p'o* soul continued to reside with the body in the tomb, surviving on offerings. Thus offerings to the dead were an essential rite needed to keep the *p'o* from becoming hungry. If these ceased, the *p'o* might become starving ghosts, returning to the land of the living, appearing in dreams, or inflicting disease as punishment for being neglected (*Ibid.*). The *wu* were also needed to help respond to such attacks.

Shamanism was institutionalized in the feudal state of Ch'u during the Eastern Chou dynasty. Shamans healed the sick, invited spirits, interpreted dreams, read omens, made the rain fall, and divined celestial signs (Wong, 1997a, 1997b). Shamanic culture remained strong in the Ch'u state even when it faded in other parts of China. Biographies of Daoist philosophers Lao-tzu and Chuang-tzu claim they were natives of different areas of the Ch'u state. Wong indicates that both were significantly influenced by shamanism, an idea many scholars do not acknowledge (*Ibid.*).[36] The "Nine Songs", part of a collection of poems titled the *Ch'u-tz'u* (Songs of the Land of Ch'u), depict "the sacredness of nature, the ecstatic union of the shaman and the nature spirits, and the flight to the celestial realm" (Wong, 1997b: 9). These themes appeared in the shamanic culture of Ch'u and continue in the spiritual tradition of Daoism.

> The Ch'u shaman's relationship with the spirits of nature was like that of a lover, and the dances and ceremonies were humanity's attempts to 'seduce' the sacred powers. The section in the *Ch'u-tz'u* titled 'Nine Songs' best illustrates the shamanic tradition of Ch'u... In the ceremony, one shaman, called the spirit-shaman (*shen-wu*), usually took on the persona of the spirit, and another shaman, who was the leader of the ceremony, played the part of the mortal (*Ibid.*: 10).

An excerpt from "Song to the Great Lord of Destiny", one of the "Nine Songs", illustrates the dialogue between spirit-shaman and mortal-shaman:

> *Sung by the Great Lord of Destiny (spirit-shaman):*
> Open wide the gates of the sky.
> I come riding on the black clouds.

---

[36] "This influence is often unrecognized, because many scholars consider the Taochia (philosophical Taoism) and the Tao-chiao (religious Taoism) as opposing branches of Taoist thinking" (Wong, 1997a:17).

I order the whirlwind to be my herald
And call the rainstorm to wash away the dust.

Sung by the shaman who is leading the ceremony:
Great One, you hover and descend to me;
I will climb and follow you
Over the heights of Kong-sang Mountain.

Sung by the Great Lord of Destiny (spirit-shaman):
This world and all its people;
Their lives, long or short, are in my hands.

Sung by the shaman leading the ceremony:
Serenely and majestically you soar in the sky;
You ride on the clear vapor of the sky and earth,
And on the breath of yin and yang.
Speedily I will go with you to far-off places,
Leading the lord of the sky to the great mountains.

Sung by the Great Lord of Destiny (spirit-shaman):
My long robes flutter in the wind;
My jade pendants, in brilliant color, dazzle in the light.
Ah, the changes of yin and yang in the universe;
None of the mortals know what I can do.
     (Ch'u-tz'u, as cited in Wong, 1997b: 16-17).

 Even as shamanism declined in the broader Chou dynasty, its prevalence in the Yang-tze river valley (the land of Ch'u) and the southeastern coast marked a division between north and south. Northerners were more reserved and sophisticated, generally abandoning spiritual beliefs associated with the land. Southerners maintained their relationship with, and respect for, nature. In the east, shamans continued to use incantations, mantras, and talismans. These regional practices of the south and east would affect philosophy, religion and spirituality throughout China's history (Wong, 1997a).

Shamanic journeying to the cosmos and underground[37] also appeared during the Han dynasty. *Bugang* – Daoist ritual walks and dances that follow cosmic patterns and the eight trigrams of the *bagua* – come from the shamanic "Paces of Yu" practice.

> The earliest preserved descriptions are found in the revealed texts of the *Shangqing* tradition, which focus on walks along the patterns of the constellations and the five planets, and especially on walks along the seven stars of the Northern Dipper... the three paces were associated with the notion of a movement through the three levels of the cosmos, leading the performer to heaven... already in the early Han dynasty, the steps seem to have been connected with the three pairs of stars that are situated under the Northern Dipper and referred to as the Three Terraces... or the Celestial Staircase (Andersen, 1990: 237-238).

(It is interesting to note that the Paces of Yu share similarities with the three Strides Visnu of early Vedic mythology, which would contribute to the development of Hinduism; the Vedic priest approached the altar with the same foot-dragging strides as the Paces). These three paces were thought to bring the god through the three levels of the cosmos, thus establishing the universe (*Ibid.*). The Way of Celestial Masters (*Zhengyi*), which later emerged as the foundation for the developing Daoist tradition, also drew on Han dynasty practices. Grave-securing writs, for example, were commands written by a Celestial Emperor to be delivered to the spirits of the tomb (Nickerson, 1987).

During the fourth century CE, The Highest Clarity Tradition transformed shamanistic practice into meditation through an original form of world-evoking visualization; "the body now became a micro-cosmos, and the practitioner journeyed within it and in the heavens... Taoists... saw themselves able to travel within the body and the heavens simultaneously" (Walsh, 2007: 161, 164). In these excursions, Daoists sought knowledge, power, ecstasy, union with a divine lover, and ultimately immortality or union with the Dao. The shamanic traveler could absorb nourishment from the stars, storing their

---

[37] Shamanic travel in the Han dynasty was not limited to ascension into the cosmos, but also going deep into the earth. Daoist Tung-fang Shuo even created a guide to journeying through the roots of China's five sacred mountains (Wong, 1997a).

essence in parts of her body (*Ibid.*). This journey into the cosmos can be facilitated by the use of mudras, or hand seals, which I explain in Chapter 10.[38]

Currently in China, the ethnic minority community of the Naxi, found in northwestern Yunnan and southeastern Sichuan provinces, practice a form of shamanism called Dongba (Wickeri & Tam, 2011). Founded by a 12th century Tibetan shaman, it blends influences of Tibetan Bön, Buddhism, and Daoism. Dongba is the name of the priests as well as the holy texts, and Baidi (White Land) in Northwestern Yunnan province is the Naxi holy land.

> The indigenous religious culture of the Naxi is similar in many respects to that of the Han... The Dongba priests act as mediators between the spirits and humankind. In different Dongba rituals, the priests communicate with spirits found in natural phenomena as well as with ghosts. They are also exorcists and ritual performers for curing illnesses and seeking spiritual blessings in the community and in personal life (*Ibid.*: 57-58).

The Dongba religion is passed down through family lineage and practiced in small groups in temples scattered throughout the region. The Naxi writing system is the only remaining pictographic script still in use. Protected by the Chinese government,[39] Naxi communities and culture are a growing tourist attraction.

6.2.2 Upheavals and Flourishing of Daoism

The eighth to third centuries BCE are known as the Classical period of Daoism, thanks to contributions by great Chinese philosophers – including Confucius, Mo-tzu, Lao-tzu, and Chuang-tzu – and a changing philosophical understanding of the Dao. During this time, the Chinese people endured the political chaos and civil war of the Spring and Autumn and Warring States Periods (Wong, 1997a). Confucius and Lao-tzu sought to articulate a vision

---

[38] In addition to these practices, Daoist shamans also perform the classic shamanic rite of acting as spirit mediums. This involves the shaman going into a trance while the spirit of another being is invited to inhabit the shaman's body. The purpose is healing and acquiring knowledge with the help of spirits.

[39] According to a timeline in the Harper Collins Dictionary of Religion, the first attempt to suppress shamanism by Chinese court officials took place in 99 B.C.E. ("Chinese Religion", 1996).

of a more virtuous and benevolent society. The latter's *Dao De Jing*[40] was the first text to advocate living in harmony with the Dao, since "changes in society must come from changes within individuals, and changes in individuals could come only from following the principles of the Tao" (*Ibid.*: 23).

> Thus adherence to the Taoist school was not a simple act of intellectual acquiescence, as in the other schools. It implied a whole way of life; it required a genuine conversion, an illumination, in which the neophyte felt himself truly changed: the psychological equilibrium which had been normal previously was upset, giving way to a totally new condition (Maspero, 1978: 308).

Their mystical roots and emphasis on developing intuitive understanding of the imperceptible made Daoist teachings unique, distinguishing them from those of Confucius and Mo-tzu.

Confucius focused instead on knowledge acquired through reason, science and study. These added up to moral perfection and the "cardinal virtue of Confucian doctrine, Altruism… The way of attaining this Altruism consists essentially in 'conquering oneself and returning to the rites'" (*Ibid.*: 291-292). Confucius' aim was to build good government by living a peaceful and harmonious life. Following the proper rituals and codes of interpersonal behavior would accomplish this; harmonizing with the natural world was not as important (Maspero, 1978; Wong, 1997a). Mo-tzu, a logician who continued the work of Confucius, was very pious and followed a very personal religion that contradicted the social religion of ancient China (Maspero, 1978). "It was at this point that he most clearly opposed the Confucians, for whom the rites had a value in themselves and who loved to carry them out, not caring to whom the worship was addressed. He [Mo-tzu] was religious, and they [Confucians] were ritualists" (*Ibid.*: 295).

In the second century CE, Daoist religion developed in parallel to Daoist philosophy, providing a framework of ritual and spiritual practice (Cohen,

---

[40] The *Dao De Jing* is the common name used for the text that was originally referred to as Lao-tzu. "*Lao* means 'old,' and *tzu* means 'wise one'" (Wong, 1997:26). Very little is known about the author(s) of this text. Some say the book was written by Lao-tzu's students or others influenced by him. Others say Lao-tzu was a fictitious character and that the book is actually a collection of teachings of other thinkers with similar ideas (Wong, 1997).

1998). Sacred texts were created, inspired by Buddhism's scriptures (Wong, 1997a).

> Buddhism in China jostled for cultural space with Taoism from the start, and as a result over the centuries the two religions interacted constantly, affecting each other in a complex pattern of exchanges going far beyond any simple borrowing... By the fourth century, we see clear signs of the absorption of Buddhist material into *Shangqing* scriptures, in the case of the *Sutra in Forty-two Sections* (Barrett, 1990: 141).

Barrett explains that Buddhist accusations of Daoist 'plagiarism' should be examined in the context of the 'common currency' of ideas, titles, and terminology traded between Daoists and Buddhists. Some even speculated that Lao-tzu and the Buddha were one and the same; Lao-tzu simply changed his appearance to express a version of his message in India (*Ibid.*).

The spiritual rituals of Daoist religion and the wisdom of Daoist philosophy combined to make Daoism a way of life. In the 10th century CE, Confucian scholars,

> embraced the quintessence of Daoism and admired the mental discipline of Zen Buddhism, but they did not want to abandon Confucian values. These scholars initiated a synthesis of Taoism, Buddhism, and Confucianism that focused on the dual cultivation of body and mind (Wong, 1997a: 81).

This synthesis accounts for the two officially recognized Daoist schools.[41] The *Zhengyi*, or Celestial Masters, grew out of southern China and are "largely lay-based, exorcistic, and devoted to martial deities" (Kohn, 2009: 154). The *Quanzhen*, or school of Complete Perfection, emerged from northern China, focused on "individual transformation and was characterized by monasticism, ascetic practices, and mystical experience" (*Ibid.*: 158).

The Way of Complete Perfection – also referred to as Complete Reality – began in the 12th century CE, and continues to be the primary monastic form of Daoism today. The efforts made to harmonize Confucianism, Buddhism,

---

[41] Other schools, as well as local cults and rituals, contribute to the dynamic practices of modern Daoism. Many modern Daoists study specific texts and lineages through individual teachers rather than adhering to one of the two main orders (Kohn, 2009).

and Daoism (Miller, 2008) proved futile, and after Daoists lost a series of debates with Buddhists in 1281, many Daoist texts were destroyed. After this setback, though, Daoism flourished under the Ming and Qing dynasties through the early 20th century. *Daoyin* healing exercises were integrated into popular religious culture and medicine to promote longevity, inner alchemy (subtle transformations of interior energies), and martial arts (Kohn, 2006). These exercises became the foundation for the Daoist practices of *qigong* and *taijiquan*.

Daoism in China has suffered greatly since 1949, especially during the Great Proletarian Cultural Revolution (1966-76), when open practice of the religion was prohibited and Daoist temples were destroyed (Miller, 2008). Its recovery began in mainland China in 1980.

> Leaders of the People's Republic of China have recognized Daoism as an important traditional religion of China and a potential focus for tourism, so many of the more scenic temples and monasteries have been repaired and reopened. Daoism is one of the five religions recognized by the People's Republic (Daoism, Buddhist, Islam, Catholicism and Protestantism). It is controlled by a state bureaucracy and the China Daoist Association... (Littlejohn 2009: 178).

The exact number of Daoist masters practicing in China is unknown, as many choose to avoid registering and training with the Chinese Daoist Association. Since 1979 there has also been an increase in Daoist practice and ritual within towns and villages of provinces such as Fujian. People visit the local Daoist master, or *daoshi,* for a variety of reasons, including requests for protection and justice (*Ibid.*).

In 1947, *qigong* was re-introduced by the Chinese Communist party as a modernized, de-spiritualized, primarily medical version of traditional *dao-yin* practice. After a young party leader recovered fully from a life-threatening ulcer via gentle Daoist exercises and breathing, the Communist party saw an opportunity for addressing the shortage of biomedical doctors.[42] "The Party adopted the idea and, in a lengthy series of committee meetings, discussed what best to call the practice: adopted from traditional patterns but to be thoroughly cleansed from all ancient cosmology and 'superstitions,' it need-

---

[42] At the time there was one biomedical doctor for every 26,000 people in China (Kohn, 2006).

ed an appropriate modern name... they settled on 'breath exercise therapy' or *qigong liaofa*" (Kohn 2006: 200; Palmer in Kohn, 2006). Since then, the nature, quality, and political position of *qigong* have continued to change according to social needs in the People's Republic of China (Kohn, 2006).

On a global scale, Daoism has thrived as Chinese people have emigrated, especially to Europe, the Americas and East Asian countries (Littlejohn, 2009). As it branches out, "the living vine of Daoism" transforms and hybridizes its history with the new context in which it roots. "The new hybrid that is produced may have stems and shoots that are short lived, but other vines may wrap themselves around new global challenges and realities and transform them and the people involved, just as the *zhenren*[43] have been made and remade for well over 2,000 years" (*Ibid.*: 183). The current form of Daoism in the United States is often presented as a New Age spirituality or perennial philosophy[44] rather than a deep and complicated Chinese religious tradition. Kohn (2006) cites the narrow perspective of American Daoist centers that rely primarily on popularized versions of the *Dao De Jing*, modified to make sense to American minds.

First introduced by Chinese immigrants, *qigong* has become widespread in the United States due mainly to its assimilation into the health and fitness movement. It also offers an alternative to allopathic medicine. Kohn (2006) places contemporary American teachers of *qigong* into four categories: traditionalists, who often identify as Daoists and claim Chinese lineage; spiritualists, who present *qigong* as a spiritual but not a religious practice; medicalists, who have studied Chinese Medicine and teach *qigong* as a preventative or restorative practice; and positivists, who emphasize the scientific proof of the many benefits of *qigong*. She offers this observation about the adaptation of *qigong* and Daoism throughout the United States and Western societies.

> Created as an intentional secularization and medicalization of religious-based practices, Qigong is absorbed back into Daoist practice both in China and overseas and contributes to its formation in the 21st century. Just as the spread of Daoist teachings and practices into Western cultures leads to a new dimension of the religions, so the growth of the Qigong movement is in the process of leading to a reinterpretation of

---

[43] *Zhenren* is one who knows the methods for nourishing and preserving life, an enlightened one (Kunio, 1990).
[44] See Aldous Huxley (1945).

the religion. It is not what it used to be, and we do not know what it will be like. Studying Qigong in America is fascinating as it shows religion in the making and cultural interchange at its rawest front (*Ibid.*: 229).

Daoism is very much 'alive' globally, taking on new meaning and application as it is received by diverse cultures. I offer yet another interpretation of Daoism and its practices, in this case in the context of their potential to inform approaches to peace.

6.3 DAOISM AS ENERGETIC PEACE: THE GREAT TRIAD

> "With respect to philosophy Taoism probably delivers the clearest, simplest, and at the same time, most mature interpretation of energetic concepts of peace" (Dietrich, 2012a: 50).

Dietrich (2012a) writes about the Daoist Great Triad – heaven, human, and earth – in which "Heaven represents the Spirit or Essence, Earth the Substance and Man the synthesis of both and mediator between them, himself partaking of the dual nature of Heaven and Earth" (Cooper, 1972: 81). The number three underscores the need for equilibrium in human nature and the importance of a harmonious balance of heaven and earth (*Ibid.*).

In this position of tension between heaven and earth, the human being recognizes unity in apparent contradictions. She manifests peace from *yin-yang* dualism; her existence is one of both spirit and substance, heaven and earth. She exhibits qualities of the earth, such as animal instincts and urges, yet also aspires to the divine. "Thus it becomes clear that peace in this worldview can only be understood as that balance and harmony between heaven and earth as it is perceivable and producible by the human being" (Dietrich, 2012a: 47). Luckily,

> by virtue of its very complexity, the human body is eminently able to charge itself with energy and thus to transmute itself. 'Of all beings, the human is the most spiritual' say the Taoist texts, for with a round head (like Heaven), square feet (like Earth), five viscera (like the planets), and so many other points of correspondence, every person has innumerable points of correlation with the surrounding universe which

can be put into correspondence with a great many spatiotemporal cycles... Thus, each person can not only live a healthy life, but also radiate energy, that is, become transcendent (Schipper, 1993: 41).

In Daoism, harmony is maintained and equilibrium restored when the human being realigns with the divine breath, the natural flow of the Dao. Dietrich integrates Kam-por Yu's etymological breakdown of the Chinese Cantonese term for peace, *he ping*. In its complete form, it can be interpreted as "calm breath in resonance[45] with the divine breath in the whole world" (Yu, as cited in Dietrich, 2012a: 48). Similarly, mythologist Joseph Campbell advises, "The goal of life is to make your heartbeat match the beat of the universe, to match your nature with Nature" (Campbell, as cited in Kumar & Whitefield, 2006: 202). By cultivating the breath, one becomes capable of following the harmony evident in the natural world. This harmony initially arises in one human being, and from there it grows to harmony with others, and consequently harmony with the whole world.

What occurs outside such harmony is a disruption to the balance between *yin* and *yang*, but such disruption is a natural, regular process. As with homeostasis, there is a natural urge and process to regain equilibrium. It is possible, however, that *yin-yang* may become unbalanced to such an extreme that the tendency towards harmony cannot be followed. "Then the two great cosmic forces fall apart to form a duality of simple good and bad, which suggests the existence of good and bad actors" (Dietrich, 2012a: 47). This duality then permeates the emotions, wishes and desires of human beings, leading to an imbalance of the system, a state of peacelessness that generates fear.

Indeed, the manifestation of peace requires more than just breath. It entails letting go of desires and the craving for control. On one level, it means offering the utmost understanding for others' perspectives and circumstances. On a higher level, it surrenders passions, *wu wei,* creating freedom to follow a path of self-actualization (Cooper, 1972; Dietrich, 2012a). In the *Dao De Jing,wu-wei* is paired with the phrase *wu buwei*, "and there will be nothing that is not done" (Kohn, 2000: 1067).

---

[45] "Chapter 6 of the Huainanzi describes resonance as being both crucial to the workings of the cosmos and deeply mysterious and hard to fathom" (Major, Meyer, Queen & Roth, 2012:8).

In this early text, non-action means retaining an inner core of quietude and letting the world move along as it naturally proceeds... In the *Zhuangzi*, non-action appears as a more psychological mode and is a characteristic of spontaneity, the main quality of the embodied Dao. It means to be free in mind and spirit and able to wander about the world with ease and pleasure, to engage in an ecstatic oneness with all-there-is (*Ibid.*).

Another aspect of non-action with roots in the cosmological concepts of the Han is the "perfect alignment with the movements of the seasons, the planets, and the times" (*Ibid.*). *Yin-yang* acts as a guide to non-action. It is less about doing nothing than doing the right thing at the right time (Kohn, 2000). Put simply, *wu wei* is about acting naturally –

> not an intentional action or an omission to do something, rather it is a way of doing things that is unique to Daoism and Daoist master sages... similar to a kind of natural or spontaneous conduct that occurs without deliberation and intention. It comes directly from the storehouse of *dao* and its limitless *de*[46](Littlejohn, 2009: 17).

Some Westerners or Non-Daoists struggle with the concept of doing what is natural, acting spontaneously. These people want actions to be guided by thorough deliberation about choices and their consequences.

> But in Daoism, moving naturally along with *dao* is not negative. It is the way out of the tangles we have created for ourselves by the institutions, rules and distinctions that clutter our minds and generate tension in our life together. The numinosity of *wu-wei* conduct lies in the fact that it accords in the situation with an efficacy that can only be attributed to the *dao* and could never have been a result of human

---

[46] *De* can be translated as virtue, power, or potentiation, and Littlejohn (2009) advises against reducing the meaning to just one translation. "If one moves in harmony with dao, he will have *de*" (Littlejohn, 2009:17). Schipper (1993) cautions that *de* should be distinguished from virtue, because virtue comes from the Latin *vir*, meaning 'male'. He states that *de*, the creative power of the Dao, is feminine. Meanwhile, in the *Huainanzi*, "Potency (*de*) is the activation of the Way in the phenomenal world... potency has the connotation of 'to accumulate'. For example, during the spring and summer, the potency of yang accumulates while the potency of yin reciprocally diminishes" (Major, Meyer, Queen & Roth: 2012:6).

wisdom, planning or contrivance… In *wu-wei*, the individual is in harmony with the *dao* and this reveals itself in a person's *de* (Littlejohn, 2009: 18).

Itinvolves "allowing the maximum of individual liberty and understanding the views of others… a yielding, primarily a yielding of the self, the ego, as that which is responsible for introducing selfishness and dissonance" (Cooper, 1972: 73). While action is often the product of endless mind chatter, a busy response to desires and self-created problems, *wu-wei* is a quieting of the rational mind that allows for clarity via intuition. The non-action of *wu-wei* is not synonymous with inaction. Rather, it is a constant return to the motionless center, from where an open mind and pure spirit can move spontaneously at any moment in any direction.

Personally, I recall several instances when a state of *wu-wei* became essential for responding to a perceived crisis situation. My work with *Los Embajadores* in Tijuana and at a drop-in center for people experiencing homelessness in Portland, Oregon, often meant being present in situations of violence and violation. As a leader in these settings, I needed to listen without reacting, pause before making decisions or taking action, and thereby serve as a source of solutions and de-escalation. In these *wu-wei* moments, I could sense myself moving involuntarily into a place of almost-stillness. I became centered and ready, my mind instantly clear, senses alert, and entire system focused on reading and receiving information in order to problem-solve. This state allowed me to become unattached to preconceived notions and judgments about what should or should not be done.

Just as Dietrich (2012a) correlates fear and peacelessness to an extended disequilibrium of the human being's natural forces, Cooper writes about the occurrence of violence when the human being drifts away from living a life of *wu-wei*. Violence in any form, whether an act of physical destruction or an impatient thought, is an expression of an infantile reaction, a symptom of immaturity. Once enacted, it is quickly exhausted and lacks sustained power (Cooper, 1972). Non-violence, on the other hand, is the product of *wu-wei*.

> It (non-violence) has sustained power as opposed to the disintegrating and dissipating qualities of violence. The incidence of violence in any of its forms is also symptomatic of a breakdown in either society or the individual, be it international murder by states, as in war, or in personal violence (*Ibid.*: 78-79).

Cooper (1972) also sees the need to let go of the false notion of security as part of *wu-wei*. When too focused on security as a preventative solution – avoiding the problems of tomorrow – the present of today may pass unnoticed. Moving beyond the desire for security and returning to the motionless center is the only real security.

Living in *wu wei* seems ideal for maintaining a non-violent society of human beings. But how is it possible? What are the ways that peace can be restored when imbalance is natural and occurs daily? Lao-tzu says,

> *Wei wu wei*
> Act without acting
> Serve without serving
> Taste without tasting
>   Big, little, many, few –
> Repay hatred with *Te*
>
> Map difficult through easy
> Approach great through narrow.
>
> The most difficult things in the world
> Must be accomplished through the easiest.
> The greatest things in the world
> Must be accomplished through the smallest.
>
> Therefore the Sage
> Never attempts great things
> And so accomplishes them.
>
> Quick promises
>   Mean little trust.
> Everything easy
>   Means great difficulty.
> Thus for the Sage
>   Everything is difficult,
> And so in the end
> Nothing is difficult.
>   (Lao-tzu, 1993: 63).

6.4 Birth, Death, and the Dao

The transformation of energy that occurs over a human's life – from its original derivation at birth from the Dao to its return to the Dao at physical death – echoes an energetic understanding of peace described by Dietrich:

> Nothing new is therefore ever created, but *energy* constantly changes its form… The striving for the sublation of dualities is founded in the belief that everything has been one at the origin and will become one again… everything is perceived to be one, the separation of body and mind is also not possible in this worldview (Dietrich, 2012a: 51, 58).

The Daoist Internal Alchemical *neidan* practice involves storing, refining, and transmuting the three different energy forms by working with the external, internal and mind aspects of the body. The goal of these techniques is to attain immortality, or for one's spirit to join with the Dao (Baldrian-Hussein, 1990). They produce the seed of original spirit, the primordial vapor of the Dao, within the body. From inside the body, this original spirit connects the human to the energy of the outside cosmos. It can be cultivated and prepared to return to the Dao when the physical shell dies. The human's essence, which gained distinction from the Dao at birth by the separation of three energies, returns to its original form upon death, re-merging with the undifferentiated energy of the Dao (Wong, 1997a). "… a *neidan* master is thought not to die, but to undergo a voluntary metamorphosis" (Baldrian-Hussein, 1990: 762). This inner process bears resemblance to Dietrich's quote (2012a, see Section 3.3.2), which names *Dasein* as the human being's defining energetic deviation from the universe.

CHAPTER 7: *YI JING,* THE BOOK OF CHANGES

> This is why the sages composed the I Ching, to explain the Celestial Tao signs, making plain therein the changes of positive and negative, fullness and emptiness, advance and withdrawal, survival and destruction. Those indications of what to aim for and what to avoid are excellent indeed (Lu Tung-pin in Cleary, 1986: 7).

Among the most influential classic Daoist texts are the *Dao De Jing, Chuang-Tzu,* and *Yi Jing*.[47] In an energetic worldview, these texts are not authoritative; they serve as pointers and sources of inspiration. "One of the purposes of Taoist literature is to help to develop this special sensitivity and responsiveness to master living situations" (Cleary, 1988: 4). Their lessons are most meaningful in practice. Imanera puts it simply: "Embodying is the important first step... be authentic, full of the deep mystery" (Imanera, 2012f). I have chosen to elaborate here on the *Yi Jing* because I have interacted most with it through embodiment of its energetic principles.

---

[47] In addition to these and other well-known books, there is also a great collection of Daoist scriptures. However, Imanera (2012f) has explained that engaging with these scriptures requires formal vows of obedience to the precepts and petitioning the spirits. Imanera states that reading hagiographies, such as that of Sun Bu'er, are pre-requisites to study of the scriptures.

7.1 HISTORY OF THE *YI JING*

The *Yi Jing*, one of the oldest Chinese texts (Cleary, 1986), has been translated and commented on by thousands of scholars from diverse fields. For my own work, I rely primarily on Thomas Cleary's 1986 introduction to the sacred text[48] because it is written from a Daoist perspective. But I also draw from the more mystical shamanic translation by Stephen Karcher (2009), known for his work in divination studies. Cleary introduces the *Yi Jing*'s power in captivating audiences for over two thousand years. "It has been considered a book of fundamental principles by philosophers, politicians, mystics, alchemists, yogins, diviners, sorcerers, and more recently, by scientists and mathematicians" (Cleary, 1986: 3). The text first received attention in the West four hundred years ago, when a Christian missionary informed a German philosopher-mathematician of the similarities between the *Yi Jing* and the binary arithmetic system (*Ibid.*). In his foreword to Richard Wilhelm's *Yi Jing* translation, C.G. Jung writes, "The ancient Chinese mind contemplates the cosmos in a way comparable to that of the modern physicist, who cannot deny that his model of the world is a decidedly psychophysical structure" (Jung, 1949: xxiv).

Four authors are credited with creating the *Yi Jing*. First was Fu Hsi, the earliest Chinese ruler on record and a "cultural prototype" recognized for having taught the basic arts of hunting, fishing, and animal husbandry. According to legend, he invented the sixty-four trigrams of the *Yi Jing* based on the patterns of a turtle shell used as a divine diagram for shamanic divination (Chia and North, 2010; and Cleary, 1986). King Wen and the Duke of Chou, models of enlightened rule, are considered the creators of the sayings that correlate with each of these sixty-four signs and the six lines of the trigrams.

Confucius is also given credit for commentaries that make up the body of the *Yi Jing*, though recent studies contend that anonymous Confucian scholars were the real authors of these commentaries (Cleary, 1986). Cooper (1972) believes that Confucius likely had a role in editing the *Yi Jing*, but that its wisdom was recorded long before Daoism or Confucianism existed. Liu I-ming, the author of Cleary's translation, "identifies the inner

---

[48] This (1986) edition is comprised of Cleary's translation of Liu I-ming's commentary of the *Yi Jing*.

component of Confucianism ('the Tao of sages') with that of Taoism ('the Tao of immortals')" (Cleary, 1986: 6). From this perspective, humanity's social development, usually associated with Confucianism, and its spiritual development, associated with Daoism, are interrelated (*Ibid.*).

The many applications of the *Yi Jing* have varied over time, but "it is a matter of verifiable record that the *I Ching* signs came to be used as a more or less esoteric notation system for describing elements, processes, and experiences in certain developmental practices involving special uses of body and mind" (Cleary, 1986: 4). From Jung's (1949: xxiv) perspective, "Just as causality describes the sequence of events, so synchronicity to the Chinese mind deals with the coincidence of events". People the world over continue to engage with the *Yi Jing*, and it remains remarkable in its versatility. It has never been designated to the domain of any specific religion or school of thought, nor is there a single approach to its usage (Cleary, 1986). Its overarching themes are change and transformation, thus its common title *Book of Changes*. Karcher explains how these themes are inherent in the very meaning of *yi:*

> Philosophically, *yi* is primordial change, the mutations or transformation that initiate the process of generation and transformation in all the Myriad Beings, *Wanwu*... Through *yi* you can seize the moment (*shi*), changing and moving as fluidly as the creative force behind it. Change and its symbols were made to connect the *yi* of the universe and the Way to your own *yi,* your creative imagination, if you choose to use it (Karcher, 2009: 2).

As a divination tool, the wisdom of the *Yi Jing* cannot be trivialized. It requires attuned concentration and effort on the user's part, and rewards with prescient self-analysis and situational assessment (Cleary, 1986).

Jung reinforces thoughtful handling of the ancient text. "The *I Ching* insists upon self-knowledge throughout... It is appropriate only for thoughtful and reflective people who like to think about what they do and what happens to them – a predilection not to be confused with the morbid brooding of the hypochondriac" (Jung, 1949: xxxiv). He advises against clinging to certitude when consulting it, and reinforces this approach with his own background in psychotherapy and medical psychology. Remember, professionals work in these fields amongst great quantities of the unknown, often utilizing effective methods without knowing exactly how or why they work.

> The irrational fullness of life has taught me never to discard anything, even when it goes against all our theories (so short-lived at best) or otherwise admits of no immediate explanation. It is of course disquieting, and one is not certain whether the compass is pointing true or not; but security, certitude, and peace do not lead to discoveries. It is the same with this Chinese mode of divination. Clearly the method aims at self-knowledge, though at all times it has been put to superstitious use (*Ibid.*).

Various translators and *Yi Jing* scholars express concern over its appropriate and respectful use. Karcher (2009) encourages going beyond reading the *Yi Jing,* to conversing with it and incorporating its insights as a guide in life. My own relationship with the text has developed through embodied castings of *Yi Jing* hexagrams, and then reflecting on their lessons and guidance.

7.2 DAOISM AND THE *YI JING*

7.2.1 Time, Change, & Transformation

For Daoists, the *Yi Jing* is not only a book of divination, but also a work hinting at the 'celestial mechanism' or 'workings of Heaven'. Heaven "commonly refers to the source of creation and direction of the universe; the Way of Heaven, or Celestial Tao, is the body of universal principle underlying all manifestations" (Cleary, 1986: 6). Coming into harmony with the Celestial Dao's design is the way to experience the purpose and essence of life. Here, Daoist interpretation emphasizes the interrelated concepts of time and change, where "… time is characterized by change, and particular times are characterized by specific relations of opposing or complementary forces taking place in the course of this flux" (*Ibid.*). Time is more about the interplay of distinct and constantly changing forces in relationship to one other. 'Celestial time' is the dynamic between a human being's present condition and her higher potential, which does not progress in a linear way. "For Taoists, to harmonize with the celestial in human life means to deal with each 'time,' each combination of relations and potentials, in such a way as to achieve an appropriate balance of relevant forces and their modes of manifestation" (*Ibid.*: 7).

This concept illuminates Imanera's remarks that time does not exist for her, only *timing* (Imanera, 2012b). Timing accounts for a choice or action corresponding or conflicting with the dynamic interplay of energies in the moment it is taken. Viewing life in terms of timing brings attention back to the present moment. "Appropriate time" (Cleary, 1986) sees feasibility or value in actions based on their surrounding arrangement of conditions. And so *wu wei* comes into play: an awareness of the need for action or non-action in order to harmonize with the current time. "One of the outstanding teachings of Taoism is the strength of weakness… The *yin* power of passivity is more enduring than the *yang* force of direct action: the one has a controlled, sustained power, the other is quickly spent and dissipated" (Cooper, 1972: 37).

In this manner, the *Yi Jing* aids realization of the Dao, especially in the practice of spiritual alchemy. Daoist mystic Lu Tung-pin described the text as the secret of the celestial mechanism, and a tool for assessing the quality of the current situation and its suitability for doing or nondoing (Cleary, 1986). It offers insights into the structure of events and living harmoniously with the "pulse of existential time" (*Ibid.*: 6-7). Eleventh century scholar Ch'eng I, a recognized figure in the Sung dynasty reformation of Confucianism, adds a specifically Daoist take on the *I* (*Yi*):

> The word *I* of *I Ching* means change; that is, changing in accord with the time so as to follow the Tao. As a book, the *I Ching* is vast and comprehensive: by following the principles of essence and life, understanding the reasons of the obscure and the obvious, and comprehending the conditions of things and beings, it shows the way to enlighten people and accomplish tasks (Ch'eng I, as cited in Cleary, 1986: 4-5).

Confucians and Daoists read the terms "essence and life" differently. For Confucians, they apply to human nature and destiny; for Daoists (who accept Confucianism but place it within a wider scope), to mind and body, or spirit and energy (Cleary, 1986).

The text's principles of transformation are of 'Heaven', because they are inherent in the design of the universe (*Ibid.*). Understood on a human level, they are reflected in the possibilities of the mind, which enables practicing the Dao. "By practice of the Tao the mind is completed by being transformed into an objective reflection of Heaven or universal law" (*Ibid.*: 8). Thus the *Yi Jing* is a guide for transformation via divine relationship with the Dao.

Imanera classifies *Yi Jing* divinations in three ways: "to connect with the spirits of change, to understand a spatiotemporal map, and to heal (including ways to communicate the symbolized alchemical ingredients in *neidan*[49] practices)" (Imanera, 2012f). She describes its sixty-four signs as holding oracular formulas that allow access to the intuitive mind. As a Daoist shaman, she engages with the *Yi Jing's* spirits of change in an embodied way – the approach she taught me. Such use clearly differs from the traditional reading of the text as a Confucian scripture (*Ibid.*).

> Daoists relate the eight trigrams to areas of the body, or more generally in the navel. Many scholars study the 'statements' or the interpretations, and lack embodied understandings. So when you learned the hand patterns of the *Bagua* you learned to embody the energetic fields. This provides you with a kinesthetic understanding of the elements/phases/patterns of energy: heavens, wind, water, mountain, earth, thunder, fire, and lake. The *Yi Jing* also is a guide to the eight nodal days of the year, the equinoxes, solstices, and the first day of each season. By meditating on these spirits the adept achieves a long life (*Ibid.*).

Considering the *Yi Jing's* vast scope of wisdom and various potential shamanic applications, my relationship with it is still very young. During my training with Imanera, I have seen the *Yi Jing* work as a diagnostic tool for treating clients, and I have practiced embodiment of the eight trigrams of the *Bagua* by meditating with mudras.[50] An introduction to the essential principle of *yin-yang* is necessary to elaborate on these specific applications of the *Yi Jing* and Daoist cosmovision.

---

[49] *Neidan* is the Daoist practice of Inner Alchemy.
[50] Mudras are discussed in greater detail in Chapter 10.

7.2.2 *Yin-yang*: an Overview

The well known *taiji* symbol shows the great forces of the universe, *yin-yang*, held in balance, with equality at the root of all manifestation. According to Wong (1997), *yin* and *yang* were originally terms used to describe the absence and presence of sunlight on mountain slopes, mutually interdependent and both contained in the all-encompassing circle of unity. Their nature is one of balance; Dietrich (2012a) and Cooper (1972) both elaborate on the significant consequences of prolonged disequilibrium of *yin-yang* forces.

> If the two forces are working in perfect balance, a unity is achieved which becomes a power in itself and has a controlled force behind it. On the other hand, imbalance and disharmony have no power, but disintegrate into total ineffectiveness. Anything out of harmony… is to be regarded as a failure in, or disturbance of, the balance of the yin-yang forces. This applies not only to human beings but to all life in the maintenance of its health and wellbeing (Cooper, 1972: 39).

The small point of white in the black, and black in the white, are no accidents. They symbolize the principle that every being holds within itself some part of its opposite, and remind us that each force can give rise to its opposite as they perpetually interact (*Ibid.*). Imanera describes the *yin-yang* similarly:

> Remember the time before you were born? You were undifferentiated but due to constant change, the two pneumas (*qi*) *yin-yang* – the two functions of the Dao – you cycled into existence. These are not absolutes because each contains the seed of the other. The *yin* of winter is transformed into the *yang* of summer… Time is *yang* and space is *yin*… These affect everything in the universe… Is time cyclical or from point A to B? It is cyclical, so perhaps death is a grand illusion? Awake is life, asleep is death or is it the other way around? Ask Chuang-tzu (Imanera, 2012f).

These dual forces are inherent in all things. "The *yin* principle is the negative, dark side and also symbolizes the feminine element, which is the potential, the existential, the natural" (Cooper, 1972: 28). *Yin* is associated with stillness, flexibility and receptivity. It is creative, the potential that gave birth to its opposite. *Yang* is the positive, light, masculine – the actual, essential, the spirit. It is associated with activity, strength, and hardness (Cooper, 1972; Wong, 1997a).

7.2.3 *Yin-yang* in the *Yi Jing*

The *Yi Jing's* founding, interacting forces can be understood as *yin-yang*. These principles hold cosmic significance as well as a presence in the phenomenal world, and the *Yi Jing* depicts their interplay and mutations (Cooper, 1972). It does not actually use the terms *yin-yang*; they are indicated symbolically and reflect many meanings. For example, *yin-yang* embody "the mundane and the celestial, the acquired and the primal, the human mind and the mind of Tao…" (Cleary, 1986: 16). In Cleary's (1986) version of the *Yi Jing*, he notes that the two are used regularly in association with flexibility (*yin,* earth) and firmness (*yang,* heaven).This dichotomy, as with most uses of *yin-yang,* applies also to the human being. Firmness is found in the real knowledge of the mind of Dao, flexibility in the conscious knowledge of the human mind. Of course, this division can be bridged through practice.

Yin-yang is used by Daoists and Confucianists alike to indicate dualism of heaven and earth in the manifest world. In Daoism, it "became the cosmic symbol of primordial unity and harmony and manifest phenomenal duality… the two great regulating forces of cosmic order in the phenomenal world" (Cooper, 1972: 27). As intermediaries, humans might unite and balance the dual forces (Cleary, 1986). This is one aspect of living the Dao, an integral part of practices such as *qigong* and *taiji*. An excerpt from the *Book of Balance and Harmony* describes this unification: "Openness is the form of Heaven, tranquility is the form of Earth… The Tao of Heaven and Earth is openness and tranquility; when openness and tranquility are within oneself, this means Heaven and Earth are within oneself" (*Ibid.*: 11). For Daoists, openness and tranquility are essential for humanity to perceive and adapt to patterns of change.

7.3 THE MAP OF THE *YI JING*

The *Yi Jing* contains sixty-four signs, called hexagrams. Each sign is made of six lines, and each line is either solid, representing *yang*, or receptive,[51] representing *yin*. The first two signs indicate heaven (full *yang*) and earth (full *yin*). The other sixty-two "illustrate particular 'paths' or aspects of the Tao in practice, again with each line of each sign showing the place of yin or yang in a given 'time' or phase of that particular path" (*Ibid.*: 21). *Yin* and *yang* take on various meanings, depending on the state of the reader and the phase of the path.

As Karcher (2009) states, the *Yi Jing* requires engagement; it involves more than simply reading a book. There are myriad nuanced interpretations of each line of the hexagrams available – based on its *yin-yang* quality, its interaction and placement with other lines, and its effects on human life. For the purpose of this book, though, the Daoist approach is most pertinent.

> Overall, Taoism uses the idea of balanced integration of *yin* and *yang* in the sense of fulfillment of the complete or whole human potential, living in the world and fulfilling worldly tasks, yet maintaining inner contact with a greater dimension, referred to as 'celestial,' which interpenetrates the worldly plane in some way (Cleary, 1986: 26).

In my own experience, I have interacted with the *Yi Jing* primarily through embodiment of the *Bagua*, the eight trigrams "held to represent fundamental elements of life through which human development can be fostered; hence in Taoist alchemy they are sometimes called the 'cauldron of the eight trigrams,' in which the refinement of consciousness is carried out" (*Ibid.*: 22). Embodiment of the *Bagua* is a shamanic practice.

---

[51] While commonly referred to as 'broken', the *yin* line can also be considered 'open' or, in the words of Imanera (2012c), 'receptive'.

7.4 Embodied *Yi Jing:* the *Bagua*

The *Bagua's* eight trigrams represent all permutations of the two lines and forces, *yin* and *yang.* They symbolize the dualism of nature, demonstrating the unity and diversity manifested in the cosmos and all its qualities (Cooper, 1972). Karcher (2009) introduces the *Bagua* as a means for entering the world of shamans and intermediaries.[52]

The eight trigrams, he explains, "embody basic energies, processes or spirits activating the world we live in and... were used to organize a wide range of cycles and associations" (Karcher, 2009: 32). They become the eight helping spirits, represented by eight forces of nature: heaven, earth, fire, water, wind, thunder, lake and mountain. Chinese medicine and magic use these spirits as effective talismans for warding off evil forces and attracting benevolent ones.

7.4.1 Soul Retrieval with the *Bagua*

I first experienced this application of the *Bagua* assisting Imanera in medical *qigong*. Client J visited her to heal various physical, energetic, and spiritual ailments. In my role as apprentice, Imanera instructed me simply to embody and meditate with energetic elements from the *Bagua*, selected based on a prior *Yi Jing* consultation. In the first of two sessions, I became the lake; in the second, Imanera asked me to be the 'mountain' but showed me the mudra for 'wind'. Thus I was 'wind under the mountain'. We later discovered that this energetic combination is a treatment for obsessive-compulsive disorder, Client J's past diagnosis that we were unaware of at the time. Excerpts from these sessions' research journals capture my experiences, as lake and as wind under the mountain.

Session 1: During the intake, J's thoughts are splintered, it is difficult for her to finish one sentence or answer a question directly. Her energy is fractured, she has visible twitches. Nervous laughter follows her numerous questions. J lies down for her session, but she is rigid, her energy fiery. At

---

[52] The eight trigrams of the *bagua*, with a representation of *yin-yang* in the center. Created by Kathleen McGoey.

first, I am sensitive to the twitches that now jolt through J's entire body, I react, I am shaken.

I am eager and inspired to do what I can to contribute to J's healing. I draw focus away from my thoughts and breathe attention into my heart. I am holding lake mudra. The sounds of Imanera's soothing voice vibrate within me. Breathing into the lake, I feel myself reaching a depth of calmness and patience. Still attentive and aware on the surface, I am submerged in a dark, luscious depth that is safe, protected. Here there is consistency and stillness, I am no longer susceptible to J's erratic, charged energy. I offer the presence of water, flushing and flowing. Water flows through J's kidneys, allowing fear to drain. ~June 19, 2012

Session 2: Consciously, I am the mountain. I have a strong, solid, weighted base. I feel rooted. My energy is flowing deeply into the earth, strong in my legs and trunk. My chest and arms are warm, I feel the air moving. I am heavy yet high, reaching through the clouds to the light. I see Imanera's hands and body moving and flowing, I sway and move with her. Then I am still. ~June 26, 2012

7.4.2 Embodying the Eight Energies: A Shamanic Practice

Like Karcher, Imanera sees the *Bagua* as a shamanic tool placing the practitioner in between earth and heavens. Engaging with one of its eight energies enables the shaman to shape-shift and travel between worlds, for healing and other beneficial purposes (Imanera, 2012b).

> To control the power of the eight elements is a mystical practice. Accessing these energetic portals allows you to change your relationship to these elements or fundamental characteristics. It must be understood on three levels: physical, energetic and spiritual. This leads to greater transformative abilities. For example, when you place the tips of all fingers together you feel the creative strength and power. This is an ancient Daoist Hand Seal for *Qian* (Heavens). It fuses energetic powers of all three treasures. It is used to dissolve into the infinite space of the sun, moon, and stars (*Ibid.*, 2012f).

I engage with the *Bagua* by meditating with *mudras,* or Daoist hand seals (described in greater detail in section 10.2). Even as a novice, I have experienced these seals as a shape-shifting technique for embodying the *Bagua'*s eight elements. Due to their power and sacred nature, Imanera explains that the wisdom of the *Bagua* and *mudras* is passed along primarily by oral tradition, and only when a student is ready.

> If a student completes a year of training we can empower the form or activate it to become real on many planes of existence, not just the physical, through rituals of star-stepping, invocations and incantations. This is not talked about because it is beyond words. When you feel the change you have a direct knowledge that it is very very real (*Ibid.*).

Daoist practitioners Chia and North write that the *Bagua* can be used in meditation for collecting, gathering, and condensing *qi,* or cosmic energy. The energy vortex created by the *Bagua* helps to strengthen a connection to oneself and form a harmonious relationship with each of the eight forces of nature (Chia and North, 2010). Though Chia and North's approach to *Bagua* meditations differs from those I have practiced, still their depiction resonates with my experiences.

As an embodied, kinesthetic tool, the *Bagua* is also a shamanic medicine wheel. Chia and North (2010) propose a Daoist wheel based on Daoist creation myth. In this model of concentric spheres, *Wu Qi* is at the core of the wheel, representing the readiness of the empty mind. Moving outward, the next sphere is the Three Pure Ones, or three *dan tians*. Then come the eight forces of the universe – the eight trigrams of the *Bagua* – followed by the twelve Chinese zodiac signs. The outermost layer contains the sixty-four hexagrams of the *Yiching* (*Ibid.*). This map inspires future inquiry into the potential for applying the *Bagua* as a medicine wheel and a tool in elicitive peace and conflict work.

CHAPTER 8: INTUITIVE WISDOM: UNDERSTANDING THE DAO

In the history of the collective as in the history of the individual, everything depends on the development of consciousness. This gradually brings liberation from imprisonment in dyvola, 'unconsciousness,' and is therefore a bringer of light as well as of healing (Jung, 1969: 271-272).

In the first chapters of this book, I described my interest in the transformative processes that open hearts and minds and attune them with an intuitive wisdom held simultaneously within every living being and the universe. I mentioned experiences in my own life when I felt a shift in perspective and became more in tune with this wisdom. This leads me to wonder: is this type of wisdom – in my understanding, synonymous with *wisdom of the soul* and *universal wisdom* – referenced in other shamanic traditions, such as Daoism? If so, how is it envisioned, and what is the language that articulates its existence?

Different philosophical, psychological and spiritual perspectives offer diverse ways to consider intuitive wisdom. This diversity reflects the variety of individual relationships with intuition. Though similarities exist, each person will ultimately experience and use intuitive wisdom differently. In this chapter, I review several interpretations of intuition, primarily from psychological and spiritual perspectives, paying particular attention to the contributions of transpersonal psychologists. I describe my own transpersonal experience of 'knowing and unknowing' myself through shamanic painting. I conclude with two sections focusing on the Daoist perspective on intuitive wisdom and *wu wei*.

8.1 Interpreting Intuition: Enlightenment and the Still Small Voice Within

Carl Jung named intuition as one of four basic psychological functions, along with thinking, feeling, and sensation (Vaughan, 1979). He notes that the word *intuition* comes "from *intueri,* to look into or upon", defining it as:

> A basic psychological function… which transmits perceptions *in an unconscious way*. Everything, whether outer or inner objects or their associations, can be the object of this perception. Intuition has this peculiar quality: it is neither sensation, nor feeling, nor intellectual conclusion, although it may appear in any of these forms. Through intuition any one content is presented as a complete whole, without our being able to explain or discover in what way this content has been arrived at… Like sensation… it is an irrational… perceptive function. Its contents, like those of sensation, have the character of being given, in contrast to the 'derived' or 'deduced' character of feeling and thinking contents (Jung, 1959: 262-263).

According to Vaughan, everyone has experienced intuition. It is a way of knowing that 'rings true', though we often do not know *how* we know what we know. She portrays the 'still small voice within' as the one telling you the truth, even when you do not want to acknowledge it; accepting this intuitive truth requires willingness from the listener (Vaughan, 1979). Similarly, Schulz (1998: 22) writes "intuition is something we see and hear and feel within, an internal language that facilitates insight and understanding".

> It [intuition] requires a suspension of your natural disbelief. Many people, perhaps most, have to go through the act of intuiting and experience the amazing sensation involved before they can begin to implement intuition in their lives… For intuition is precisely that: another unique language created by the brain and the body to help us gain insight into and understanding of our past and to provide solutions for the future and help us create stronger, more pleasurable lives (*Ibid.*).

For some people, the intuitive sense is boundless, not limited to the typical sensory channels. Their intuitive perception becomes an avenue for accessing infinite realms through precognition, clairvoyance, telepathy, artistic inspiration, and mystical religious experience (Vaughan, 1979).

Spiritually, a deep connection to intuitive wisdom is often referred to as 'enlightenment', a change in perspective and appreciation for the simplest aspects of our lives. Moments of enlightenment might occur during seemingly mundane activity. "When you become enlightened it can come about through a very small or ordinary thing. You see, the most difficult thing for someone to accept is the plainness of their life. To discover the magnificence in every moment of a simple life is truly life's greatest reward" (Ni, 1997: 20). Enlightenment often arises as an experience of illumination, changing how the perceiving subject views the world around her. "The state which is called enlightenment or illumination is an intuitive experience wherein one penetrates behind appearances, to see things as they really are, to know them from within, through identification of the knower with the object known" (Vaughan, 1979: 175). Walsh adds, "Metaphorically it (enlightenment) refers to a dramatic sense of insight and understanding; literally, it refers to an experience of being illuminated or suffused with light" (Walsh, 2007: 67).

The association between reaching a new level of understanding and the sensation of being filled with light is familiar to many religious traditions. Vaughan refers frequently to Buddhist traditions' valuing of intuition, where enlightenment does not occur by following fixed teachings, but by a spontaneous and natural intuitive process. In Buddhism, enlightenment comes to a silent mind as an intuitive knowing of the truth. The systematic development of intuition is one of the aims of yoga, too (Vaughan, 1979). In the Daoist tradition, intuition is similarly cultivated through the practice of *qigong*.

Enlightenment is not the only term that describes an elevation of spirituality.

> These higher reaches are known by many names: *enlightenment* and *liberation, salvation* and *satori, fana* and *nirvana, awakening* and *Ruah Ha-qodesh*. Different names, but all point to the highest human possibility, which, paradoxically, is simply the recognition of who we really are (Walsh, 2007: 28).

Conceiving of this "highest human possibility" may be limited by a human being's propensity to favor rational faculties. Walsh alludes to this limitation, stating that in "who we really are" the 'who' may be "not only more than we think, but more than we *can* think" (*Ibid.*).

Theories about intuition's source have always varied. Ancient Greeks believed intuition was a message from the heavens and gods. Modern science would dismiss that idea, ascribing intuition to the seemingly infinite capacities of the brain. But Schulz, a medical doctor herself, offers examples of humans expressing extraordinary knowledge that, examined through a scientific lens, cannot be attributed to brain function. "We've always believed the brain is the repository of knowledge that we take in consciously on a rational level, but is it possible that the brain is also a *transmitter* of knowledge that comes to us unconsciously on a nonrational level?" (Schulz, 1998: 24). She returns to the ancient Greeks, and specifically Pythagoras, who offered an oxen sacrifice to the god Apollo after conceiving his famous theorem:

> … the station that broadcasts to our intuition is something external. It's a god outside of us – the soul or the divine consciousness… The divine consciousness speaks to our human consciousness, offering us quick, keen insights into the problems of everyday life and suggesting potential solutions through the language of intuition – the language of the soul (*Ibid.*: 25).

This interplay between divine and human consciousness helps decipher the role of intuition in *Yi Jing* divination. While the source of intuition appears external, as Schulz writes, tools like the *Yi Jing* help us crack the code to uncover the wisdom of spirits and ancestors found within us.

Ervin Laszlo, a leading systems theorist, coined 'the Akashic experience' to describe "a real, lived experience that conveys a thought, an image, or an intuition that was not, and very likely could not have been, transmitted by our senses either at the time it happened or at anytime beforehand – at least in our current lifetime… a lived experience in the extra- or non-sensory mode" (Laszlo, 2009: 1). The roots, source, and substance of this experience is the Akashic field, which exists beyond brain and body, and was long recognized in traditional cultures.

> In ancient India the Sanskrit word *Akasha* meant 'cosmic sky,' similar to our concept of space. But Akasha referred not only to space in the modern sense but also and above all to the higher spheres of life and existence. The Hindu seers believed that all things arise from, and re-descend into, the cosmic source they called Akasha. Akasha was seen as the first and most fundamental of the five elements… (*Ibid.*: 5).

The Akashic experience involves a sense of non-dualism, where the experiencing subject becomes aware that she is linked in "subtle but real ways" to other humans and the cosmos (*Ibid.*: 2). This quality of oneness is a trait of most transpersonal experiences.

8.2 AWAKENING INTUITION

Although often disregarded or undeveloped, intuition exists in everyone. "A Course in Miracles"[53] furthers the belief that the illumination of enlightenment emanates from within, and cannot be sought externally: "Those who seek the light are merely covering their eyes. The light is in them now. Enlightenment is but a recognition, not a change at all" (Vaughan and Walsh, 1983: 1). Intuition cannot be produced or sought in a forced manner. But a shift in valuing *how* we perceive and *how* we attend to what we know may aid in the recognition of intuitive wisdom's presence within us.

Intuition is a rich resource; it can play an integral role in creativity, problem-solving, and interpersonal relationships. (In Chapter 11, I describe intuitive ability as key to unlocking creativity otherwise restricted by rational objections). Yet, misunderstood, it is often discounted. "Intuition occurs when we directly perceive facts outside the range of the usual five senses and independently of any reasoning process... Scientists... have tried to rank it as cognition, a part of the rational mind, the thinking brain. But intuition is a perception, of seeing or hearing or feeling rather than thinking" (Schulz, 1998: 19, 22).

The unexpected options people access through intuitive wisdom make it relevant to transrational approaches to peace. Vaughan (1979) recommends a series of exercises that help suspend critical judgment, thus allowing intuition to emerge. She clarifies that awakening intuition does not imply removal of rational functions, which are needed to check intuitive perceptions and processes. Like *yin-yang*, intuition and rationality work together: the former emerges from a collective unconscious, and the latter plays an important role in interpreting and applying this wisdom on the personal level.

---

[53] http://acim.org/Lessons/index.html

At any given moment one is conscious of only a small portion of what one knows. Intuition allows one to draw on that vast storehouse of unconscious knowledge that includes not only everything that one has experienced or learned, either consciously or subliminally, but also the infinite reservoir of the collective of universal unconscious, in which individual separateness and ego boundaries are transcended (*Ibid.*: 4).

The challenge in awakening intuition for many is to temporarily *suspend* the rational voice that dominates our thoughts. Vaughan acknowledges that the idea of *learning* to elicit intuition is paradoxical. Intuitive experiences usually occur spontaneously, and excessive effort generates resistance that interferes with the intuitive process.[54] Therefore, awakening intuition is not about *making* experiences happen, but rather *allowing* space for them. Vaughan cites meditation as one of the most effective methods of tuning in to intuition, since most forms of meditation direct attention away from rational, analytic thinking, thereby allowing the intuitive voice to be heard.

Hua Ching Ni also suggests meditative concentration as an exercise for becoming aware of inner wisdom. "Concentration… is obtained by keeping your awareness upon the subtle actions that occur inside your thoughts, inside you, and inside your environment… Having intuitive power is attained by relaxing one's nervous system and quieting the active intellect. This masterly energy will spontaneously respond to a situation and give the advice you need" (Ni, 1997: 27-28). With regular practice, the meditative state gradually melds with one's everyday mindset. Eventually, sustained changes in consciousness occur which transform the practitioner's way of experiencing herself and her universe (Vaughan, 1979).

In his texts on energy medicine, biologist and biophysicist James Oschman (2003) illustrates this interaction between rationality and intuition. The first of our two major forms of consciousness is 'neurological consciousness', derived from the operations of the nerves and brain. The second is 'connective tissue', or 'continuum consciousness', which is more rapid and precedes neurological consciousness. Connective tissue consciousness operates "via the continuum pathway in the living matrix… (and) arises because the living matrix is an *excitable medium*, just as nerve

---

[54] Vaughan (1979) notes that the conscious mind, or ego, is at the root of this interference. The mind and ego are discussed in more depth in Chapter 9.

cells are excitable" (Oschman, 2003: 56). So, through connective tissue or continuum consciousness we essentially 'plug in' to the living matrix and a 'precognitive consciousness'. It may be in this intuitive, transrational state that artists and athletes do their most outstanding work. Neurological consciousness – or the rational filter – kicks in to help us integrate and function in our daily lives.

8.3 TRANSPERSONAL EXPERIENCES

> I now believe that consciousness and the human psyche are much more than accidental products of the physiological processes in the brain; they are reflections of the cosmic intelligence that permeates all of creation. We are not just biological machines and highly developed animals, but also fields of consciousness without limits, transcending space and time (Grof & Grof, 1990: 26).

If reason is the lens for perceiving at the *personal* level, intuition perceives at the *transpersonal* level. "Transpersonal experiences may be defined as experiences in which the sense of identity or self extends beyond (*trans*) the individual or personal to encompass wider aspects of humankind, life, *psyche*, and cosmos" (Vaughan & Walsh, 1993: 3). In this beyond-personal state, rational confines of time and space are transcended. The *personal* consciousness, on the other hand, sees the world as a series of separate objects and events that pertain to contexts of time and space. Both perspectives are valuable.

> In fact, both these levels of consciousness are part of human experience, and both are necessary for the fulfillment of human potential… direct experience of the transpersonal level affirms and evokes the intuitive mode of knowing. The task at hand is not to reject either of these views in favor of the other, but to expand our understanding and experience of consciousness to include both (Vaughan, 1979: 52-53).

Receptivity to subjective experience is the most crucial component of awakening intuition and transpersonal experiences, beyond even external stimuli. For Stanislav and Christina Grof, the "trigger" of such experiences is often a change in balance by which the unconscious suddenly gains the upper hand over ordinary awareness.

> The most important catalyst for spiritual emergencies is a deep involvement in various spiritual practices… in active forms of worship, such as trance dance, Sufi whirling, powerful drumming, gospel singing, or continuous chanting… (or) by less dramatic forms, such as sitting or moving meditation, contemplation, and devotional prayer (Grof & Grof, 1990: 33).

They propose opening energetic channels to cultivate receptivity to the transcendent, just as Imanera (2012d) teaches untying psychic knots and severing energetic cords to open energy gates and restore *qi* flow. Equally helpful is maintaining a non-interfering awareness in the midst of distracting ideas, sensations, and emotions, and trusting in the process of intuitive knowing (Vaughan, 1979). Many personal narratives in this book portray my own attempts at this challenging practice of non-interfering awareness.

The transpersonal experience enables a transcendence of boundaries between subject and object, knower and known (Vaughan, 1979). This allows the knower to unite with the known, understanding it via identification *with* it rather than information *about* it. "The process of awakening this non dual awareness, however, involves *disidentifying* from internal states and observing them" (*Ibid.*: 24). Such experiences are typically characterized by dissolution of distinctions between inner and outer, which are replaced by a sense of oneness with everything.[55]

> What these experiences have in common… is a universal affirmation of the human capacity for transcending ego boundaries and the limitations of the rational mind, and the fact that the essential truth of reality can only be apprehended intuitively. It is this direct apprehension of truth which characterizes, pure, spiritual intuition (*Ibid.*: 65).

This mystical experience is the form of intuitive awakening that most directly produces sensations of wellness and harmonious oneness.

---

[55] I endeavor to describe a personal experience of this nature in section 10.7.

> With this mystical intuitive power, you know everything, including the sufficiency of your spiritual nature. This is the way to master your life... you can allow all things around you to be what they are. In this way, everything can smoothly reach the Subtle Origin. You join the transformation, but at the same time you maintain the centeredness which is untouched by transformation (Ni, 1997: 27-28).

This corresponds to the *wu wei* practice of the *Dao De Jing*,

> The Sage...
> Leads people
>   Away from knowing and wanting;
> Deters those who know too much
>   From going too far:
> Practices non-action
>   And the natural order is not disrupted.
>   (Lao-tzu, 1993: 3).

Humanistic psychologist Abraham Maslow (1971) illustrates how a transpersonal sense of non-dualism can take shape in many different ways, including via the "highest love between man and woman", or other human relationships:

> While this transcendence of dichotomy can be seen as a usual thing in self-actualizing persons, it can *also* be seen in most of the rest of us in our most acute moments of integration within the self, and between self and the world. In the highest love between man and woman, or parent and child, as the person reaches the ultimates of strength, of self-esteem, of individuality, so also does he simultaneously merge with the other, lose self-consciousness and more or less transcend the self and selfishness. The same can happen in the creative moment, in the profound aesthetic experience, in the insight experience, in giving birth to a child, in dancing, in athletic experiences, and others which I have generalized as peak experiences (Maslow, 1971: 165).

Scientists, psychologists, and other researchers have named the transpersonal experience differently based on the focus of their studies. "These Akashic experiences can often encompass what William James called mystical experiences and what Abraham Maslow later referred to as peak experiences, and also what Carl Jung considered to be encounters with the numinous... They can take the form of a deeply rooted, embodied sense of unity, an awareness of great love, and a fundamental sense of interconnection" (Schlitz, 2009: 170).[56] Whether they are filled with pain or beauty, transpersonal experiences are often transformation catalysts. The state of revelation and cosmic consciousness they elicit quells doubts and replaces them with sensations of bliss, awe, and joy. Even a fleeting moment of such clarity produces a sense of illumination which a person may then choose to value, expand upon, and integrate – or to deny and repress (Vaughan, 1979).

Maslow coined the term "peak-experiences" to name the personal mystical revelations known by every high religion, including Buddhism, Daoism, Humanism, and Confucianism. He equates these with "ecstasies" or "transcendent" experiences (Maslow, 1970: 19-20)[57] and lists twenty-five religious aspects of peak-experiences, including:

- ... the whole universe is perceived as an integrated and unified whole... one is a part of it, one belongs in it...
- ... tremendous concentration of a kind which does not normally occur. There is the truest and most total kind of visual perceiving or listening or feeling.
- ... cognition of being (B-cognition) that occurs in peak-experiences tends to perceive external objects, the world, and individual people as more detached from human concerns... he (the perceiver) can see it (nature) in its own Being (as an end in itself) rather than as something to be used or something to be afraid of or something to wish for or to be reacted to in some other personal, human self-centered way.
- ... perception in the peak-experiences can be relatively ego-transcending... desireless, detached... it becomes more object-centered than ego-centered...

---

[56] Numinosity, wrote Jung, "is wholly outside conscious volition, for it transports the subject into the state of rapture, which is a state of will-less surrender" (Jung, 1954: 57). He describes numinosity as sourced from the contents of the unconscious (*Ibid.*).
[57] Maslow goes on to say that, "this intrinsic core-experience is a meeting ground not only, let us say, for Christians and Jews and Mohammedans but also for priests and atheists, for communists and anti-communists... for men and women... athletes and for poets, for thinkers and for doers" (Maslow, 1970: 28).

- The peak-experience is felt as a self-validating, self-justifying moment... so great and high an experience that it justifies not only itself but even living itself (*Ibid.*: 59-62).

Maslow believes it possible that "all or almost all people have or can have peak-experiences" (*Ibid.*: 29). Cleary describes "peak-experiences" in terms of the dynamic interplay of *yin-yang*. "... [P]ure *yang* may be used to allude to a peak experience, after which there is a reintegration of this enlightenment into life in the world, again balancing *yang* with *yin*... Pure *yang* refers to pure unbound consciousness... represented as spiritual immortality" (Cleary, 1986: 26). Embodied and interpreted through the *Bagua*, pure *yang* energy is Heaven, thus a peak-experience in Daoism holds the energetic qualities of the creative cosmic force.[58]

Grof and Grof describe certain transpersonal experiences, which they call "spiritual emergencies", as intensely challenging periods that impact the individual greatly. Spiritual emergencies are:

> critical and experientially difficult stages of a profound psychological transformation that involves one's entire being. They take the form of nonordinary states of consciousness and involve intense emotions, visions, and other sensory changes... often revolve around spiritual themes... feelings of oneness with the universe... In the most general terms, *spiritual emergence* can be defined as the movement of an individual to a more expanded way of being that involves enhanced emotional and psycho somatic health, greater freedom of personal choices, and a sense of deeper connection with other people, nature, and the cosmos (Grof & Grof, 1990: 31, 34).

They also acknowledge the divine quality of some spiritual emergencies, such as those of athletes and meditators reaching transcendental states. Grof and Grof emphasize the importance of spiritual emergencies' aftermaths, asserting that these transformations should ideally be integrated through a natural process of inner growth over a period of years. They concur with Vaughan (1979) and Maslow (1970) that the capacity for spiritual emergence

---

[58] "Pure yin" and "pure yang" are specialized terms that place *yin-yang* as opposites. "Pure yin refers to the mortal, earth-bound material dross, which must eventually obey the laws of matter" (Cleary, 1986: 26).

herent in all human beings, just like physical growth. When understood atural developmental processes that are sometimes difficult, spiritual emergencies can be sources of emotional and psychosomatic healing, positive personality shifts, and new problem-solving perspectives.

Maslow and Grof propose various methods for eliciting transpersonal experiences. Maslow (1970) suggests that psychoactive substances such as LSD (Lysergic Acid Diethylamide) have the potential to produce peak-experiences for study and observation. Monitored administering of psychedelic drugs might also offer a way to introduce ecstatic experience safely to non-peakers. Psychologists like Stanislav Grof have observed these states without the use of psychedelics, stimulated through techniques such as Holotropic Breathwork.[59] Grof refers to particular nonordinary states of consciousness as:

> *Holotropic* (literally, 'moving toward wholeness,' from the Greek *holos* = 'whole' and *trepein* = 'moving toward'). What makes these states a fascinating object of study is their heuristic, therapeutic, and evolutionary potential... Holotropic states cover a rich spectrum from those that shamans experience in their initiatory crises and use in their healing practices, native people induce in rites of passage and healing ceremonies, and initiates experienced in ancient mysteries of death and rebirth, to extraordinary experiences that occur in the systematic spiritual practices of yogis, Buddhists, Taoists, Kabbalists, Sufis, Christian hesychasts, and Desert Fathers, as well as those that are found in the accounts of mystics of all countries and historical periods (Grof, 2009: 194-195).

Regardless of *how* transpersonal realms are accessed, Maslow (1970) maintains that mankind might be divided into two religions: peakers and non-peakers. The former have peak-experiences, and accept and make use of them. The latter either have peak-experiences but repress them – and

---

[59] Holotropic Breathwork is a transpersonal modality using music, rhythm, and breathing that, by allowing access to non-ordinary states of consciousness, emulates the effects of drugs like LSD. Holotropic Breathwork offers the advantage of enabling the practitioner to be able to get out of a bad 'trip' if needed, because the change in consciousness is produced without consumption of drugs or medicine. I have had the good fortune of personally experiencing deep, unpleasant and uncomfortable transformation and awakening through this method of self-discovery. http://www.holotropic.com/index.shtml

therefore cannot apply them for personal therapy and fulfillment – or simply never have them.

8.4 NON-PEAKERS AND COGNICENTRISM

Throughout my research, I have witnessed occasional resistance to talking about transpersonal experiences, to the point of being dismissive about their very existence. I have become curious about such skepticism regarding the topic. It is important to first acknowledge that, as Walsh (2007) states, there is no proof that all sources of inner vision are relatable or similar in nature. It is possible some of these sources are aspects of the individual mind, while others are transcendent, either within or beyond us. "... [I]nterpretations of phenomena in general, and of spirits in particular, are determined by their 'world hypothesis': their fundamental assumptions about the nature of the world and reality" (*Ibid.*: 148). Peoples' ideas regarding intuitive wisdom, enlightenment, higher human potential, or universal consciousness are determined by their foundational beliefs.

Vaughan (1979) emphasizes the influence of attitudes and beliefs on whether or not one is willing to consider new ways of knowing and experiencing. If someone does not believe it possible to quiet her mind and expand her consciousness, she will probably not be successful in doing so. In the long run, beliefs and disbeliefs are subject to change, but in the present moment they are difficult to suspend.

> Choices are also made about levels of awareness. If you choose to change your attitude about something, your experience will change even when circumstances have not changed... What you choose to believe shapes your reality, and beliefs are invariably chosen intuitively. Rational decisions about beliefs are rare; generally, rational faculties are used to rationalize beliefs (*Ibid.*: 40).

Moreover, some may not be willing to accept what their intuition tells them because they would rather not acknowledge such insights; in this case the rationalizing process may obstruct formation of intuition-based beliefs. Intuition offers a path to a different form of truth, but it demands a willingness to confront self-deception.

These are Maslow's "non-peakers": not just people *unable* to have peak-experiences, but those who renounce or repress these experiences for many reasons. He identifies several reasons in his direct observations. The non-peaker's personal character may be extremely rational or mechanistic, or exhibit obsessive-compulsive tendencies, so she regards her transcendent experience as insanity, overwhelming, or a loss of control. She might cling instead to stability, reality, and a need to command or deny personal emotions (Maslow, 1970).

Maslow also addresses a phenomenal link between non-peakers and organized religions. Religion might be considered an effort to communicate peak-experiences to non-peakers. In this context, the task of teaching peak-experiences is typically taken on by non-peakers. But, "the peak-experiences and their experiential reality ordinarily are not transmittable to non-peakers, at least not by words alone, and certainly not by non-peakers" (Maslow, 1970: 24). This leads to a systematic concretizing of symbols and ceremonies, which in time honor the sacred objects and rituals themselves, rather than the original revelation.[60] Maslow summarizes this distortion, and the ensuing loss of original meaning, as "idolatry which has been the curse of every large religion" (*Ibid.*). Set in their concretized ways, religions may become hostile toward the very mystical experiences and prophets from which they originated.

Grof and Grof explain how the spiritual emergency may be interfered with by the protective ego. This biologically useful mechanism nonetheless produces fear in people that they are unprepared for – or perhaps unworthy of – such experience. Equally troublingly, some may see their everyday lives as lackluster in the wake of awe and ecstasy experienced in a transpersonal vision. Addressing resistance to non-ordinary states of consciousness (such as the shamanic 'trance'), Grof refers to Michael Harner's *cognicentric* bias in Western psychiatry and psychology:

> By this he means that these disciplines formulated their theories on the basis of experiences and observations from ordinary states of consciousness and have systematically avoided or misinterpreted the evidence from non-ordinary states, such as observations from psychedelic therapy, powerful experiential psychotherapies, work with individuals

---

[60] From my personal experience, this theory strikes a chord with how I have perceived certain aspects of Catholicism.

in psychospiritual crises, meditation research, field anthropological studies, or thanatology. The paradigm-breaking data from these areas of research have been either systematically ignored or misjudged and misinterpreted because of their fundamental incompatibility with the leading paradigm (Grof, n.d.: 5).

In cognicentrism, "... it is not the narrowness of someone's *cultural* experience that is the fundamental issue, but the narrowness of someone's *conscious* experience..." (Harner, 1990: xx). Harner introduces cognicentric bias as an analogue to ethnocentric bias,[61] both of which plague how modern industrialized civilizations understand the human psyche.

Perspectives on and comfort levels with altered states of consciousness and their potential benefits vary by culture. Harner argues that, in terms of natural selection, the naturally occurring presence of consciousness-altering drugs in the human brain (such as dimethyltryptamine[62]) indicate that altered states contribute to human survival. "It would appear that Nature itself has made a decision that an altered state of consciousness is sometimes superior to an ordinary state" (*Ibid.*: xxi).

Also contributing to the value of altered consciousness is overall cultural perception. Anthropologists place cultures into two categories: *monophasic* and *polyphasic*. Most shamanic cultures are *polyphasic*, meaning they are aware of and utilize multiple states of consciousness, including dreams and meditative states (Walsh, 2007). They value these states for their insights into the mind, humankind, and the cosmos. *Monophasic* cultures, including most of the modern West, do not recognize many healthy altered states, instead developing their understanding of reality primarily from the ordinary waking state. In these societies, the majority of the population is skeptical and often critical of alternate or unfamiliar states. Any healing or spiritual potentials found therein are also discounted.

Like Maslow (1970), though, Walsh (2007) maintains that the popularization of LSD and other psychedelics, and the research they have prompted, has increased awareness in the Western world of the value of altered consciousness. The diversity of spiritual practices flooding the West has also

---

[61] Ethnocentric bias entails judging another's culture based on the standards of one's own.
[62] Trace amounts of dimethyltryptamine, or DMT, exist naturally in plants and mammals. When ingested as a drug, DMT produces psychedelic states.

brought openness to methods such as yoga, meditation and contemplation. Perhaps the Western world is on the path to a more polyphasic culture.

8.5 Spiritual Intuition: A Shamanic Perspective

The shaman accesses and utilizes transpersonal consciousness to serve her community (Grof & Grof, 1990). I spoke with three shamanic teachers about intuition. Imanera (2012d) describes inner wisdom as innate, belonging to the state of the congenital mind prior to taking on acquired emotions. As we go inward searching for intuition, she believes, it emerges from somewhere other than the rational mind. The message of the intuition, or original mind, is sourced from perennial wisdom, present and true since the beginning of time.

Peter Kirschner (2012) explains that messages from our intuition are very clear. But as they pass through the brain and layers of our consciousness, they are disrupted, so that in our conscious state we cannot detect their true meaning. This is why he teaches entering into "holy silence", a state of pure mind, of no thought, which serves as a vehicle to carry us through these veils of consciousness. As we learn to exist in holy silence, we receive messages clearly from our intuitive mind. In his course "The Rememberer I" (the first in a four part series), Kirschner introduced me and other students to holy silence as a platform from which to approach the spirit world.

Ixeeya,[63] shamanic dancer, healing guide and artist, offered a very embodied response when asked about her own understanding of intuitive wisdom (Ixeeya, 2012a-b). Like Grof (1990, n.d.), she poetically described being part of a "vast universe of intelligence" in constant communication "with us, through us and as us" (Ixeeya, 2012c).

> The experience of energy I feel in and around my body while entranced with the earth and in shamanic movement is an obvious state of guidance and interconnection... It is a thickening of the air around me. A slowing down of my experience of traditional time. A shift out of 'worldly' concerns and limitations. The thoughts in my mental body

---

[63] Ixeeya is the alias of Stephanie Beacher.

> slow down and fade away and are replaced with 'intuitive wisdom'. This reveals itself as visions, metaphors, bodily movement and shaking, jolting, clear understanding of what 'to do' next, without analysis... Wisdom that is clear and clean of my personality imprinting. There is no hesitation or doubt; it just reveals itself with no judgment or attachment (*Ibid.*).

Ixeeya elaborated on how personal practice and aligning with the universal has led her to doorways into the realm of infinite perennial wisdom.

> I have come to know these states as moments of deep listening. As I practice the shamanic and yogic lineages these moments happen more and more often, to where now I can control entering them. I have noticed perennial/universal wisdom does have doorways. Doorways that are always available in some capacity but wider at certain moments, to name a few: during full moons, quarters and cross quarters of the year cycle, birthdays – moments of alignment in nature, with the earth's seasons and celestial beings. As we learn how to navigate the ego we have more choice and opportunity to experience this (*Ibid.*).

In writing this book, Ixeeya's classes and sacred ceremonies honoring moon phases and year's quarterly cycles have inspired me. Her shamanic painting courses have introduced me to transformative embodied experiences connecting with nature and spirit.

8.5.1 Shamanic Painting: Knowing and Unknowing

I believe my "complex path of knowing and unknowing myself", which I first articulated in my Peace Studies journey, has been a process of revealing inner wisdom. *Unknowing* is freeing up a channel for that wisdom to emerge. *Knowing* is listening to and trusting it. When I first wrote that "writing offers the possibility of illustrating something that my spirit and soul know, that words have not yet found a way of sharing", the feedback I received was: "Could a process that strikes this balance, between the indescribable ineffable experience and the human desire to express it, be one that pays equal attention to both 'knowing' and opening the space for 'unknowing' oneself?".[64]

With a shamanic painting class called "The Rattle and the Brush", I was offered deeper insight into this concept of knowing and unknowing. As a result, I can now rephrase my expression, "*Painting* offers the possibility of illustrating something that my spirit and soul know, that words are still finding a way of sharing". Vaughan echoes these sentiments, stating that the spiritual dimension of intuition, where there is no duality between knower and the known, "cannot be described in words, since words invariably posit duality or separation from what is described. The intuitive experience of reality is not an argument that can be proved, it is simply a reality that can be experienced" (Vaughan, 1979: 186). This aligns with Imanera's portrayal of Daoist shamanism: it cannot be taught, only realized when embodied through direct experience.[65]

Art is a medium through which I have only just discovered this unknowing. For most of my life, making art was an authentic experience of freely exploring color and creativity, guided by (original) limitless inner vision. But my personality, my ambition, and my human conditioning, made art cerebral during high school – a tendency that only intensified at university. I listened to instructions and trained my mind to *know* what to do, how to create so that my artwork looked as it 'should'.

"The Rattle and the Brush" led me on a journey of *unknowing* the ways in which I had become a 'prescriptive' artist. I shifted my approach to rely on 'elicitive'[66] capacities: quieting of the mind, and letting go of expectations and rules. I returned to the limitless inner vision of the transpersonal realm.

> The intuitive faculty leads the artist into new ways of expression and, whatever the medium, serves as the link between the individual and the universal experience given expression in a work of art. Thus, the source of true art is always an intuitive cognition of reality (*Ibid.*: 48).

Visionary artist Alex Grey speaks directly to this universal experience and how it inspires his work. He refers to a "Universal Creative Force connecting

---

[64] My thesis supervisor, Norbert Koppensteiner, offered this insightful inquiry.
[65] I have chosen transpersonal methods of intuitive inquiry and embodied writing to express my own intuitive experiences of reality for these reasons.
[66] In Chapter 11 I discuss peacework in terms of prescriptive versus elicitive approaches.

all beings and things, a source of love and wisdom that can be drawn from and revealed through the creation of works of art" (Grey, 2009: 134). In my process of *unknowing*, I began to channel this force and became receptive to a new (for me) intuitive source of vision and creativity.

Ixeeya (2012a) introduced shamanic painting as a process of channeling spirit guidance using the sacred tools of the rattle and the brush. She accurately diagnosed my situation: painting can be an activity like any other where we become trapped in our minds. She encouraged connecting with the energies of earth and air, letting them move through our whole bodies and out through our hands to these sacred tools. Before beginning, Ixeeya demonstrated how the energetic medicine of the rattle is used to smooth energy or break it up. The first passage from my research journal gives an account of my receiving a 'rattle bath' from a partner. Ixeeya had asked that each of us hold an intention as we received the rattle bath; mine was to let go of expectations pertaining to painting and to be open to guidance from spirit.

I lie on the earth and I am lulled into the soothing calm of the soft rattle. Drifting into that meditative state of mindlessness, I only see color. My mind wanders in its typical way – this time distracted by the fact that my brother is giving me the rattle bath. "How is he? ... Does he like this class? ... What is he sensing in my energy field?" But the soft shush-shush-shush of the rattle eases those thoughts, they fade... then SHASH SHASH SHASH the rattle shakes loudly just above my face. It feels abrupt, disruptive – interrupting my calm, quiet state. My mind jumps in, "he doesn't know what he's doing. Why is he doing it like that? Come on, just let me relax." I observe these thoughts as they appear, and luckily, the rattle bath continues in the exact same way. Some lulling, calming, then SHAKE SHAKE awake! There is to be no deep drifting away in this process. I sense that I am actually being rattled out of my mellow state. I am unattached. Accepting, receiving. My body remains still and relaxed, I do not tense, I do not pursue those thoughts.

When the rattle stills I sit up, eyes open, and something has changed. Something in the energy around me, the air against my skin feels thick, some subtle vibration has shifted. I feel refreshed, my vision sharp and clear. That rustling up of energy, that movement, washes through all channels of my being, attunes my focus, ceases the distracted wanderings where my mind tends to go, my typical patterns of perceiving are absent. I am here and only here, in this moment. My whole self is permeable, vision soft. Around me, in me, through me the vibration changes, there is that charge in the air, subtle but evident. Spirit reveals itself, my question is answered, my intention held.
~May 17, 2012

The next class began with a discussion of the shamanic roots and experience of making art. Painting is a practice that reminds us that we are part of the earth, said Ixeeya; thus, connecting with the earth and expressing that connection is our birthright. Yet we are connected not only to the earth, but also to spirit and, through shamanism, we ourselves become the bridge between the two. Shamanism is connecting with unseen beings and asking for guidance, she explained. Art helps make this guidance and presence visible. We can journey to anything because everything is vibrational and holds a life force, including color. As dancers, we translate vibration with our bodies; as painters, it passes from our bodies through the brush to the canvas.

Ixeeya described how the base layers of our paintings are shamanic because we act as open channels, translating messages from spirit, letting the color choose us rather than the other way around. The next steps would require serious non-attachment, since in the second and third layers, we started with a previously expressed experience, not a blank canvas. But the key was not to be attached to preserving what had already appeared; rather, we should continue to channel openly, not intervening with mind-driven preferences. "Put your mind in the backseat and make way for the wisdom of the universe… ancient wisdom" (Ixeeya, 2012b). This recalls Vaughan's (1979) advice about awakening intuition: excessive effort inhibits it, generating resistance that interferes with the process. To continue painting, the challenge would be to let go of the past and make room for the present.

During the next class, I learned to paint and mark-make with the elements of fire and water. Fire, igniting and burning, corresponded with a technique of flinging paint off the brush with a 'splat'! Water, on the other hand, soothing and flowing, corresponded to a smooth, fluid 'smear' on the canvas. The class integrated sound, as we painters shook our own rattles, sometimes accompanied by drumming, violin, and our own voices. We began to move to our own rhythms and colors.

I stand at the canvas and rattle, I open up. I open up and I am swept into trance. I am seeing and sensing differently. There is a soft give in my vision, mind supple and receding, simultaneously expansive and focused. I see the muddled darkness, I splash in the light. The light grows too bright and I drag through the current of dark. Thinking red, the brush lands in yellow. I let it go. Instead I work in value now. I work in value now. ~May 24, 2012

As I turned away from my painting and noticed the sensations in my body, then turned again to discern the changing forms emerging in my painting, I was flooded with elation in my own relationship with art. The moment prompted me to recall the concept of knowing and unknowing myself, and I poured these reflections into my journal:

The process of relying too much on the brain in creative expression has a lot to do with trust. Do I trust this intuitive knowledge? Do I trust that I will produce something beautiful even if I let go of control? Do I allow myself to take the risk and simply be playful and let my body move and groove as it delights, lay the paint down without a plan, and then... Let go? Feel fine with what is produced? Remain unattached to what I might love as each new layer veils the last?

How long have I been conforming to the rules of art? They were presented as a formula. I learn the techniques, I follow them, I get better. I do what they say, I respond to critiques, everyone likes what I do. I prove what I can do by demonstrating that I did what I was supposed to, the way I learned, what the instructor told me... and yeah, in the end, I always make it look 'right', according to plan. The final product would always be 'good', even great.

But where was I in the finished version? I was there as that 'known' version of self, carefully pruned as someone who has neatly put the pieces together. At some point, my art began to emerge via a calculated process that would produce successful results through a prescribed formula. I was trained to be attached to outcomes, and not just in art. Get it right! Perfect it in each moment! Make the team. Get the best grades. Look good.

And what if what I see is not necessarily about what others like? What if my painting makes no sense, is ugly, remains chaotic and unclear... what if, as a channel versus an authority of creation, I don't smear, lay the paint smooth like water – what if, shaking with the rattle, drumbeat resonating, staying in a flow, the force vibrates through me, cascading over my shoulder rushing down my arms shooting out my fingertips to the brush that is flung with a fiery SPLAT!? It feels like angry release. How did I lose sight of THIS option?! No more cool calculated containment, evenly paced precision. Instead, again! SHOUT! RELEASE! SPLAT! No confines of contentment and control. I do not need to be the one who follows the formula, who knows the steps to the dance. What is interesting about that? Where are the limits pushed? Where is the discovery? ~May 24, 2012

This photograph portrays my painting, although it is not complete, after that second class of fire and water. The following stage is more an oracular process of meditating with and seeing what exists within the painting, looking deeply for all the life forms it holds. The last stage will be to draw out those forms, staying true to the shamanic expressions of channeling and translating that brought the forms into being. I named the painting after Ixeeya's quote from the end of class, one which reflects my journey in art and many other aspects of life: "We all know nothing and we all know everything" (Ixeeya, 2012b).

"We All Know Nothing and We All Know Everything" (with Detail)

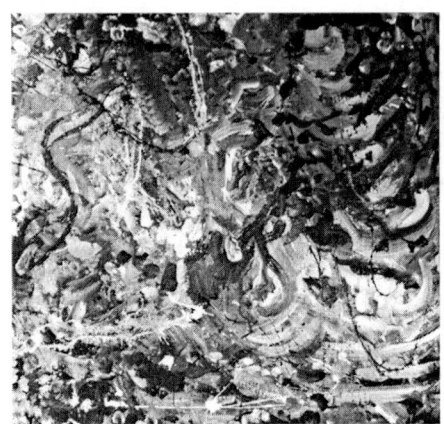 

8.6 THE WISDOM OF THE DAO AND *WU WEI*

> The Grand Master said, 'Tao covers and supports all things. How overflowingly great! The ruler should cast away his [selfish] mind. To act without taking an (unnatural) action means Nature. To speak without any action means virtue. To love people and benefit all things means humanity (*jen*). To identify with all without each losing his own identity means greatness. To behave without purposely showing any superiority means broadness. To possess an infinite variety means richness. Therefore to adhere to virtue is called discipline. To realize virtue means strength. To be in accord with Tao means completeness. And not to yield to material things is called perfection. If a superior man understand these ten points, he surely makes up his mind and all the world will come to him like rushing water' (Chuang-tzu, as cited in Chan, 1963: 205).

Wong (1997a) indicates that intuitive wisdom is synonymous with the Dao, the source of life. This wisdom is part of life's flow and the resonance between humans, earth, and heavens. The variable in the human experience is whether or not we attune to this flow, which determines how easily we may access that wisdom and pursue our full potential.

Individual qualities persist even when one shared essence unites. This duality is possible through the Dao, illustrated here as a source of spirit illumination that must be discovered, not taught, by each person for herself.

> Those who believe it possible to teach inspiration and genius, to enclose beauty, virtue and truth in formulae, to impose from without what can only be born from within, are blind; the illumination of the spirit, the revelation of the Tao has never enlightened them. Each man must find in himself his own truth, his own beauty, his own virtue; the salvation of the soul, like genius, can neither be bought nor taught. Everything is unique, though the essence of all things is one. All undergo perpetual change, perpetual creation (Hovelaque, as cited in Cooper, 1972: 15).

In the *Huainanzi*, self-cultivation through meditative techniques brings about this illumination. It is directed at "refining and controlling one's store of vital energy to attain a state of authenticity that is a manifestation of 'quintessential spirit' (*jingshen*)... One consequence of self-cultivation can be the achievement of 'spirit-illumination' (or 'spiritlike illumination'), an ability to see deeply into matters hidden from the perception of ordinary humans" (Major, Meyer, Queen & Roth, 2012: 8).

In Daoist practice, being free from thought – empty, still, at rest – is necessary to access the "awakening of the whole human potential" (Cleary, 1986: 9-10). Emptiness is not an end, but a means to such awakening. It opens the way for receptivity to reality by stilling personal tendencies and allowing unbiased understanding and action. Rest creates space for unattached awareness and therefore deliberate action, an essential Daoist practice described in the *Book of Balance and Harmony*: "When one is open, the mind is clear; when one is tranquil, the mind is pure. When one is imbued with purity and clarity, the principles of Heaven become evident... the truth and falsehood of people can be discerned by observation of their concrete manifestations" (Cleary, 1986: 10). Cleary compares the embodiment of openness and tranquility to polishing the mirror of our being, allowing it to reflect clearly. This clarity provides not only everyday insight, but also increased sustainable consciousness.

Notions of freedom, emptiness, and stillness deserve closer attention. Being free from thought is not synonymous with completely eliminating rationality or one's shadow aspects. This would be an impossible endeavor. A classic saying from the *Dao De Jing* reminds us that *yang* always contains a trace of *yin*, and vice versa. "Knowing the white, keep the black; be an exemplar for the world" (Lao-tzu, as cited in Cleary, 1991: 26). In one annotation, Cleary elaborates: "Here, the 'white' is the everyday world and the rational faculty; the 'black' is formless abstraction, the nondiscursive 'dark side' of the mind" (Cleary, 1986: 12). Daoism understands rationality as providing useful lessons for one part of the human totality, just as *yin* must always be present in *yang*. When neither the 'white' nor the 'black' is rejected nor allowed to dominate, the 'illumination of spirit' may arise spontaneously.

Emphasis is placed again on this 'illumination of spirit' coming 'of itself'. It is not contrived, nor produced through concerted effort. "To the extent that it involves effort – which means that there is a split within the mind – even the practice of stillness is regarded as a barrier to realization" (*Ibid.*). Another Daoist book of sayings, *Directions for Blessings* by Lu Tung-pin, cautions against intentionally seeking stillness.

> Concentration in stillness is not a matter of intentionally keeping the mind on something while remaining quiet. If you intentionally seek stillness while quiet, once you move or act your mind will again be aroused. When stillness culminates, there is spontaneous movement – this is the force of potential. If you can seek stillness while active, your mind stays on truth, so you can act without error. Then there is no further concern when quiet (Lu Tung-pin, as cited in Cleary, 1986: 13).

Even in stillness there is subtle, spontaneous movement, potential energy. So stillness itself is not a goal or benchmark along the path to quieting the mind. Stillness may be experienced as the mind becomes clear, a helpful state to evoke while in the midst of a chaotic or disturbing environment. Accessing this state is particularly beneficial for the peaceworker; I explore this further in Chapter 11.

The fundamental concept of *wu wei* is also key in deciphering how inner wisdom is interpreted in Daoism. According to Cooper (1972: 73-74), *wu wei* allows for a "sudden flash of intuition" that occurs only when the mind is inactive and a "spontaneous recognition of reality" takes place. A state of *wu wei* is conducive for intuition to arise because *wu wei* is being open to spontaneity and a natural flow. "In the *Huainanzi*, it [*wu wei*] generally does not refer to a state of utter inaction but to the ability of a person (especially a ruler) to be so attuned to the Way and therefore so filled with potency that his desires are translated into reality without any visible effort on his part" (Major, Meyer, Queen & Roth, 2012: 8). Accessing intuitive wisdom through *wu wei* is integral to the human experience of harmonizing energies and living in peace.

8.7 THE AIM OF DAOIST PRACTICE

"The work of Taoism is, as in all mysticism, to make man realize he is this true Self, the Tao, and to unite him with it again" (Cooper, 1972: 54). Any other self, such as the ego, is part of the mundane world alone and "disappears like a reflected light when the great source of all light is recognized" (*Ibid.*). Whereas much of Western philosophy seems intended as fuel for academic discourse, Eastern philosophies' purpose is to be applied to human behavior, to affect and influence character, to create the Sage, the Perfect Man, the True Man, the one who has attained 'The Great Whole'. Wholeness is a requirement of the Daoist sage. He is the epitome of human possibilities, the union of earthly and divine qualities.

> The Sage is the result of the gradual withdrawal from the illusions of the senses into the reality of the Tao, of the attainment of wisdom, of enlightenment, of a profound gnosis which, too, is 'beyond life and death' and implies a complete acceptance of all things as they are… (*Ibid.*: 57).

The master Daoist text *Chuang-tzu* states, "His glory is to know that all things are One and that life and death are but phases of the same existence" (Chuang-tzu, as cited in Cooper, 1972: 57). Poem 10 of the *Dao De Jing* informs the cultivation of such a life:

> Can you unite your spirit with the One and not let it leave?
> In concentrating on your breath, can you make it soft like an infant's?
> Can you purify your thoughts and clarify your mind
> So that they are spotless?
> Can you love your country and people without effort?
> In opening and closing the celestial gate,
> Can you become the female?
> In understanding everything in the universe,
> Can you do it without using knowledge?
> Give birth to them and nourish them,
> But do not possess them.
> Help them know that they are not dependent on you.
> Guide them but do not control them
> This is the most profound virtue.
>
> (Lao-tzu, as cited in Wong, 1997a: 31).

The Sage is not concerned with fame and recognition, nor even accruing the worldly knowledge of the scholar. His life is marked instead by a natural return to quiescence and simplicity (Cooper, 1972).

> The emphasis on the natural in Taoism must not be mistaken for any 'back to nature' movement. One cannot go back to what one already is. It is, rather, 'to find one's true nature', to get rid of the layers of the artificial and bring to light that which has always been there… the Nature which man can observe is only the kaleidoscope outward manifestation of the great inner power behind manifestation (*Ibid.*: 64).

Cooper sees this state as something akin to paradise, one where human nature is in balance and harmony with all life. The human is capable of reaching this state of perfection here and now; "it is an internal state which, at the moment of enlightenment, can be brought to actuality. It is to realize, to the fullest extent, the sum of all spiritual and metaphysical as well as human possibilities" (*Ibid.*: 64-65).

Living in harmony implies full consciousness and cooperation with surrounding conditions and life forms, maintaining balance between head and heart, reason and feeling. This Daoist ideal contrasts the general tendencies of the modern human, who stands apart from his environment, assessing it analytically, breaking it down into categories and labels. Cooper sees this rationally-minded existence as implying a split personality; it seems impossible to live in accord with a world regarded as distinct from oneself. "The merely analytical approach is the masculine, *yang*, by itself an arid intellectual function, while that of pure feeling is the *yin* 'humid' reaction" (*Ibid.*: 65). Analysis and feeling must be kept in balance: "head and heart, reason and feeling, dry and humid, are all equally useless and destructive of harmony unless held in equilibrium. The observation of nature, however acute and detailed, is not the same as entering into understanding through intuition and being" (*Ibid.*). Harmonious connection with nature is formed not simply through thought and observation, but also through open awareness, receptivity, and authentic presence.

Efforts to transcend dualistic tendencies and 'see oneself in the other', to deconstruct categories of 'us and them', align with Daoism. Dissolving boundaries between self and nature, self and others, and entering social interactions via intuition and 'being with', the human being engages in *wu-wei*. She holds great awareness of others while not completely letting go of herself. Losing one's sense of interrelation with all things, feeling distinct from nature, paves the way for destruction of both nature and of human spiritual life. "The natural man is one who 'is always in accordance with Nature, and does nothing to increase artificially that which is already in his life'. Nor does he 'inflict internal injury upon himself with desires and aversions'" (Chuang-tzu, as cited in Cooper, 1972: 66).

8.8 ADDRESSING THE CHALLENGES OF LIVING IN THE 'WESTERN' WORLD

Attachment to efficiency, ambition, and material desires presents a significant obstacle for people living in modern Western societies. Lin Yu-tang's criticizes these values as an 'American' way of life; Cooper responds that they are actually common throughout the Western world, not just the United States. Since the industrial revolution, some societies have placed such value on material abundance that many of their citizens have lost awareness of the impact humans have on the natural environment. The result is devastating disequilibrium. This external imbalance, writes Duane Elgin (1993: 246), mirrors the internal: "Our outer world reflects our inner conditions". Conforming to the values of a modern, industrial lifestyle, particularly in regards to time, means losing the glory of a beautiful, idle afternoon. Worse, it turns the human being herself into a clock (Cooper,

1972). These critiques resonate with my own after my first immersion experiences abroad.

Fortunately, many perceive a growing interest in 'alternative' ways of life in parts of the modern West, with attention shifting towards communal mindfulness and ecological awareness and away from thoughtless consumption. But the challenge of how to resist the demands of contemporary life remains. Somé (1993) presents a correlation between increased technological reliance and decreased spiritual presence. The former offers the desired benefits of increased productivity, allowing for material abundance, but also results in societies being controlled by tools devoid of spiritual strength.

> Technology can and is supposed to be attentive to what liberates the person toward taking care of the higher level of existence. But, to me, the role of technology must be to attend to the lower part of human existence, since a thing devoid of the spiritual cannot help reach out to the spirit. The spirit liberates the person to work with the things of the soul. Because this reaching out to the spiritual is not happening, the Machine has overthrown the spirit and, as it sits in its place, is being worshipped as spiritual. This is simply an error of human judgment. Anyone who worships his own creation, something of his own making, is someone in a state of confusion (Somé, 1993: 59).

How to live within the systems and demands of modern society and maintain harmony? Somé advises that each person may initiate her own spiritual emancipation through ritual. Ritual takes place in sacred space and is characterized by the following elements: invocation (inviting non-human presence); dialogue (with spirit and with ourselves); repetition (of actions and structures); opening (through invocation); and closure (by thanking and sending spirit away).

For a Daoist, life will always be *yin-yang* balancing. The challenge is to harmonize the presence of dialectic forces, to avoid being swayed by any particular influence. Cooper's Daoist Sage exemplifies this balance. The Sage delights in a life of *yin-yang* harmony in all aspects, including social environment and relationships.

> The Sages, artists and poets who retired to the wilds seemed to have a genius for friendship, sharing their wisdom, music and poetry and delighting in company just as often as enjoying solitude, and so, in their

lives, maintaining the *yin-yang* harmony of inward and outward movement (Cooper, 1972: 67).

This Sage teaches by example, holding her knowledge firmly within, instead of arguing to convince others. In this way, she attracts others to her without effort or exertion, and is influential without words, without need to teach or perform.

In an exemplary natural way of life, knowledge for knowledge's sake is useless, as it produces complacency and superiority. Wisdom, however, incorporates wholeness. "Wisdom demands a fluid attitude of life-understanding and is dynamic and, being concerned with life in its entirety, it cannot be divorced from the spiritual" (*Ibid.*: 68). In Daoism, the task is to work towards conscious cooperation while remaining integrated in society. This way of life resonates with an embodied approach to energetic peace, where peace begins internally and spreads outward, through society and the universe. In the following chapters, I explore practices for developing this great human potential for peace, which involves change (*yi*), letting go (*wu wei*), and balancing *yin-yang* in a state of harmony with the Dao.

CHAPTER 9: MEDITATION AND THE MIND

> The mind of the perfect man is like a mirror. It does not lean forward or backward in its response to things. It responds to things but conceals nothing of its own. Therefore it is able to deal with things without injury (to its reality) (Chuang-tzu, as cited in Chan, 1963: 207).[67]

Meditation is a holistic practice that brings all aspects of the human being into harmonious resonance with the natural world. From an energetic peace perspective, the human sensorium capable of experiencing peace comprises the body, senses, and spirit (Dietrich, 2012a).[68] There is no division between mind and body, and meditation helps dissolve that perceived separation.

> Part of the art of being human is also, and mainly, the corresponding use of this sensorium, which wants to be learned and practiced. The method is mostly called meditation… If the human being, with all her faculties, wants to bring herself into harmonious resonance with the macrocosm of the universe to experience peace, then she has to mobilize all those aspects of herself that can resonate. According to experience these are breath, voice, and movement. It is for this reason that these are the central

---

[67] Chan adds the following: "The mirror is an important symbol for the mind both in Zen Buddhism and in Neo-Confucianism. The difference is that with Buddhism, external reality is to be transcended, whereas with Chuang Tzu and Neo-Confucianists, external reality is to be responded to naturally and faithfully, like a mirror objectively reflecting all" (Chan, 1963: 207-208).

[68] These elements echo Imanera's (2012a) physical, energetic, and spirit bodies.

means for energetic rituals and celebrations of peace, out of which emerged music, dance, and theater... (*Ibid.*: 60).

Meditation is fundamental to shamanism. Before describing specific shamanic meditation forms and their use in peacework, I elaborate in this chapter on the mind and brain, their interrelated functions and potentials, and how meditation activates and trains new pathways for these functions, thus altering the human experience.

9.1 MEDITATION'S MANY FORMS

> Meditation is the inward focus of attention in a state of mind where ego-related concerns and critical evaluations are suspended in favor of perceiving a deeper, subtler, and possibly divine flow of consciousness. A method of communicating with hidden layers of the mind, it allows the subconscious to surface in memories, images, and thoughts while also influencing it with quietude, openness, and specific suggestions (Kohn, 2008: 1).

While my own meditation described in this book is rooted primarily in the Daoist tradition, there exist a cornucopia of meditative forms. Indeed, meditation as a technique for inner peace is so effective in part because the meditator has so many practices to choose from. Her culture and belief system will help determine how she practices; certainly there is no 'one-size fits all' method for meditation. Similarly, the mystical experience accessed by the practitioner is also influenced by her personal cosmovision.

The word 'meditation' itself connotes a wide variety of activities and ideas. One option for sub-classifying the broadly defined act is to consider each form's processes and outcomes. Meditation typically involves attention regulation, or concentration, but different types utilize different entryways to such concentration: breath, body, mantra, prayer, visualization, or sense of stillness, to take the most common examples (Gawler & Bedson, 2010). These mechanisms may aim to produce different outcomes: therapeutic results, nonattachment to experiences, stillness of mind, psychological acceptance, transcendence of thought, oneness, spiritual insight, or enlightenment. Additionally, meditation can be understood via its physical effects, "physiological, biochemical, hormonal immunological or neurological" (*Ibid.*: 372).[69]

For Kohn (2008), both the practice and effects of meditation are culturally determined, and whatever the practitioner seeks in meditation, she will eventually find. Subtle differences in experiencing "union and inherent oneness" result from the seeker's individual intentions and perceptions. These personal preferences determine the specific form of meditation, the approach to accessing the subconscious, transformation of the mind, and consequences of the practice. Kohn believes positive results will come faster and easier when the practitioner follows the method best suited to her own capacities. Those wishing to meditate might consider 'trying on' various techniques before devoting themselves to a particular practice.[70]

Even a few examples of meditation terminology reveal its richness across various spiritual traditions:

- *Dhyana* is the generic Sanskrit (the ancient, sacred language of India) term for meditation that, in the yoga sutras, refers to both the act of inward contemplation in the broadest sense and, more technically, the intermediate state between mere attention to an object (*dharana*) and complete absorption in it (*Samadhi*)…
- *Gom* is the most common Tibetan word for meditation. It is related to the word *com*, which translates as 'getting used to' or 'becoming accustomed to doing something so that it is a part of oneself.' What one is getting used to is the true nature of the mind.
- Christian meditation is often associated with prayer or scripture study. It is rooted in the Bible, which directs its readers to meditate… This brings us in close touch with God's reality, power, grace, faith and miracles…
- [Judaism] In the Old Testament, there are two Hebrew words for meditation: *hagâ*, which means 'to sigh' or 'to murmur,' but also 'to meditate,' and *sîhâ*, which means 'to muse' or 'to rehearse in one's mind.'…

---

[69] Gawler and Bedson (2010) give credit to several sources that provided input for the creation of this definition of meditation: Pauline McKinnon, Dr. Craig Hassed, Ian Gawler, Paul and Maia Bedson, Dr. Ruth Gawler, Robyn Jones, and Seikan Cech.
[70] Some meditation traditions I have 'tried on' besides Daoist are Vipassana, Brahma Kumaris, and several self-designed methods since childhood.

- [Islam] Meditation in the Sufi traditions is based largely on a spectrum of mystical exercises, varying from one lineage to another. Numerous Sufi traditions place emphasis upon a meditative procedure similar in its cognitive aspect to... the Buddhist traditions... described above as shamatha ['calm abiding'] practice (Gawler & Bedson, 2010: 375-377).

- In the language of India in the time of the Buddha, passanā meant seeing in the ordinary way, with one's eyes open; but vipassanā is observing things as they actually are, not just as they appear to be... This is Vipassana: experiencing one's own reality by the systematic and dispassionate observation within oneself of the ever-changing mind-matter phenomenon manifesting itself as sensations (Goenke, 1980: 9)

- [In Taoist meditation practice] the body, through the inner vision of the divinities, is seen as a complex of a higher dimension; thus the meditator's understanding of the universe is reorganized and his worldview reconstructed. With all attention focused on the deep inner life of the body, a series of mental exercises centering on a symbolic and nonrational vision of the world is undertaken (Robinet, 1989: 159-160).

Kohn proposes categorizing meditation's many forms "according to the venue they use to access the subconscious mind". She classifies them using primary modes of human perception: visual (visualization), auditory (mantra), and kinesthetic (body awareness). "Underlying all these different modes of meditation is elementary or access concentration, commonly reached through a sustained focus on the breath" (Kohn, 2008: 7). Kohn identifies three additional modalities: observation, immediacy, and body energetics, any of which may be used alone or to supplement the three primary modes.

9.2 COMMON FEATURES OF DIFFERENT MEDITATIVE PRACTICES

Meditation schools share many fundamental characteristics: use of breath, alignment with an ethical process, acknowledgment of the dualistic nature of human existence, to name a few (Kohn, 2008). They differ from one another in other aspects: cosmovisions, the human being's role in the universe, notions of mind and body, the importance of the teacher or master, techniques for advanced practitioners, and even the ultimate goal of meditating. But the common attributes of meditative techniques persist.

First, the use of the breath, a technique that not only links body and mind, but is also connected with emotions, nervous conditions, and peace. "The more the breath is deepened and calmed, the quieter the mind becomes and the easier it is to suspend the critical factor and enter into the serenity of the meditative state" (*Ibid.*: 10). Joining mind and breath is a fundamental aspect of many approaches. In Daoism, it clears the mind; in Buddhism, it serves as a remedy to the mind's predisposition to become distracted and scattered (Cleary, 1986: 11). The late 19th century Daoist text *Alchemy for Women* emphasizes the need to join the two harmoniously in practices of self-refinement. "This means that the mind rests on the breath, and the breath too rests on the mind. But what is most important is harmony… This harmony is not apart from balance, and balance is not apart from harmony" (*Ibid.*: 12).

Sakyong Mipham notes that the Buddhist viewpoint sees humans as inherently peaceful. Unfortunately, humans become accustomed to chasing the mind's thoughts and emotions. Though the overwhelmed mind is untrained, still it holds built-in meditative capacity: "the natural process of becoming familiar with an object by repeatedly placing our minds upon it… We begin to see that we have to work with these intense emotions because if we don't, they'll grow. Once they grow, we act on them. When we act on them, they create our environment" (Mipham, 2003: 24-27). Mipham teaches "peaceful abiding", placing the mind on the breath, and maintaining it there, instead of allowing it to leap from one object, desire, or emotion to the next.

> This is how we shift our allegiance from the bewildered mind that causes its own suffering to the mind that is stable, clear, and strong… Ordinarily we just can't handle the natural joy of our mind, so we end up churning up intense emotions… 'Peaceful abiding describes the mind as it naturally is… The human mind is by nature joyous, calm, and very clear. In shamatha meditation we aren't creating a peaceful state – we're letting our mind be as it is to begin with. This doesn't mean that we're peacefully ignoring things. It means that the mind is able to be in itself without constantly leaving (*Ibid.*: 25).

Another common aspect of most traditions is the relationship of the meditative practice with an ethical process. Regardless how the worldview's central force is named or understood, it is out of our reach until we have cultivated a certain degree of internal 'purity' or divinity. This typically involves adherence to some set of basic moral rules and precepts, such as those against killing, stealing, lying, and sexual misconduct. Other more specific codes exist along with each tradition (Kohn, 2008). Mipham recognizes this ethical aspect as an attribute of an enlightened society, which is not a utopia of enlightened beings, but a "culture of human beings who know the awakened nature of basic goodness and invoke its energy in order to courageously extend themselves to others" (Mipham, 2003: 197). Through meditation, we are able to ride the "windhorse", experiencing this basic goodness with the energy of an enlightened mind.

In "The Tao of Personal and Social Transformation", Elgin envisions this transformed society as a 'new frontier' of human and social possibility, where both individual and institution take responsibility for their collective fates. "First is a Self-Realization Ethic, which asserts that each person's proper goal is the evolutionary development of human potential... Second, we must develop an Ecological Ethic, which accepts our earth as limited and recognizes the underlying unity of the human race as an integral part of the natural environment" (Elgin, 1993: 250). Meditation stimulates the development of ethics that unite self-realization and ecological and social sustainability.

A further commonality between different meditative practices is, as Kohn puts it, "the dualistic vision that the mind we carry in our ordinary life is not the pure mind necessary to realize oneself or the divine" (Kohn, 2008: 12). In Daoism, the tendency to perceive the conditioned consciousness as the real mind is referred to as "mistaking the servant for the master". Some conditioning is useful for everyday survival, but unwanted problems appear when habits conquer decisions and behaviors. Stifling mind habits limit a person's greater potential (Cleary, 1986).

> Buddhist philosophy would explain these habits of thinking as being driven by craving and aversion, desire and fear, or running toward some imagined future happiness and success, and away from perceived suffering and failure. In either case, craving and aversion keep us running. Through the practice of mindfulness [meditation], we choose to stop 'running,' anticipating and planning, and instead pay attention to what is around us and inside us right here and now (Gawler & Bedson, 2010: 124-125).

To break such habits, meditative methods enhance observation of the customary patterns of the mind, and provide tools to enable transformation of those tendencies.

Finally, different mediation traditions help develop compassion, calmness, equanimity, peace, and joy (Kohn, 2008). In their writing on Mindfulness-Based Stillness Meditation, Gawler and Bedson (2010) describe "intentional meditation" as that which is actively directed towards certain hopes and goals. They mention specifically the qualities of acceptance, humility, simplicity, patience, presence, trust, compassion, and right action. These qualities move the practitioner away from blame, guilt, self-criticism, and pain, and open the way for gratitude and loving kindness. The meditator broadens her perspective of self and others, thereby cultivating a response from others of kindness and understanding instead of judgment or aggression.

Most meditative traditions state that the pure mind, closely related to the divine, is inherent in us. By transforming our own mind we achieve this state and live the enlightened life we are meant for. For Daoists, transformation of the mind is about moving towards balance. It is the human's gift and task to accept and integrate both dark and light *yin-yang* forces (Cooper, 1972). We are never entirely free from our shadows as long as we live. Thus, the Daoist aim of 'pure state' is understood as one where *detachment* from problematic mind patterns facilitates the inherent connection with a divine source.

This requires some dissolution of the ego and heightened awareness of our existence in the here and now.

> The mental calmness [meditation] provides and the access it offers to the subtler levels of consciousness serve to awaken a greater power or universal force – the 'divine,' defined in different traditions as God, Dao, *atman,* Buddha nature, and so on. Meditation suspends conscious and ego-related thinking and thereby allows the divine or cosmic powers to come to the fore (Kohn, 2008: 8).

Walsh describes the loss of previous identity as part of this spiritual emergence: "Spiritual practitioners must be willing to confront not only physical death but also ego death. This is the demise of an old, outmoded identity so that from its ashes can arise a new identity appropriate to spiritual life" (Walsh, 2007: 71). Liberated from interfering distractions of the conscious mind and ties to formerly held notions of self, the practitioner is free to develop wider vision and understanding. She begins a journey of transformation from ordinary existence to a sagely or enlightened one (Kohn, 2008).

9.3 SUSPENSION OF EGO AND SHAMANIC TRANCE

Kohn identifies this key shared meditative attribute – "the suspension of ego-related concerns and critical, intellectual evaluations in a state of self-hypnosis" (Kohn, 2008: 9) – as appearing in shamanic practices as well. She critiques contemporary practice directed at self-improvement and healing, stating that critical evaluation is only slightly interrupted during the actual meditation and returns to normal strength otherwise. The whole meditation effort has been motivated, she believes, by "egotistic concerns and personal interests, the vision of a well-adapted, successful, and sexy self" (*Ibid.*).Though I understand her point regarding some 'self-help' meditation, I am inclined to see the situation differently. Even if the initial motivation for practice involves the ego, meditation can still lead to the cultivation of peace and harmony far beyond the self. Gawler and Bedson address this concern with the following advice:

> We need to temper the natural desire to experience all of this [outcomes of meditation] with the mindfulness that is required to actually allow it to happen. What helps is to combine the positive intention to do the exercises as described with the right attitude – one where we deliberately let go of expectations, judgments and reactions. Approach this exercise with that open curiosity… (Gawler & Bedson, 2012: 227-228).

Working on oneself *is* the initial step. Meditating cultivates seeds of peace. From its inception as embodied *inner* peace, the force contained in these seeds grows, affecting the meditator's surrounding spheres of life with harmonious resonance. Gawler and Bedson stress the importance of intentions and attitude. When done with clear intentions, meditation's transformational impact reaches beyond self-centered goals.

Working with the subconscious requires a unique combination of "active effort and passive surrender" (Kohn, 2008: 17). Active methods for subconscious communication include muscle stretching and relaxation, energetic movement, breath control, creative imagination, visioning, and chanting. To be truly effective, these methods require serious commitment and regular practice. But they should not be sought with excessive ambition, creating a meditation-based ego that feeds feelings of superiority or inferiority based on progress or lack thereof. "Attainment in meditation appears on its own; one has to surrender to the process to let it happen. Yet one has to keep the process moving with a steady effort to ripen awareness" (*Ibid.*: 18). It is counterproductive to pursue meditation with attachment to its possible outcomes and transformation. Instead, meditation – and therefore life – are approached with complete equanimity.[71]

9.4 UNDERSTANDING THE MIND AND EGO

With 'mind' and 'ego' so central to meditative practice, it bears a moment to reflect on their meanings. Psychologists from Freud to Jung to Pavlov have conceived of the mind on their own terms (Kohn, 2008). Each meditation tradition also has its own way of explaining the mind, its functions, and how to change it.

One way the mind can be understood is as a pyramid composed of three interrelated parts: the unconscious, subconscious, and conscious. At the base of the pyramid is the unconscious, responsible for physical coordination, posture control, and instincts. It manages the inner organs and breathing, physical responses to emotions (fear, anger, etc.) and potential change through systematic conditioning (*Ibid.*). The next level 'up' the pyramid is the subconscious mind, which holds memories, emotional connections and ingrained belief systems. Easily molded, the subconscious protects the body, discerning what is beneficial or not, and can be accessed through imagery, metaphors, music, and visualizations. It controls habits and automated responses, and holds emotions in both their present form and as past memories.

At the top, the conscious mind serves as the 'command center', controlling language, critical reasoning, and decision-making. Through it, we know what we perceive. It, too, protects us – albeit by rational analysis of

---

[71] As is taught by S.N. Goenka through Vipassana meditation. http://www.dhamma.org/

information. The conscious mind "works with set patterns that create projections of ideal or fearful situations, often distorting actual facts, then sends signals to all other agencies that either excite or inhibit their actions" (*Ibid.*: 15). This conscious aspect allows for intelligent focus so we may think clearly and make decisions.

Chang San-feng (a Daoist adept recognized for creating the practice of *taijiquan*)believed that the duality of the conditioned conscious mind versus the primal unconscious mind is not permanent, that the 'true' mind might bring them together.

> The true mind is broad and luminous; where the true mind abides is peace and freedom. When you manage your affairs with the true mind, everything is integrated; when you seek the Tao with the true mind, myriad differences are of the same root. But if people want to use the true mind to deal with affairs, they need to foster it so that it is strong, and to keep it calm and uncluttered. Then it can work without weariness, and be responsive even while tranquil (Chang San-feng, as cited in Cleary, 1986: 16).

San-feng's "true mind" is commonly referred to as the "mind of Tao" – in Cleary's translation of the *Yi Jing*, for instance. Whereas the human mind is connected to "mundane" *yin*, characterized by instability and acquired conditioning, the mind of Dao is associated with "celestial" *yang*, or primordial real consciousness (Cleary, 1986). Jung writes about the interplay of conscious and unconscious while interpreting the hexagrams. "If the *I Ching* is not accepted by the conscious, at least the unconscious meets it halfway, and the *I Ching* is more closely connected with the unconscious than with the rational attitude of consciousness" (Jung, 1949: xxxii).The Daoist mind, attuned to true reality, is often clouded by the human mind, which is tied to thoughts and emotions related to objects. "Taoists practice what they call 'repelling yin' and 'fostering yang,' overcoming the human mind and promoting the mind of Tao" (Cleary, 1986: 17). The *Book of Balance and Harmony* teaches:

> Although there is the mind of Tao in the human mind, and there is the human mind in the mind of Tao, it is just a matter of persistence in the midst of action and stillness: If the shining (Tao) mind is always maintained, the straying (human) mind does not stir; the unstable is stabilized, and the subtle becomes apparent (*Ibid.*).

The two minds are not divorced, and neither should be eliminated. Rather, the human mind may be regulated so that the conscious light of the Dao mind guides.

Great liberty has been taken in defining, interpreting, and applying the concept of 'ego' proposed by Sigmund Freud. Freud introduced it as an organizing principle of processes necessary for coherent mental functioning (Freud, 1960), and presented psychoanalysis as an approach for working with this part of the psyche. The ego, he explained, represses or excludes certain forms of effectiveness and activity from consciousness because they stand in opposition to it.

'Ego' is used slightly differently in relation to meditation. For example, 'dissolution' or 'bypassing' of the ego during meditation would, in the Freudian sense, signify a complete cessation of existence. "There are now several misconceptions about the key Buddhist notion of *annata*, or egolessness. To begin with, many new meditators mistake egolessness for the abandonment of the Freudian ego" (Epstein, 1993: 121). Epstein provides a list of popular misconceptions about egolessness that ultimately imply "that the ego, while important developmentally, can in some sense be transcended or left behind" (*Ibid.*: 122). It is not the Freudian ego that is targeted in Buddhist insight and other forms of meditation:

> It is, rather, the self-concept, the *representational* component of the ego, the actual internal experience of one's self that is targeted. What is being transcended here is not the entire ego. Rather, self-representation is revealed as lacking concrete existence. It is not the case of something real being eliminated, but of the essential groundlessness being realized for what it has always been. In the words of the Dalai Lama, 'This seemingly solid, concreted, independent, self-instituting I under its own power that *appears* actually does not exist at all' (*Ibid.*: 123).

Thus, meditation's goal is not so much to abandon the ego as it is to move beyond belief in the ego's solidity, to let go of identification with the ego's representations. Meditative practice is actually aimed at "a restructuring and reintegration of the personality, leading to 'an authentic individuality that is not compulsively driven by conditioned tendencies from the past' but encompasses a dimension envisioned as divine" (Kohn & Welwood, as cited in Kohn, 2008: 16). Several authors' interpretations shed light on understanding the ego in this context.

For Kohn, "... 'ego' describes the various regulatory and integrative functions of the personality, the constructs that surround conceptions of self and what cognitive psychologists call the 'self-schema'" (Kohn, 2008: 15). Located mostly in the subconscious and partially in the conscious mind, the ego consists of fixed beliefs and deeply ingrained emotional reaction patterns. Likening the ego to a spoiled child, Kohn writes, "it enjoys power and does not like change; nor does it like quietude, calmness, and rest" (*Ibid.*). The ego demands certain behaviors according to its automatic patterning and need for predictability. It challenges the meditative process with constant requests for control and compulsive, deep-seated responses. Many traditions teach ego dissolution as deautomatization of these set reactions and behavior. Personally, I envision the ego as a referee governing conscious reactions according to its own rules.

As a Buddhist, Mipham (2003) refers to the concept of 'me' in place of 'ego'. With meditation and the development of *prajna*, he explains, we begin to see that the forms our conscious and subconscious minds once perceived as solid are actually fleeting. Thus the classic Buddhist lesson, "form is emptiness, emptiness is also form",[72] (as cited in Mipham, 2003: 192). This concept of emptiness applies equally to the 'me'.

> Seeing the reality of no self is a preliminary understanding of profound emptiness... Our relative wisdom – causal prajna – takes us beyond the concept of 'me,' directly into the reality of our experience. It creates the conditions for the final result, which is nonconceptual understanding... It's the intuitive insight that knows the truth directly, not through reason or logic, but beyond the realm of thought (Mipham, 2003: 190, 192).

Dissolution of the 'me' opens the door for the intuitive insight that takes us beyond the conceptual mind. There we uncover basic goodness and begin to glimpse the entirety of the heart of the universe, which is reflected in our human hearts.

From a Daoist viewpoint, Bock-Möbius (2012) encourages us not to identify with the ego, but to instead recognize connections, so that we experience mystical union. To her, the ego is a mask, a societal role we play, while our true core resides beneath. Even as the soul becomes aware of its quest toward mystical union, the ego may interfere. "Ego-fixations, self-

---

[72] This mantra is taken from the Prajna Paramita Hridaya Sutra, or, the Heart Sutra.

attachments, and avoidance of transcendence and spirituality are ways of rejecting integration into a greater reality" (*Ibid.*: 43). In the transpersonal experience, though, a transformation occurs where "the individual perceives deeper connections of human life and enters a state of consciousness in which he or she is no longer a mere ego, but purely awake and present. Awakening, clarity, and presence are similarly the goals of qigong practice and are described in similar terms" (*Ibid.*: 50). Overcoming of ego is relatable to *wu-wei* nonaction, since as we step outside of "ego-consciousness", we no longer impose a way of being that obstructs the natural way of life, the Dao.

9.5 The Brain and Meditation: A Western-Science Perspective

Although brain function in the contemporary medical sense is not my focus here, recent scientific validation of meditative practice bears mentioning. Change in brain waves resulting from meditation is among the most interesting of this evidence. The conscious mind operates primarily in beta waves. When quieted through meditation, it shifts to alpha waves, a phenomenon frequently found even with beginners. In advanced practitioners, theta waves "indicate a deeply calm, yet conscious state unique to meditation. Less frequent but also observed were delta waves, usually associated with deep sleep and hypnotic somnambulism" (Kohn, 2008: 19).

Scientific analyses of meditation also report on its psycho-social effects, such as increases in extroversion and self-esteem and improvement of verbal creativity. Positive psychological upshots include greater empathy, (healthy) assertive behavior, autonomy, and overall happiness. Social and interpersonal effects – reduction in conflict level, improvement in social functioning, and overall enhanced everyday living – also benefit (Ospina et al., 2007). In general, through fixed attention, calmed thoughts, and focused breathing, meditative concentration affects brain chemistry in such a way that tensions are reduced and the body relaxes. In this state, practitioners are fully engaged in the present and reduce tendencies to juggle, strive, and get ahead (Austin, 2006).

Equally significant in understanding meditation's effects on the brain are the "two-way street of causality between mind and brain" (Kohn, 2008: 23) and the brain's amazing neuroplasticity, or capacity for change and transformation. "Neurological regeneration and reorganization are thus not only desirable but distinctly possible" (*Ibid.*) through perception and attention training. "Closely intertwined with consciousness, attention serves to filter out perceptions, balance multiple data, and attach emotional significance to them" (*Ibid.*: 23-24). Evidence of "synchronization or coherence between different cortical areas" has led some Transcendental Meditation researchers to link the act with enhanced creativity and psychological growth (Walsh, 1993: 63). Through Western science, we now know it is possible to retrain the brain.

Walsh refers to the mind's neuroplasticity in contemporary psychological terms even as he discusses shamanic death, dismemberment, healing, and rebirth:

> With conditioning and dynamics dissolved, reorganization can be guided by the mind's innate holotropic drive toward health and wholeness. For one of the most hopeful of all contemplative and clinical discoveries is that the psyche is inherently self-organizing and self-optimizing, and under supportive conditions it can be not only self-healing but also self-actualizing, self-transcending, self-awakening, and self-liberating. The result can be a reconstructed psyche and identity that are unbound from the past, and therefore less conflicted and less symptomatic, and consequently more healthy, integrated, and whole. The death of the old self allows birth of the new (*Ibid.*, 2007: 75).

The key challenges are to allow this 'death of the old self' and to stimulate the psyche's self-liberating capacities.

Of course, evidence of the mind's innate ability to move towards wellness is not new; it is found across time and cultures, though sometimes with different terminology.

> These innate tendencies for the mind to flower, unfold, and develop its potential had been recognized before in both East and West, psychology and philosophy. Long ago Plato spoke of Eros and Tibetan Buddhism of the self-liberating nature of mind. More recent recognitions include neuroanatomist Kurt Goldstein's 'actualization,' Carl Rogers' 'formative tendency,' Carl Jung's 'individuation urge,' Abraham Maslow's 'self-transcendence,' Erik Erikson's 'self-perfectibility,' philosopher Ken Wilber's 'eros,' and Aldous Huxley's '*moksha* drive' (Walsh, 2007: 274-275).

Walsh notes that psychological growth is often marked by periods of pain or confusion resulting from this development. Clarity can be deceiving. Often mistaken as a cue for certainty, it may actually signify that we are clinging to old, comfortable understandings of ourselves and the world, avoiding our lives' constantly changing novelty and uncertainty. Meanwhile, when unsettling spiritual and psychological crises are navigated successfully, their disturbances may also make space for new, life-affirming beliefs and goals.

In the following chapters, I reference this self-optimization through Daoist insight meditation, which works not only with the brain, but with the practitioner's entire energetic reorganization. Through this reorganization, the limitations of body-rooted identity and critical evaluation no longer apply; a state of no-body and no-mind supplants them. This allows for the "calm apperception of the true nature of the self" (Kohn, 2008: 87). As Imanera (2012b) teaches, moving beyond our *jing* physical body to know our *qi* energy body is part of the path to our *shen* spirit body.

Kohn addresses one more recent scientific find: the happy outlook, compassion, and ethical concerns commonly found in serious meditators, and the salient discovery that positive emotions can be cultivated through mental training (Begley, as cited in Kohn, 2008). "Advanced experiences include profound peace, concentration and joy, intense positive emotions of love and compassion, penetrating insights into the nature of mind, and a variety of transcendent states that can run the gamut of classical mystical experiences" (Walsh, 1993: 61). With training aimed at a more positive life, emotions like compassion are nurtured, eventually leading to a more caring and supportive, rather than competitive and distrusting, population (Kohn, 2008).

9.6 MEDITATION: AN ENERGETIC PERSPECTIVE

Worldview plays an important role in peoples' desire and ability to align with a particular meditation form. Kohn notes that a worldview common to many traditions entails a quantum perspective: reality is not comprised of solid objects, but vibrating matter interconnected through a network of energetic fields.

> Often this worldview encourages an awareness of the vibratory nature of the body and the close integration of the body-mind. This, in turn, matches the understanding of quantum physics, which has shown that

matter is made up of vibrating energy and fields that change their state very rapidly – trillions of times in one second... Body and mind consist of the same vibrating atoms that are constantly oscillating, arising and dissolving: all empty, no solidity, no firmness (Kohn, 2008: 27).

Masami Saionji, chairperson of the Goi Peace Foundation and the World Peace Prayer Society, describes his Akashic experience:

> When I go into meditation, I simply concentrate on oneness with the essential universal vibration. My breathing becomes deeper, slower, and more spiritualized. My body cells become more spiritualized as well. I can feel my cells expanding through the surrounding space until there is no dividing line between me and space, nor between me and others. My consciousness still recognizes that I am Masami Saionji, but there is no borderline to my existence. I am one with the universe, one with Earth, one with all living things, existing beyond time and space (Saionji, 2009: 150).

This conception corresponds with an energetic worldview and energetic approach to peace. Reality is understood as an "interlocking web of fields that each pulsate at their own rate... These interlocking fields of vibration can come into harmony with each other and mutually support and increase their amplitude" (Kohn, 2008: 27). Daoists and Chinese medicine practitioners describe these fields as *qi* flow patterns. But the energetic fields do not always vibrate in harmony. They also interfere with each other and cause disturbances that may ripple out through other energetic fields.

Imanera (2012f) describes *qi* as the universe's primordial formative energy. We can direct and play with *qi*, she teaches, forming a relationship with it that promotes health, longevity and immortality. Specific *qi* forms are identified as Source *Qi*, Ancestral *Qi*, Central *Qi*, Constructive *Qi*, Defensive *Qi*, and *qi* that pertain to each organ. "In medical and self-cultivation contexts, *qi* means 'vital energy' or 'vital breath,' the animating principle of a living body. The principal aims of various techniques of self-cultivation are to refine the body's *qi*, to attain deep states of insight, and to control and direct the flow of energy within the body" (Major, Meyer, Queen & Roth, 2012: 6). In Daoist shamanic healing, *qi* is guided to refresh energetic flow along the meridians and the *dan tians* of the body (Imanera, 2012f).

The flow of these interlocking energy fields applies equally to body, mind, and universe. In meditation, practitioners attune with vibrations that far exceed the limits of their own individual form. They actually 'plug in' to cosmic energy.

> Just as bodily transformations are of unlimited possibilities, so the mind is ultimately nonlocal; it can be anywhere and exchange information with anything else instantaneously... Engaging in meditation exercises, practitioners thus connect to the energy-fields of the greater universe and, as traditional mystics have claimed all along, establish a deep harmony with the essential energies of the cosmos (Kohn, 2008: 27).

The Daoist meditator clarifies and stabilizes her mind, opens herself to energy fields, and brings the microcosm of her being into harmonious resonance with the macrocosm of the universe. As she embodies these spheres of heavens and earth, the practitioner becomes the intermediary.[73] With specialized skills, she may then take on the shamanic duty to venture further into various realms, gathering information to be translated for her community's benefit.

Attunement to universal resonance may be refined into a crucial tool for shamanic traveling between worlds. The trance enables the shaman to travel in varying physical forms to perform healing work. "Sometimes the journey is for the explicit purpose of communing with powerful beings who live in a different reality from the physical, in order to get their help in a healing process or conquer them in a shamanic battle on the invisible planes" (Noble, 1991: 131). The shaman may also communicate telepathically and gain knowledge of the future. "Methods of entering and achieving trance states vary from culture to culture and include a spectrum of diverse practices from quiet meditation to wild drumming and dancing, from fasting and purification to the ingestion of psychotropic substances" (*Ibid.*).

Grof and Grof depict the shamanic journey as one form of spiritual emergency, a "dramatic episode of a nonordinary state of consciousness that marks the beginning of the career of many shamans" (Grof & Grof, 1993: 140). Death and subsequent rebirth are typically at the core of this experience. "Initiatory dreams and visions include a descent into the underworld under the guidance of ancestral spirits, attacks by demons, exposure to unimaginable emotional and physical tortures, and finally complete annihilation. This is then typically followed by sequences of rebirth and ascent to super-

---

[73] Details about practicing this embodiment through 'Drawing down the Heavens' *qigong* are included in Chapter 10.

natural realms" (*Ibid.*). For the shaman to be accepted, she must integrate the transpersonal crisis of this rebirth, and demonstrate the ability to function in daily life.

Shamans are not alone in utilizing alternate states of consciousness to access wisdom and aid others.

> Meditators, yogis, contemplatives, and mystics also seek them and claim that it is these states that birth the deepest realizations. Mystical traditions have therefore developed techniques for altering consciousness in systematic ways, and these techniques constitute a *technology of transcendence* and a *technology of the sacred* (Walsh, 2007: 182).

Indeed, across various philosophical, psychological, and spiritual disciplines, there is common acknowledgement of the value of ego suspension to create space and silence for a different source of intuitive knowledge to surface. This does not eradicate the ego or abandon the rational mind; rather, it balances actively between dual forces, *yin-yang*.

9.7 MEDITATION AS A TRANSFORMATIVE PROCESS

As a transformative process, meditation works primarily with the subconscious mind. But the subconscious is not easily reached, due to the barrier of the critical conscious mind. This is why most practices begin with concentration techniques that enable the conscious mind to become still (Kohn, 2008). It is normal at the beginning of a practice to experience racing thoughts, jumping wildly from past memories to present concerns to future expectations. This behavior is often referred to as the 'monkey mind'. Through focused awareness on the breath, the conscious mind is given a rest from this seemingly uncontrollable rush of thoughts. In this rest, practitioners yield to the subconscious mind. "Gently drawing out the patterns of emotions and old habits, they release deeply ingrained ego-structures that were often accompanied by physical tension and unpleasant sensations" (*Ibid.*: 16). Oschman discusses the extraordinary perception and action that may occur in such transcendent states of consciousness.

> Recognizing our competing impulses more clearly, we can more freely choose among them, suppressing or sublimating some while acting up-

on others. To the extent that religious, moral, or therapeutic disciplines succeed, a person's many wills tend to become one will, single but articulated. As they are integrated, once-divergent intentions produce stronger results… If successful, transformative practices extend the capacity for purposeful action produced by animal evolution. They can strengthen the capacity for one-pointed behaviors evident in earlier forms of life while providing more options for creative behavior. They can make us better animals and better humans at once, as it were, more single-minded when we choose to be, but more various in our realized intentions (Murphy, as cited in Oschman, 2003: 48).

Removing old patterns, new options are recognized and considered with stronger intention. Meditation aids informed decisions in place of random impulses. New personality traits emerge.

> Thoughts are changed toward positive, well-meaning patterns, toward views in line with the teaching, such as nonaction in Daoism, impermanence in Buddhism, immediacy in Zen, deities in tantric Buddhism, or the true self in yoga. Negative emotions are eliminated and positive feelings installed, typically involving inner peace, calmness of mind, trust, gratitude, generosity, compassion, sympathetic joy, and the like… (Kohn, 2008: 17).

Memories and pain stored deep within the psyche and body are drawn out and acknowledged as important parts of the past that no longer hold meaning for the present. The practitioner can then leave behind these past associations that may have inhibited her from reaching a fuller human potential (*Ibid.*). The meditation tradition's worldview is crucial at this point, helping the transformed 'new person' to orient herself on her new path, free from ingrained patterns and past habits.

Mipham encourages observing one's journey on this path through balanced aspects of awareness, *sheshin* (presently knowing), and insight, *vipashyana*.

> The power of awareness tells us how the mind feels, what it's experiencing, the quality of our meditation, and how we're conducting it. It notices the transitory and illusory nature of thoughts, emotions, and concepts. Insight is the higher view that draws conclusions about what awareness sees. It penetrates phenomena, our mind, confusion – all that

we encounter – and sees its true nature, its meaning. At this point, an amazing transformation takes place (Mipham, 2003: 189).

The awakening and cooperation of these two capacities, awareness and insight, begin to develop *prajna*, the mind's natural intelligence and sublime knowledge, the "ability to know what *is*" (*Ibid.*).

A transformed mind and the leaving behind of old memories, emotions, and ingrained evaluations allows for immersion in a:

> state that goes beyond ordinary consciousness but pervades all levels of the mind. This superconscious level is called no-mind, wisdom mind, true self, Self, Big Mind, or cosmic consciousness. It is part of the divine that underlies the universe and connects the person with all existence. The ultimate state to be attained is what mystics describe as union or unitive consciousness, where oneness prevails and the common separations no longer apply (Kohn, 2008: 18).

"Cosmic consciousness" is known by many names, but various traditions describe the common experience of surpassing ordinary intellectual, emotional, and spiritual bounds to connect with an all-encompassing source. "Anchored in the joyous awareness of the infinite and firmly established in wisdom, they (meditators) are constantly aware of their true cosmic nature and remain undisturbed by the polarities of success and failure, pleasure and pain" (*Ibid.*). A new channel opens within the practitioner that allows her to align differently with the flow of life, a 'source' or 'intuitive wisdom'. Free from the burdens of attachment, she lives more fully in the present moment.

Meditation is also essential for integrating challenging or unsettling peak experiences such as Grof and Grof's 'spiritual emergencies'. "The general strategy here is to create situations in the everyday life where it is possible to fully confront the emerging material, such as periods of meditation or introspective experiencing facilitated by music. This seems to clear the remaining time in everyday life from the intrusion of unconscious elements" (Grof & Grof, 1993: 144). Whether blissful or troubling, meditation transforms insights and awareness, creating balance between conscious and unconscious input.

The *Book of Harmony and Balance* elaborates on how transformation helps humanity find its place in the larger cosmos. "Freedom from thought and freedom from contrivance are the substance of transformation; sense and response are the function of transformation. When you know the function you can fathom the substance; when you comprehend the substance you can sharpen the function" (Cleary, 1986: 9). Direct perception of change without subjective interference and sensitive response free from arbitrary action – the "function(s) of transformation" – come forth openly, untouched by thought and contrivance. They "represent practical expressions of two complementary modes of existence, movement and rest" (*Ibid.*). The *Book of Balance and Harmony* explains this perennial Daoist theme: "Rest is the foundation of movement, movement is the potential of rest. When you do not lose the constant in movement and rest, your path will be illumined" (*Ibid.*). As with rest and movement, other balances – stillness and action, receptivity and creativity – are recognized as complementary and interdependent. All are inherent aspects of being human.

9.8 My Research Journal: Quieting the Monkey Mind

Accessing concentration is the first step in focusing the mind and calming the senses. Focusing with steady awareness on the breath's movement in and out of the body facilitates this. In mysticism studies, concentration is described as an introversive or enstatic experience. The *Dao De Jing* encourages 'guarding oneness' and mental quiet, though it does not provide specific methods (Kohn, 2008). The Han dynasty's *Guanzi* (works of Master Guan) devotes a chapter to 'inward training', offering practical instructions and noting that generative energy (*jing*) is a concentrated form of *qi*.

> *Qi*, it says, is bright and dark, vast and lofty, and – like Dao – cannot be halted by force or controlled by rational thinking and speech. However, it can be secured by virtue or inner power (*de*) and brought into the self with the help of awareness or intention *(yi)*, the gentle conscious force that guides the *qi* through the body (as cited in Kohn, 2008: 44).

My own meditative encounter with and dismissal of 'monkey mind' brought me into the 'vast and lofty' *qi* described above. At the time I recorded this experience, I had been committed to a daily practice of meditation with mudras for about two months.

> *I close my eyes, form diamond mudra at my lower dan tian and my mind gets going- who I need to email, what I need to do before I leave for Austria. The usual. I've been struggling to quiet my mind recently because I've been in such physical discomfort from a painful infection in my mouth. Without*

practice to keep it quiet, my mind is a runaway train. A wave of frustration passes over me, taking me further away from the profound calm depth that I know awaits. I play the singing bowls again to bring me back, and I breathe. I raise the diamond mudra to my heart. I breathe and I bring my attention only to my breath... There it is. Like a cloth over a birdcage, a veil is dropped, soft and dark, muting and clearing. Today it feels like a soothing blanket that has smothered the flame. Ah, comfort. In my head I feel a pleasurable sinking, a respite, warm embrace. I am reclining into the dark simplicity of no thoughts. My body feels alert...

I sense a nagging tap on the shoulder, it is time. Time on my mind. How much time do I have? I breathe into that nagging question and it vanishes... My mind falls back into cushiony, velvety silence. Cloaked in this blanket, I find comfort. I sense I am receiving what I need. Nourishment, as though I'm leaning into a hug I long for, hearing the heartbeat of my lover, soothing, constant, reliable and deep. Connection. A soft ripple, a slight vibration, subtly passes through my body. ~June 28, 2012

The ability to regulate the mind to stay in the present moment eventually extends beyond just meditation; the process of keeping distracting thoughts at bay is the same. The following journal entry describes a powerful, novel, spiritual experience I underwent in a ritual for activating magic tools[74] with Imanera.

I reach the precipice panting from the climb. The sweet fresh aroma of pine fills my nostrils and mouth. Around my body is a blanket of heat, the warmth of the sun trapped under my long robe... As we begin to call in the directions, our robes flap and billow and the wind picks up, blowing hard. The sudden force of the wind surprises me, my body tingles. The atmosphere changes, as though a switch has been flipped. I feel weightless and grounded at the same time. My focus is keen, all senses alert. I pick up my stones and step back. The wind shifts. It no longer blows long gusts, it is whipping around, choppy, blustery. My hands are shaking visibly, my body trembles. I feel like a vessel and something else is coursing through me, like my blood holds a new charge. Fear briefly washes over me. I hold the lotus mudra and begin to shift my weight, seeking pressure on my joints. I sway slowly, grounding. The wind jumps around me, brushes up against me, bumps me.

---

[74] In this case, the tools being activated were minerals.

In rushes the familiar lure of thoughts, inviting me to 'snap out of it'. An invitation to the fastest way out – to follow those thoughts to another place, another story, just to get away from this confusing vulnerability, and to seek illusive security in another place, in distraction. I know the potential ease and comfort of dismissing what I am experiencing. But the gentle tremble of my body is not something I want to ignore. I want to know it, to stay in it. I am drawn to the anticipation and thrill of these sensations even though they surprise and scare me.

Imanera is here and her red robe is flapping. The sun shines warm on my cheeks. Mind recedes. I am the vastness in me. I let the energy rise. ~May 16, 2012

CHAPTER 10: DAOIST PRACTICES

> The active Taoist undertakes a certain representation of the universe, of the body, and of himself or herself. This representation comes alive, it becomes visible to the mental eye and is perceived by the inner being of each and every adept. The aim of the practice is to integrate personal individuality into a coherent and harmonious unity. More than that, the representation as it is actively and consciously produced by the practitioner and his or her living experience has to be encompassed in the greater unity: respiratory and visionary practices provide a new and newly integrated understanding of the body as well as of the divinities who cause it to be alive (Robinet, 1989: 159).

The ultimate goals of Daoist forms are the prevention of disease, aging, and death. In this chapter, I discuss these practices and traditions, and the Daoist perception of our physical, energetic, and spirit bodies, interspersing excerpts from my research journal that reflect my own experiences with the forms.

For Imanera (2012d), Daoist practices fall into three categories: literati, organized, and longevity. Literati practice entails contemplative study, research, and translation of Daoist texts, painting, and calligraphy. Organized practice involves group rites, rituals and ceremonies, and work with talismans, poetry, music, and star-stepping. Longevity forms focus on self-cultivation across many acts: breath regulation, healing shamanic sound, visualization from Highest Clarity, *dao-yin* (now known as *qigong*), self-massage, meditation (sleeping, sitting, standing, walking, and with stick, fan, sword, whisk, or animal frolic tools), tendon-changing and bone marrow washing, *neidan* for transmutation, external *qi* healing, mudras, tea, dietetics, and *fungshui*. Imanera's highest form of practice unites all three categories within the shaman's path.

Daoist practices that integrate body and universe go beyond simply a transformed *perception* of self to realize a fully transformed self in all aspects.

> The newly developed perception creates an utterly new body, a body that consists as much of the physical body proper as of the idealized image actively created. The physical body is the basic working material of the Taoists, their *materia prima*: all Taoist practices begin with the body, and one may well say that this is a characteristic common to all the various schools of the religion. The aim of the practice is therefore to establish the perception of a new body, called the 'spiritual body' by Tao Hongjing in the fifth century and the 'yang body' in the texts of operative and inner alchemy... In addition, it results in a new personality of cosmic dimensions, where the physical and the imaginary body, the individual and the cosmos, are intimately merged... Undergoing a gradual progress, he [an adept of Taoist meditation] attains unity or the One, a state of primordial oneness that nourishes and sustains the numerous diverse manifestations of being (Robinet, 1989: 160).

Such practice stimulates not only spiritual and imaginative facets, but also the physical. They transform the meditator's being to reflect her unique makeup as a microcosm of the universe.

10.1 BREATH, *QI*, AND THE *DAN TIANS*

Deepening the breath and focusing attention inward are fundamental to most meditation practices. Breathing calms the mind and connects to the universe; the breath is a source of cosmic energy that gives life to all beings (Kohn, 2008). Daoists view it as a manifestation of greater power, the life force of *qi*.

> *Qi* means both 'matter' and 'energy'. Everything that exists is made of *qi*, and every action is a manifestation of *qi* energy. *Qi* comes in various textures... Ethereal *qi* is heavenly, and coarse *qi* is earthly. Spirits are made of highly refined *qi*, but ordinary physical matter is made of coarse *qi*. Highly refined states of consciousness such as tranquility and clarity are manifestations of ethereal *qi*. *Qi* consequently serves as a

vibrating, resonant medium that conveys responses to stimuli (Major, Meyer, Queen & Roth, 2012: 7).

By recognizing *qi* as the substance of divine and earthly material, we begin to see the human's unique position in the Great Triad. Her body and breath are comprised of *qi*; thus divine and earthly energies unite in the human form.

We envision *qi* flowing in a system of waterways throughout the human body and nature. Keeping its flow smooth and balanced is of utmost importance. "*Qi* is the root of the human body; its quality and movement determine human health" (Kohn, 2008: 32).It can also be understood as electromagnetic energy, a current circulating through the body. Some adept *qigong* meditators believe the light perceived in their eyes and mind during practice is a transformation of electric *qi* (Yang, 1997).

There are three bodily *dan tians*:[75] lower, middle and upper. The lower is located just below the navel, storing generative energy, or *jing*. "Jing, best translated as Essence, is the Substance that underlies all organic life. It is the source of organic change. Generally thought of as fluidlike, Jing is supportive and nutritive, and is the basis of reproduction and development" (Kaptchuk, 1983: 43). *Jing* can be refined into vital energy – *qi* – which is stored in the middle *dan tian*, located near the heart.

Qi, in turn, can be transmuted into spirit energy – *shen* – residing in the upper *dan tian*, often referred to as the third eye. "*Shen* is best translated as Spirit... the Substance unique to human life... Shen is the vitality behind Jing and Qiin the human body. While animate and inanimate movement are indicative of Qi, and instinctual organic processes reflect Jing, human consciousness indicates the presence of Shen" (*Ibid.*: 45). This spirit energy is the form that might eventually merge with the primordial vapor of the Dao. Each *dan tian* has a gate that must be opened in order for the three body energies to be worked with and transformed (Wong, 1997a). We call *jing*, *qi*, and *shen* the Three Treasures, and they can be thought of as ice, water, and steam: all comprised of the same basic elements, but existing in different states due to their varying concentration and arrangement (Cohen, 1997; Imanera, 2012d).

---

[75] The *dan tians* are also referred to as 'cauldrons'.

The chakra system of bodily energy points is perhaps more familiar, and I raised the question with Imanera about the differences between *dan tians* and chakras. *Dan tians* are energetic pools, she explained, located in three distinct *qi* "reservoir" areas of the body. Chakras, on the other hand, are energetic vortexes spiraling out from the body-center *taiji* pole, and extending through the *wei qi*, the protective sphere of *qi* around the body (Imanera, 2012b). "The degree to which the individual chakras are open or obstructed determines the way one experiences the world and relates to it" (Grof & Grof, 1990: 34).[76] Imanera added that meridians are rivers of energy running through the body. In Chinese medicine, there are eight extraordinary and twelve primary meridians, and the functions and energy forms of each are different. The *dan tians* store and transform energy, the chakras protect, and the meridians circulate energy between inner and outer organs (Imanera 2012b).

Throughout life, humans gather *qi* from their food and air, and their sexual, emotional, and social interactions. We also lose *qi* by polluting our bodies with environmental conditions, improper nutrition, or negative interpersonal interactions. By controlling the breath, *qi* can be managed and cultivated, leading to physical wellness, longevity, and deeper spiritual experiences (Kohn, 2008).

> When *qi* resides in the body, the spirit is calm and the *qi* is like an ocean. If the *qi* as ocean is full to overflowing, the mind is at rest and the spirit centered. When this centering is not lost, body and mind are gathered in tranquility. Tranquility then grows further into deep concentration, and the body can exist for years eternal (*Ibid.*, 2008: 43).

In Daoist meditation, we draw breath deeply into the abdomen – the 'Ocean of *Qi*' in Chinese medicine terminology, or the lower *dan tian* in Daoism (*Ibid.*). The abdomen expands upon inhalation and contracts upon exhalation so that maximum breath, and therefore *qi,* reaches the organs. Such breathing allows for a focused mind, as *qi* gently fills the whole body.

In my work with Imanera, I have learned to harvest *qi* in the natural environment via *qigong* and meditation with mudras, or hand seals. I present these techniques here in passages from my research journal, which serve as a

---

[76] To do a self-analysis of your own chakras, see Appendix A.

'before and after' synopsis of some aspects of my Daoist practices. The first is taken from an entry recorded in early June, when I was still new to *qigong*.

Looking around me at the sleek rock wall towers encircling Chasm Lake, I sense the energy spiraling up like a gentle cyclone. My chest opens and weighty, stuffy, pieces of me evaporate softly into the air, lifted upward in the swirl. With my feet firmly on the ground, I am floating on that eddy, riding lightly on the wind as it circles the surface of the lake, then rises along the canyon walls. I meditate with diamond mudra, holding it first at my lower dan tian, then at my heart, and eventually up toward the heavens. I breathe deeply. I am part of this place. Its movement moves in me. ~ June 1, 2012

In the next passage, I reflect on my transition returning to town and my desire to prolong the calming effects of nature's *qi* in my daily urban life.

Moving at an urban pace, my mind keeps running and I fill the space with choppy, quick thoughts and distracting sounds. I want to remain in the place within me where I listen longer, where silence carries me lightly from moment to moment. I wish to ride the gentle river of qi down the mountain and flow smoothly into the valley, continue through the streets. Engulfed in qi, I look around slowly and deliberately, in my own rhythm, without notion of beginning or end. My thoughts are quiet and clear. ~June 2, 2012

The next account is dated September 10, 2012, at which point *qigong* had become a well-ingrained daily practice, and I saw firsthand how *qigong* was contributing to my wellness. It depicts a similar challenge to the above. I wonder how to absorb the soothing tranquility of nature and carry it with me, instead of feeling sadness or detachment knowing I will have to depart from that environment and the sensations it elicits in me. In this case, I have found techniques to help me meet this challenge.

Often when leaving the wilderness I react with anxiety: how can I possibly leave this place behind? How can relish in it 'enough' to be ready to move on? I have this yearning to somehow see enough, touch enough, get enough time in the place to be able to 'soak it in'. I am not sure if it is greed or desperation or perhaps just a longing that results from a lack of contact to the simple beauty of nature in my daily life. Here, my everyday preoccupations give way to the sweet taste of mountain air, the lush scent of pines, the curious intrigue of birdsongs, and deep hues of forest greens highlighted by golden patches of Aspen.

I am discovering that qigong offers a way to overcome that longing. Movement and visualization help to dissolve the perceived barrier between my surroundings and me as I merge the qi. Through qigong I fulfill the need to deepen my connection to place on levels far beyond mind and senses. I am not just walking by, I am not just sitting and looking. I slow down to stillness, then select forms dedicated to engaging and harmonizing with the energy patterns of the lake, the mountains. I break free from the thought that I cannot stay in this moment forever. I'm relieved from this clinging because my mind is quiet.

My attention is on my breath. I lower the bamboo curtain. I hold lake mudra as I meditate and I become the lake. I feel the cool, dark, slow depths within me, I bask in the warm, bright reflection at the surface. I am harvesting lake qi. With bear qigong I gather qi in my kidneys. I hold tree posture and send my roots deep. I close with 'Drawing down the Heavens' to merge heavens and earth within me, sealing the qi at my lower dan tian.

All of these forms help me to connect with nature and replenish my energy. The qi flow is restored, invigorating my cells. I am delighted. I continue walking with a light heart and rested mind, my steps buoyed by qi. ~September 10, 2012

10.2 MUDRAS

One of the first Daoist techniques I learned was mudra meditation, a sacred practice which involves shaping the hands into forms representing elements of nature – those of the *Bagua*, or the constellations of the Chinese zodiac, for instance – to connect with cosmic energy. Imanera describes mudras as 'mind stamps' and 'hand seals' and explains that they invoke a shape-shifting experience that cannot be taught, only learned directly. Meditating with the mudra for 'heavens', for example, enables the practitioner to tune into original, creative, divine energy. Meditating with the 'lake' mudra brings clarity. "After activation, hand dances in Daoist rituals are communication forms, magical tools and portals through the universe… Basically, the universe is in our hand" (Imanera, 2012f). As a novice, my mudras still serve as a bridge between physical and energetic realms; more advanced practitioners activate portals in their hands to bridge energetic and spirit worlds.

Chinese studies scholar Mitamura Keiko (2002) writes about the history of mudras, linking them to ancient shamanic techniques that also utilized hands and fingers in ritual contexts.

> Combined with spells and talismans, Daoist hand signs engaged the good spirits of the otherworld and banished the bad. Originating in

finger techniques that activated certain cosmic points in the body, they are deeply rooted in ancient indigenous practice and only secondarily evolved into their formal patterning under the influence of Buddhist mudras (Keiko, 2002: 247).

Shamanic dances, chants and other forms were also adapted by *fang-shi*, magical practitioners, and transmitted to Daoism. "Daoist hand signs (*shoujue*) have been used in personal and communal rites since the Six Dynasties for a variety of purposes, including the exorcism of evil forces, control over spirits, and healing of diseases" (*Ibid*.: 235). Primarily passed down orally as a secret sacred tradition, few written sources describe their history or present use.[77]

The more formal patterning of Daoist mudras was eventually influenced by their Buddhist counterparts, although Daoist mudras continued to develop on their own. They are thus divided into two main groups: the Buddhist influenced mudras, and the uniquely Daoist. The signs for 'lotus', 'bridge', and 'sword', for instance, imitate Buddhist mudras in name and execution, but take on additional meaning in Daoist texts. "Here, unlike in Buddhism, each finger segment was linked with the larger cosmos by being associated with the eight trigrams, seven stars of the Dipper, or twelve zodiac positions" (*Ibid*.: 236, 239). Though even uniquely Daoist mudras appear later than the Buddhist-inspired, indicating the possibility that they, too, may have been adapted from Buddhist techniques.

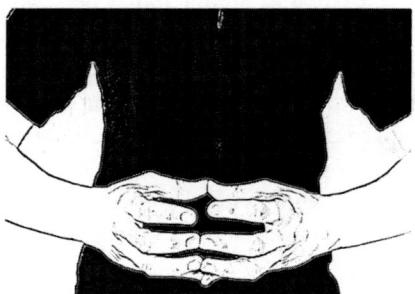

Lake Mudra
(energetic embodiment of the *Bagua*)

---

[77] All images in Chapter 10 are photographs taken by Imanera and modified by Aaron Stueck. Reprinted with permission, 2013.

Diamond Mudra   **Rooster Mudra**
(centering)   (looking out to look in)

Daoist mudras are formed using both hands, one hand, or hand movements. Finger techniques are essential in developing the practitioner's bodily integrity and harmony, as well as increasing and maintaining cosmic powers and protection. "In all cases, the transformation of the body into a locus of contact with, and merging into, the otherworldly realm of the Dao is a key element in the rites, and sacred hand gestures serve to empower and enhance this transformation" (*Ibid.*: 237). The mudra is usually held at the lower *dan tian*. Moving it adjusts its energetic response and produces different sensations in the meditator: the lower *dan tian* elicits a kinesthetic response; the middle *dan tian*, an empathetic one; the upper, intuitive (Imanera, 2012a). In section 9.8, I observe the subtle changes moving the diamond mudra from my lower to middle *dan tian*.

Master Liu He (2009) explains the power of the diamond mudra: "True intelligence depends on emotional stability. The Diamond Mudra helps you attain inner strength and teaches you persistence. Even when difficulties arise, this simple posture helps you center yourself and continue on" (Liu He, 2009: 152). This description resonates strongly with my own experience. In my initial training, I meditated with diamond mudra for 100 consecutive days. Imanera explains why she asks her students to do this:

> We are teaching them (students) how to transform *jing* into *qi*. Prenatal *jing* is cultivated and stimulated by meditation. *Jing* is one of our treasures; it is our essence, it is in our bone marrow. *Qi* is our bioelectricity and a vitality in the Universe. The *shen* is our spirit. We need to have a strong relationship with our growing spirit so nothing can harm us. To raise vibrational rate, energy moves from *jing* to *qi* to *shen* to *Wuji* to Dao like ice to water to steam. Diamond mudra meditation leads to a clear, peaceful mind (Imanera, 2012f).

In the following passages from my early weeks of Daoist training, I feel the profound effects of the diamond mudra.

Holding diamond mudra brings comfort. My body warms and relaxes. Worries melt away. My mind is peaceful, I can maintain this feeling of centeredness, of here and now, of trust. Trust it will all work out. I want to stay in this space, perhaps I need to be here longer to nurture and sustain it. But the truth is I can return at any moment, anytime, anywhere. ~May 1, 2012

I meditate with diamond mudra. I feel warmth in my lower dan tian, heat radiating throughout my body. I sense the energy pulsing, feel sensations soaring through my limbs. Like I've been plugged into a socket, I am recharged. Effortless. I do no work to sit up straight: drawing energy from the earth, my spine is guided gently toward the heavens. I relax my shoulders, my third eye. My mind is calm, rooted. I am not distracted or agitated. The rising anxiety of a moment ago is relieved. My thoughts have retreated. I dissolve in this moment. Here I am, I am here, and all is well. My mind need not interfere. ~May 10, 2012

Other Daoist *mudras* involve the practitioner exerting thumb pressure on one or more joints of the other fingers, a technique unique to China and not found in India. This indicates a departure from Buddhist-inspired static symbols toward "indigenously Daoist hand movements and Cosmic functions" (Keiko, 2002: 244). The mudras for the Chinese zodiac are formed with this technique. Here, I meditate on the energy of the seasons with monkey mudra, an aid for letting go, and rooster mudra, my star sign (I was born in the year of the rooster).

It is the end of the month of the monkey, soon we will move into the month of the rooster. At the end of summer, we are in the harvest, gathering energy, storing it like squirrels. We are preparing for the contraction that will begin with approaching winter. With monkey mudra, I embody letting go of what does not serve me for this transition into Autumn. Clean slate. I feel liberated, like those tendrils attaching me to worry are severed. My mind is clear, my heart round and whole, I am centered, open. I grow my roots into the earth, three times my height, and feel the energetic connection through my soles. ~August 23, 2012

10.3 MY MEDITATION CHALLENGES

Though most of the journal entries I include portray 'successful' meditative endeavors (these sessions are certainly more inspiring to write about), I have also experienced many days when the task of uniting mind, body and breath feels almost impossible. Developing meditative concentration requires regular, dedicated practice and, according to Daoist master Sun Simiao, it will progress in stages. At first, the practitioner experiences agitated, wandering thoughts and little tranquility. She will later begin to experience moments of calm, leading to a state of half agitation and half tranquility. Simiao believes the mind eventually recognizes the benefits of rest and will more readily reach greater tranquility and only slight agitation. Finally, one enjoys a mind of complete purity and tranquility void of agitation (Simiao, as cited in Kohn, 2008).

In the next two journal excerpts, I face uncertainty, physical exhaustion, anxiety, and emotional turbulence.

I find my physical self to be quite fatigued this evening, recovering from last night's Beltane celebration. In forming diamond mudra in front of my heart, I feel some disconnect, distress. Slight anxiety arises, level 2 (out of 10), pertaining to the questions: is this where I should be... why am I here? ~May 2, 2012

My anxiety is here, reaching climactic points. Family changes bring on acute sadness. My new interests and lifestyle create what feel like obstacles and changes in relationships with old friends, straining communication as I'm uncertain how to connect openly and honestly. Tension comes and goes in my household as roommates voice their needs, confront differences, and work to understand and restore flow. In the throes of these scenarios, I am emotionally overextended. My heart reaches out to people and circumstances, too far. Too committed. In this overextension, I feel incapable of focusing on this project. I am drained. I feel pressure to reach an impossible deadline, an insurmountable barrier. I feel desperate – meditation helps but it is so hard to find my center because I am so scattered. I hold diamond mudra but in exhaustion and unsettled emotions, I lose focus. ~June 21, 2012

In retrospect, I wonder about my breath: was I aware of and utilizing it? Key to facing such challenges is not allowing criticism of perceived failures or setbacks to take over. This happens easily, and feeds the meditation-based ego, which gauges and judges based on the 'progress' of practice. Inevitably, the mind wanders from the breath, and it is necessary to refocus again and again without succumbing to frustration or self-criticism. The goal remains "to allow everything to come up, with all its energy: all of, for instance, your anger and loneliness and despair, to allow these things to arise and be transformed by the light of awareness" (Rosenberg, 1999: 7). Not being taken for a ride by emerging emotions requires a combination of effort and surrender, refraining from expectations and evaluations, and remaining completely present to access the subconscious (Kohn, 2008).

Kohn makes clear that a tranquil mind requires a holistic lifestyle commitment. Removing heavy foods and grains is advised, along with regular exercise conducive to opening the body's *qi* channels – *qigong* and *taiji*, for example (*Ibid.*). A 'well-ordered' mind allows *qi* to flow through these channels so that all aspects of life are filled with its power. At this point, the adept Daoist practitioner enjoys complete balance of body and mind, allowing her to let go of the ups and downs of life, to detach from constricting emotions, and to experience harmony, peace, and alignment.

10.4 Transforming Emotions into Virtues

Imanera teaches that "virtue is the structure of the Dao, and original mind is its function" (2012b). At birth, when the human being still exists in the purity of original mind, she possesses Dao virtues: kindness, joy, trust, integrity, and wisdom. Over time, humans absorb emotions resulting from 'templates of wounding', such as rejection and abandonment. These emotions – nervousness, anger, fear, grief, and worry – fester as energy stored in specific organs.[78] When they appear in excess or preoccupy the mind, they bring harm to internal organs and disturb *qi* (Cohen, 1997). While they can arise at any time, certain emotions are more likely to appear in particular seasons (Imanera, 2012b).

Acquired emotions[79] let us know where we are in relation to our center. But they are also detrimental to health, dispersing or consuming *qi*. The most effective coping mechanism for these emotions is to sublimate them into virtues,[80] which instead heal the organs (Imanera, 2012b). Dissipating emotional vibrational charge allows for stillness, where we again find balance

---

[78] For example, fear is trapped in the kidneys, grief in the lungs, anger in the liver, worry in the spleen, and nervousness and shock in the heart.
[79] Chart reprinted with permission from Imanera (2012b).
[80] "The Chinese word for virtue (de) was originally written with the same character as the word 'to plant,' suggesting that virtue is a power that can be cultivated" (Cohen, 1997: 236).

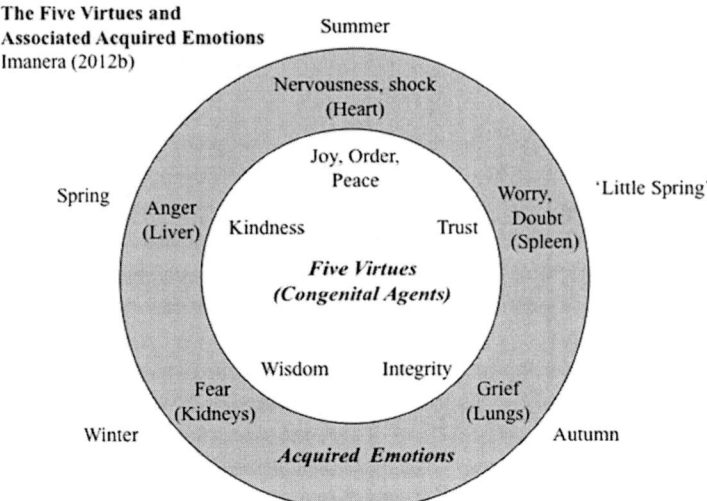

between expansion and ecstasy on the one hand and contraction and depression on the other.

As previously discussed, meditation works with the subconscious to release old patterns of perceiving and judging, opening space for the practitioner to reach her highest potential and experience the Dao's flow. Insight practice is one meditative form that can change emotional patterns and structures.[81] It begins with access concentration and is aimed at creating, "a detached observer at the center of consciousness... It similarly encourages the transformation of emotions, supports a detached attitude toward the changes of life, and acknowledges that there is no permanent entity that makes up the self or affords a solid identity" (Kohn, 2008: 85).

Insight meditation works with the Daoist interpretation of the mind as it relates to the five major organs.

> ... Daoists understand it (the mind) as consisting of several dynamic functions associated with the five inner organs, further assisted by a va-

---

[81] Daoist insight meditation is also referred to as "inner observation", "concentration and observation", or "true observation" (Kohn, 2008: 85).

riety of energetic forces understood as different aspects of *qi*. The main mental aspects, as also defined in Chinese medical literature, are: 'The spirit soul in the liver; the material soul in the lungs; the essence in the kidneys; the intention in the spleen; the spirit in the heart'... The intention at the center, associated with the spleen, then, is the force that connects the mind with outside reality and governs its interaction with the world (*Ibid.*: 86).

In Daoism as in Chinese medicine, various bodily components such as blood and saliva are seen as forms of cosmic *qi* that support the organs as energetic entities (*Ibid.*). These forces comprise important parts of the mind and are essential to spiritual and emotional transformation. The transformative aspects of insight meditation are aimed not only at altering perception and emotions, but also a:

> Complete energetic reorganization of the person... The practice of calming the mind and establishing a witness consciousness accordingly serves to overcome the limitations of a personal, body-motivated identity and of the critical, judgmental nature of the mind in favor of a state of no-body and no-mind... This state of no-mind in due course becomes the foundation for the calm apperception of the true nature of the self (*Ibid.*: 87).

Anxiety falls under the same category as worry. Similarly, it can be transformed into, or by, the virtue of trust. Personally, I have worked to manage anxiety in this book's various research stages; so when I notice myself becoming anxious, I often recite a mantra about trusting. This journal entry describes one such process of visualization and embodiment of trust.

I begin my day with focused clearing. A clearing of all those voices and emotions pulling me in every direction. I breathe into this project. I breathe into what I want my body to feel, the sensation I know will course through me when I am successful in writing. I hold that vision, that sensation of accomplishment, I breathe into it. And in that way I empower myself – from muscles, to emotions, to a prayer to my guides – to succeed. The anxiety is kept at bay when I am able to trust, not merely <u>think</u> trust, but to embody trust, to breathe it into my cells. I pause in this embodiment. Then I proceed. ~June 21, 2012

10.5 *QIGONG* – BODY AWARENESS

A large component of my Daoist practice is *qigong*, a technique in the meditative category of body awareness. Unlike other meditation forms, body awareness involves slow, conscious movements and poses.

> Body awareness, the subjective consciousness of body sensations in mental absorption, is similar to concentration and insight meditation in that it, too, requires deep and steady breathing and the development of a detached observer in the mind… accesses the subconscious mind through kinesthetic apperception… The point of the practice is to access and release past conditionings retained in the muscles and joints while enhancing the body's natural wisdom, creating inner peace, freedom, and ease as well as an ultimate connection to the divine (Kohn, 2008: 154).

The animal dances of the *wu*, the ancient Chinese shamans, exhibit the first evidence of *qigong*-like exercises (Cohen, 1997). In the second century C.E., the famous physician Hua Tuo explained the value of the Five Animals Frolic, one of the early healing exercises and a widely known *qigong* form today:

> The body needs a certain amount of movement. This movement serves to properly balance right and left and to redistribute and assimilate the various grain energies; it also causes the blood to circulate smoothly and prevents the arising of diseases. The human body is like a door hinge that never comes to rest. This is why Daoists practice healing exercises. They imitate the movements of the bear, which hangs itself head down from a tree, and of the owl, which keeps turning its head in different ways. They stretch and bend the waist, and move all the joints and muscles of their bodies in order to evade aging (Kohn, 2006: 165).

In India, body awareness appeared as the yogic tradition. In ancient China, it was originally known as *dao-yin*, now called *qigong*. In this case, *dao* means 'to guide' or 'direct', and *yin* 'to draw a bow', which suggests building tension while also activating strength. *Qi* translates as 'life energy', *Gong* as 'daily effort' (Kohn, 2008).

> In self-cultivation… [*dao-yin*] implies to guide the *qi* through the body in order to establish harmony with Dao, realizing the inherent polarity of yin and yang and aligning oneself with the cosmos… *Qigong* is a

system of slow body movements done in coordination with deep breathing and the mental guiding of *qi* that releases tension, effects healing, and contributes greatly to overall well-being (*Ibid.*: 155, 177).

Qigong is distinguished from Indian yoga because it involves mostly standing and works with continuous movements versus held poses.

Both yoga and *qigong* draw a connection between strength and flexibility and well-being, longevity and spiritual attainment, recognizing that many psychological and spiritual traits are rooted in the body's physical tissue. Body awareness meditation takes the larger Chinese worldview that the entire universe, including the human body, is composed of *qi*, which is always in motion. "… [I]t [*qi*] divides into two aspects *yin* and *yang*, which signify its phases of resting and moving, slowing and accelerating, descending and rising… and so on" (*Ibid.*: 171). *Qigong* increases this flow of life energy through the joints, stimulating an opening and release that helps access new levels of emotional and spiritual life. It also harmonizes *qi* flow through the eight extraordinary and twelve primary meridians, moistening and distributing nutrition, and balancing internal *yin* and *yang*.

Regular body awareness practices help overcome the tendency to form splits in our bodies, rebalancing the right and left sides, or upper and lower body. Isolation of the head from the rest of the human is a common scenario; people are either completely stuck in their minds, following only logic, intellect, and rational thought, or they move through life 'headlessly', responding blindly to emotions and intuition (*Ibid.*). In *qigong*, practitioners develop greater awareness of such splits and, through poses and movements, begin to integrate their distinct sides.

Cohen divides body awareness techniques into two categories. In dynamic or active *qigong*, the whole body is in motion from one posture to the next. Or one posture is held while the arms enact different positions. In tranquil *qigong*, the body is still, and "the *qi* is controlled by mental concentration, visualization and precise methods of breathing" (Cohen, 1997: 4). But these categories are not strict. It is important to find balance between their relative principles: stillness in action and action in stillness, seeking to balance *yin-yang* forces.

10.5.1 *Qigong*: Variety in styles and approaches

Qigong techniques have evolved over time, changing with the worldview, intent and background of the teacher and practitioner. For one, its purpose may simply be to improve health. Another may wish to unify *jing, qi,* and *shen* (Cohen, 1997). I have read about a *qigong* form from the Chinese government's perspective, and then learned the form of the same name from Imanera, where it takes on a very different look and feel in its shamanic incarnation. What's more, multiple *qigong* forms exist to express one intention, such as harmonizing heavens and earth, giving the teacher and practitioner a wide range of options.

Qigong is one of the primary techniques Imanera teaches. Its goal, she believes, is to transform energy and, therefore, to increase consciousness. "Everyone is born with *qi* and everyone has the potential to use *qi*... [T]he skill to use *qi* is trained, not born. Once a person is trained how to reach the *qi*, he or she can then use *qi* for martial arts, dancing, pilates, hiking and medical self-healing" (Imanera, 2012a). Imanera practices and teaches not just as a healing technique, but also for its original (*dao-yin*) intention of finding cohesion between physical, energetic, and spirit bodies, while harmonizing with the Dao's divine energy. Her approach revives *qigong*'s ancient shamanic roots through embodiment and transmutation of energy, and travel between heavens and earth.

Take the Eight Piece Brocade, the most recent *qigong* form I have learned in preparation for 100 consecutive days of practice. Imanera has shown me the direct link between this *qigong*'s various movements and the energetic patterns of the eight elements of the *Bagua*. It thereby becomes another practice for embodiment of the *Bagua's* forces, leading to shamanic shape-shifting for energetic healing, and opening up the eight extraordinary meridians. Breathing techniques are adjusted for each year of Eight Piece Brocade practice in order to stimulate energetic transmutation: natural breathing in the first year, abdominal breathing[82] in the second, and reverse abdominal breathing[83] in the third. Breathing changes are crucial in *neidan* inner alchemy practices for the transformation of *jing, qi,* and *shen* energies (Imanera, 2012e).

Eight Piece Brocade *qigong* is also taught and practiced as a *wushu* martial arts form – the technique the Chinese government approves. This version emphasizes posture repetition graded according to exact replication of its teaching (*Ibid.*). Discussion of the *Bagua* or inner alchemy are removed from

---

[82] "In abdominal breathing the lungs are expanded and contracted by the muscles of the diaphragm and abdomen, rather than the chest muscles" (Yang, 1997: 128).

[83] Reverse abdominal breathing is often called "Daoist Breathing... [W]hen you inhale, you draw the abdomen in and hold up your Huiyin (Co-1) cavity or anus. When you exhale, gently push out your abdomen and Huiyin cavity or anus" (Yang, 1997:129).

the equation, and the form becomes a strategy for well-being and defense, not an art or *neidan* practice. The pictures below demonstrate the movement differences that distinguish the *wushu* approach. Image A shows the right index and middle fingers pointed skyward. Image B illustrates the form I learned, with those two fingers extending straight out, parallel with the arm; this allows *qi* to flow to the fingers' extremities, then circulate back. Imanera believes the bent right wrist of the *wushu* form may crimp this flow, preventing its full cycle.

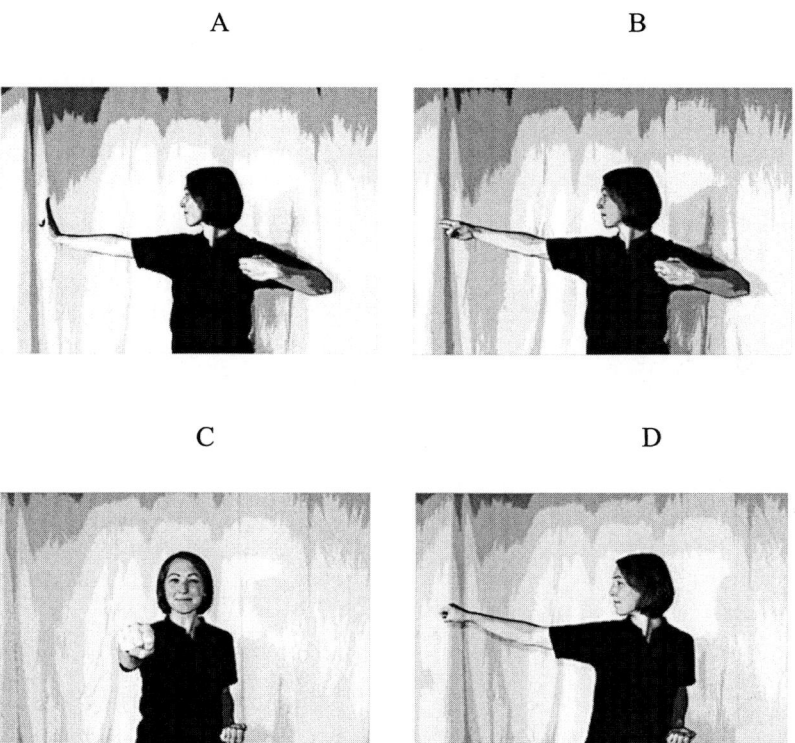

Cohen's *wushu* style of "Punching with Angry Gaze to Increase Qi and Strength" (Cohen, 1997: 193) is depicted in Image C. In Imanera's teaching of this form, the arm and fist extend straight out to the side and the gaze follows (Image D). This version readies the practitioner for defending herself, but in a less aggressive style.

Qigong forms harmonize heavens and earth within the human being, in part via internal alchemy's visualization techniques (Cohen, 1997). Drawing

Down the Heavens *qigong* harnesses the energies of the Great Triad, merging the heavens' openness and earth's tranquility through three simple gestures. Drawing the hands up, palms to the sky, signifies "I am heavens". Drawing them down, palms to the ground, indicates "I am earth". Finally, drawing them down the central axis of the body expresses "I am intermediary". The cosmic and earthly *qi* gathered after nine repetitions is sealed at the lower *dan tian* (Imanera, 2012a).[84]

10.5.2 Peace *Qigong*: Effects

Among the first forms I learned with Imanera is a series called Peace *qigong*. I currently practice this form daily, though I have yet to complete 100 consecutive days. Imanera taught this form to a group of students, asking us to quantify our inner peace before and after the series.

	Inner Peace Rating (scale 1-10) **Before** Peace *Qigong*	Inner Peace Rating (scale 1-10) **After** Peace *Qigong*
Practitioner A	7	10
Practitioner B	2	8.5
Practitioner C	8	10+
Practitioner D	3.5	7

---

[84] In *qigong*, *qi* is sealed at the lower *dan tian* to help students experience the important first step of feeling centered and grounded, to develop a root. *Jing gong* and *shen gong* are other Daoist practices for generating the energy forms *jing* and *shen*, but are, respectively, too sexual and too difficult for most beginners. Since the three energy forms are different manifestations of the same essential elements, the 'elixir field' of the body is able to integrate and harmonize all (Imanera, 2012d).

Practitioner E	9	10

The following further describes my personal experience with the form that day:

We practice the peace qigong series. Repetition, prayer, breath, slow movements. This combination is rich, seductive. It is both empty and full. Empty in that there is nothing to be 'done' but follow the steps and breathe. Full because it engages every bit of my awareness. I am drawn in, lulled into each smooth movement and breath. Upon completion we are asked: what is peace? Peace is nowhere but in the present moment. And in the present moment, I feel confidence and trust. I feel secure, patient. I sense I am doing what I am meant to do, on a path. My inner peace climbs from a 7 to a 10. ~June 28, 2012

The following photos portray the basic movements of Peace *qigong*. Each movement is accompanied by an inhalation or exhalation, and visualization.

 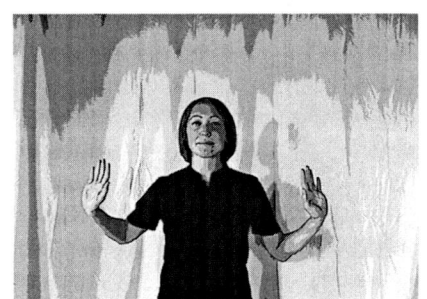

 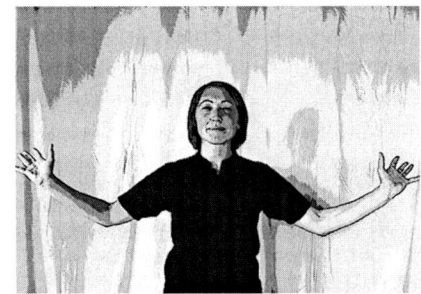

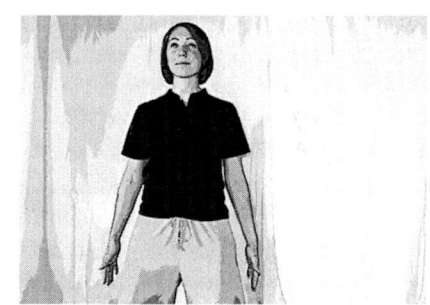

Completing the Peace *qigong* set, Imanera asked us to consider what the form means for us, and for peace. My reflection led to the relationship between personal and universal consciousness.

What does it mean to have engaged in this process? What happens when my energy shifts from worry, fear, grief, mostly about what <u>could</u> happen, to a calm, grounded sensation that right now, in this moment, I am well, I accept all as it is. How does that energy affect the frequencies of people and places around me? My human consciousness manifests in how I treat others, how I think and act. It influences each decision I make. And what about a global level, and beyond? A universal consciousness? If my consciousness is more closely attuned to peace, if my priority is inner peace, and I feel free to explore extremes, then return to a peaceful center, doesn't this shift, ever so slightly, the priority of a consciousness much larger than my own? ~June 28, 2012

In writing this book, I purposefully curtailed a *wu wei* state of spontaneity. Acceptance with receptivity is a fundamental aspect of *wu wei* non-action, and typically preferable over will. "Will is the basis of most Western thought, hence the preference for action" (Cooper, 1972: 77). This preference for action ignores the possibility that, in many scenarios, it may be better not to *do* anything, but instead permit the situation to "develop naturally without gratuitous interference" (*Ibid.*: 77). Cooper writes, "'the active essence of non-action and the passive essence of action' runs through all alchemical tradition as the spiritual work of transmuting and ennobling the soul, the soul being the 'substance' worked upon, the spirit expressing itself in form" (*Ibid.*: 87). When the idea of changing this book's theme from shamanism in general to Daoist shamanism first occurred to me, I felt 'turned inside out'. I was exasperated, since I had already invested significant time and effort developing the initial theme. Fortunately, I remembered to 'practice what I preach', and employed transformative techniques to consider this change in a different light.

In the library, I am panicking. My heart beats faster. I'm flushed and annoyed. I rush out of the library and walk toward the grass. My steps are hurried and impatient but I slow down once I'm off the sidewalk. I walk to a tree and sit close to its trunk. I form diamond mudra. I breathe into the sunshine. I breathe into the warmth, the green, the clear sky, the bright light of the day. I smile, my forehead relaxes. My irritation fades, slowly. I breathe my way into clarity. I stay with my breath as the worry wanes. I begin to feel comfortably heavy, drawn to the earth. I lie belly down in the grass and roots and my heartbeat reverberates in my body, deep, loud thumps. Constant, continuous. I listen and my whole body is wrapped around the earth, our heartbeats are one.

Resting, it's as though a sea of cloudiness is parting in my mind. I see with wider, clearer vision. What am I trying to force? Why be willful and rigid with expectations when solutions reveal themselves naturally along a way, and I may simply choose to accept? ~August 20, 2012

With so much of my energy directed towards analyzing, organizing, processing, and writing, I succumb to the very head-body split I research. Imanera (2012b) presented another option to address the dilemma. Scholarly work produces fire in the mind, so she advised me to send the attention that tends to stick in my head down to my toes. In the eight trigrams of the *Bagua*,

> The human mind belongs to fire, which is based on the body of heaven… The mind of Tao belongs to water, which is based on the body of earth. This is the jade pond, containing the water of celestial unity as real knowledge; this is that in which the hardness and firmness of heaven is balanced in the center – that is, the original innate knowledge (Cleary, 1996: 43).

Visualization and energetic redirect create space for new insights. This more spontaneous form of perceiving requires my directed attention and intention, and so action and non-action, acceptance and will, remain constant companions on my path.

Alteration of the body's energetic sensations through *qigong* leads many to think of *qi* as an electromagnetic current. Yang explains that electromotive force (EMF) is required for a current to exist, and one of the four causes of EMF in the human circuit is the mind and *shen* (spirit). The *qigong* meditator uses her mind to send this 'electricity' to the limbs and "energize the muscle tissues", creating more balance in the human circuit. (Yang, 1997: 55).

In my own case, it enables my mind to calm and my focus to return as I distribute fire energy down to my toes. Peace *qigong* allows me to transition into a state of *wu wei* and facilitates a shift from fire to water energy. By pausing to break from habits of willfulness, I problem-solve better and trust a clear intuitive voice more deeply. Cooper sees this *wu wei* process as an unfolding rather than forced exertion.

> Until he has achieved spontaneity his actions are the result of the will, or the deliberations of the rational mind and therefore are artificial and strained and out of harmony with the 'motions of Heaven'. Movement should be an unfolding, not an exertion; it should be involuntary (Cooper, 1972: 74).

In my journal, I process my rational mind ignoring the growing fire and pressing on with work, even as the intuitive voice wishes to redirect energy to Peace *qigong*'s non-action.

I have been working for about three hours. I was feeling motivated and energized because writing was going well. But the fire has been growing – that heat and intensity that starts building at the back of my head and spreads. It's that burning sensation of focus that will perpetuate itself, it is relentless because its message is, if you lose me, you will lose momentum. When writing, there is an extra degree of pressure involved, trying to integrate all these ideas and make every next sentence fit with the last. The intensity, burning, is all-consuming. Every cell of my body is convinced that I have to keep feeding the fire. But I know the consequences. The fire produces smoke and the smoke changes everything, it is deceivingly transparent but hot, thick and heavy. It becomes a barrier to thinking clearly, disturbs the water-like quality of fluid thoughts. It limits perspective, disrupts qi flow, and I become fed up, exhausted.

So I interrupt the burning drive to continue. I choose to stand up and go outside, wander down to the creek. Smiling with other people along the path breaks the tension. Gradually, my mind and eyes open up, I hear the creek and feel the flickering sun and shadows on my cheeks. The fire begins to subside. I am walking. I hear my breath. The embers of the fire linger. This point is familiar and vulnerable. This is the exact scenario where I can fall into the trap of my own patterns: if I push it, if the fire is stoked by some de-

mand, it will flame up with irritability. And in those cases it spreads and becomes unbearable. But now, I am alone and aware, with no one but myself to attend to. I move closer to the creek's edge.

I listen to the water and watch the ripples. The ducks are so playful. I breathe. The remaining heat of the fire dissipates. I begin to relax, the skin across my forehead softens, my shoulders drop, my belly softens. My legs feel strong and solid. I am calm, but where is my energy? It has just staved off the fire. To help the creek's coolness fill me, to bring in the water, I do peace qigong. Ten repetitions. I am finding my heartbeat, following the river's rhythms. I send a blossoming lotus flower to the sky, I note its perfect color and form. I cradle the heavens and merge with the earth, I am bowing in humble honor of the beautiful position I hold between heavens and earth. I am sending ten prayers to the sky, I know I am not alone. I am breathing, bending, energy is circulating. The cool qi is invited to move through all my limbs. When I finish, I am still. I swallow, seal the qi, close the practice. I am at rest. The heat of the fire is just a memory now. I smile, soaking in nourishing qi, letting it sink into my bones. I transition with a little shake, and return to writing. ~September 4, 2012

10.5.3 Confidence in Creative Expression

Peace *qigong* helps me step outside my usual tendencies, to 'reset' and experience energetic refreshment – what Kohn describes as harmony with the flow of life. Persistent body awareness practice unravels common body-mind patterns, making the practitioner aware of her own interactive and experiential options. "What the Indian tradition describes as the true self and the Chinese express in terms of harmony with Dao is thus felt by people today as a sense of integration and inner well-being, complete with the courage to express oneself individually and creatively in the world" (Kohn, 2008: 162). Awareness of options and confidence in courageous, creative expression are essential aspects of peacework. A mediator must develop a broad range of perspectives to see many possibilities and to proceed confidently in articulating and exploring them. *Qigong* and other body awareness methods help develop these qualities.

I taught Peace *qigong* to friends during a visit to Innsbruck, and found that sharing the practice with others fostered my confidence and improved the quality of my interactions with my 'students'.

I am speaking and holding myself in a place of calm trust. I am open and receptive, a vessel. I teach peace qigong with confidence in my own practice, and curiosity about others' responses. Whereas in the past, I would have been self-critical and nervous about whether or not my friends would enjoy it, now I proceed with teaching without that doubt. I teach from my heart rather than from my head, thanks to regular practice and a kind of pruning of the mind, a quieting of that self-critical voice. I ground down by meditating with diamond mudra. From the warmth generated in my lower dan tian, I speak with smooth strength and fluidity. I am teaching while holding intention, instead of concern about others' reactions. When I raise my face to send the lotus flower to the heavens, I pause to feel the sun, to resonate with prayer and my environment. In peace qigong, the heart and breath lead the movements, there is little place for the mind to dictate what should or should not be. With a quiet mind, I allow prayers to spontaneously arise.

As we move and breathe together, I feel a different sensation from practicing alone. The movements flow through my limbs more smoothly, more fluidly as I sense the others moving in unison. My breaths sink deeper as I hear others' exhalations. And in these rhythms I feel the series become effortless, as though I am carried by the qi flow amongst the three of us. The initiation of each movement is no longer prompted by my energy alone.

With enhanced awareness, I remain more available to help others ground and process without losing connection with myself. I can be in the rhythm of the group while maintaining my own beat. I am sharing insights with friends about finding peace and balance based in my own experiences and observations. The time I need to surface, to be outward after going deeply inward, has shortened. Likewise, the transition between reaching out, pushing my own limits to explore something new, and coming back to balance, to center, in order to integrate and process that stretch, has become smoother. I feel buoyed back to center. ~August 11, 2012

10.5.4 *Qigong* in Support of Others

While Chapter 11 explores in more detail how Daoist shamanic practices assist the elicitive peaceworker, it first bears mentioning the ways that *qigong* practice helps anyone wishing to improve the health or quality of life of others. Those in fields such as peacework and social work often experience emotions of anger, sadness, and frustration when confronted with the magnitude of challenges within the communities and clients they support. The *qigong* practitioner can work directly with the energetic patterns of her and her clients' emotions, grounding her emotional field to become a shining light for all. She can also serve as a leader of transformation in her community. In response to a recent Colorado tragedy that filled people with fear and anger and led families to keep children indoors, Imanera suggested we invite the public to practice *qigong* together. By gathering in a safe community space and identifying with animals and nature through *qigong* movements, people may transcend fear, anger, and grief to get in touch with the sense of freedom they have lost. This transcendence allows for reintegration of mind, body and spirit to restore wellness to the overall population.

This is in part because *qigong* operates through "coherent resonance" (Imanera, 2012e). When person A is in the field of another person B practicing *qigong*, person A will actually begin to feel the effects of B's gathered *qi*. This produces inner tranquility, and can be a very effective *wu wei* practice to support severely traumatized people, for instance. In this sense, *qigong* is a means to care for others. Advanced practitioners of Chinese medicine can even heal by transmitting *qi*. This practice takes significant training, though, since it requires mastery of many skills: reaching, gathering, purifying, directing, and transforming *qi*.

Though *qigong* is typically a solitary or group practice, some *taiji* forms involve interacting with one other person. Partner *qigong* is a powerful technique for cultivating interpersonal sensitivity and modifying perception of others (*Ibid.*). Harmonizing movement and breath with another living being relieves self-centered focus and attunes us with fellow human life.

10.5.5 *Taiji*

The martial arts' expression of *dao-yin* is *taijiquan*, which develops "openness, fluidity, and energetic harmony" (Kohn, 2008: 174). It keeps muscles relaxed through a series of movements typically enacted in an upright position with feet planted. "*Taiji* means 'Grand Ultimate'. It is the force that generates two poles, Yin and Yang... *Taijiquan* [is] a Chinese internal martial style which is based on the theory of *Taiji*" (Yang, 1997: 297). I have not experienced *taijiquan*, but I have been introduced to some of its forms while practicing *qigong*. In both, all movements are directed by *qi*; it is responsible for moving the muscles, rather than the actions being forced by mental or physical exertion. If *qigong* is the grandmother, *taiji* is the grandson (Imanera, 2012a).

10.6 Visualization and 'Fusion of the Five'

Visualization is another meditative technique that accesses the subconscious mind and retrains brain patterns, transforming emotional reactions. It dates to the Han dynasty, where records show "activation of the five inner organs with the help of color visualizations" (Kohn, 2008: 128).

> The term for visualization in Daoism is *cun,* a verb that basically means 'to be,'… and is here used in its causative mode: 'to cause to exist'… It thus means that the meditator by an act of focused intention causes certain energies to be present in the body or makes specific deities or scriptures appear before his mental eye… An early form of concentration through visualization is called 'guarding the One' (*shouyi*), first described as focusing the mind on the organs as centers of primordial *qi*… The *Taiping jing* (Scripture of Great Peace)… describes it as full mental fixation on the inner light of the body which represents the cosmic forces of creation (*Ibid.*: 129, 132).

This inward gaze offers another method for bridging mind and body, and finding peace and healing in that cohesion.

Through Fusion of the Five *qigong*, I have used visualization to nurture my organs with colored light. Its movements align with the five directions recognized in Daoism: South, North, East, West, and Center. Attention may be placed on certain aspects correlated with each direction: colors, animals, internal organs, and virtues, for example (Imanera, 2012c). The South is the direction of the red bird, where emphasis is placed on the heart and the virtues of peace and joy. The North is the direction of the black turtle and snake, the kidneys, and the virtues of wisdom and will. The East is the green dragon; focus is directed to the liver, and compassion. To the West lies the white tigress, the lungs, and integrity. The center is home to the golden dragon, where trust is cultivated in the spleen and stomach. "[Each colored light] is, moreover, the radiance of the centered harmony of the universe and signifies true peace" (Kohn, 2008: 133). The goal of most Daoist practices I have experienced is to bring the five spirits into harmony to create peace and good health.

Though my practice has been less consistent with this form, I aspired for 100 days with it.

This morning I begin the day with fusion of the five virtues qigong followed by peace qigong. When I wake up knowing that my day will be propelled forward by the demands of writing the pages of this book, and beyond that there are countless smaller items to accomplish, there is temptation to immediately focus on these things, piecing my schedule together like a puzzle. Starting the day that way is like handing over the reins to this busy mind pattern: looking ahead, with attention directed outward into the future, my day becomes a broken up series of events, of expectations, and my outlook is about making sure all these things happen as planned. I lose the pleasant ease of the present moment because I am focusing on what needs to be done next. But, today is my fourth consecutive morning with fusion of the five virtues, outside in the late summer air.

I walk out and feel the wet dewy grass under my feet. My skin detects the temperature – it's warmer than yesterday, warmer than I expected. My senses wake up. Nature greets me. I see the pods of seeds hanging heavy and low from the branches, the sunflowers wilting, bending toward the earth. The sounds of birds and sprinklers and the smell of grass and earth fill me, so that my mind actually cannot rush ahead, it is silent as I begin to trace my breath moving through my body. I begin loosening my joints – the seven star points – opening the qi flow. My neck softens, shoulders relax, knees warm. Today my heart expands as I step to the south, the direction of the red bird, the virtues of joy and peace. I am pulsing my hands above my head, aligning the rhythm of my breath with the movement of my hands. All feels still, within, without. Simply drawing attention to each virtue elicits a profound sensation of peacefulness.

I breathe into my liver the multiple shades of green from the full lush foliage. I taste sweetness in my mouth, as though my saliva is honeyed and begs to be swallowed. The waking sounds of birdcalls and rustling leaves help me integrate inner and outer worlds as I come to center. Trust. Trust in the center. Relief washes over me. Anxiety and worry have no place here. I relish in quiescence. ~September 7, 2012

Visualization is one approach to soul retrieval, a transcendent shamanic practice. In medical *qigong*, this technique restores health to the organs by allowing the spirits who usually reside in those organs, but have fled, to return. To accomplish this, the acquired emotion held in each organ is visualized as an orb of light. The energetic cords connecting those orbs to the organ are severed by one's intentions (Imanera, 2012d).[85] For two straight weeks practicing Fusion of the Five *qigong,* I had noticed constriction and heaviness in my chest as I turned to the West, the direction of the lungs. During my first soul retrieval by Imanera, I followed the above process and severed energetic cords attached to grief, without any import placed on where they came from, or why they were still there. Afterwards, I felt no trace of the former tightening in my chest; ease and warmth took its place.

The *Taiping jing shengjun bizhi* ("Secret Instructions of the Holy Lord of the Scripture of Great Peace") describes how visualization restores health. After a basic level of concentration is reached,

> A radiance or light will arise. It will shine brilliantly in the four directions... When the light first arises, make sure to hold on to it and never let it go. First it will be red, after some time it will change to be white, later again it will be green, and then it will pervade all of you completely. When you further persist in guarding the One, there will be nothing within that would not be brilliantly illuminated and the hundred diseases will be driven out (as cited in Kohn, 2008: 133).

As a sacred peace scripture, this text deserves closer attention. According to Imanera, it:

> ... refers to stability of social life and denotes a condition of training the self, like you are going through right now, while relying on the spontaneous workings of the heavens. It teaches that the central harmony of *yin-yang* nourishes all people and brings contentment. Over time the mistakes made by people are inherited by future generations. This is the concept of inherited burden. This is a reason for epidemics, wars. So then the question of how to break these chains arises. Wise people learn to perform rites that advance peace. These healing rites rid the body of disease, with plant medicine, talismans, acupuncture, breathing practices and music as a means of healing (Imanera, 2012f).

---

[85] The energetic cords can grow back, requiring additional attention.

Visualization meditation is practiced in myriad ways with multiple outcomes: holistic wellness of body and mind, removal of acquired emotions, and opening of *qi* flow to restore balance and harmony.

10.7 MY MEDITATION ENSTASY[86]

'Sitting in Oblivion' is a contemplative Daoist meditation technique for advanced practitioners involving "a state of deep meditative absorption and mystical oneness, during which all sensory and conscious faculties are overcome and which is the base point for attaining Dao" (Kohn, 2010: 1). This 'oblivion' recalls Cooper's (1972) "paradisical" state of harmony, balance, and perfection in the here and now. Guo Xiang offered this perspective:

> In a state of oblivion, what could there be not forgotten? First one forgets the outward manifestations, then one forgets that which causes these manifestations. On the inside one is unaware that there is a personal body; on the outside one never knows there are heaven and earth. Only thus can one become fully vacant and unify with the changes, and there will be nothing that is not pervaded (Xiang, as cited in Kohn, 2008: 104).

This interpretation suggests a twofold process: forgetting about external conditions, then reaching complete oblivion regarding those conditions'sources, be they the perceiving agent (self) or of cosmic origins (Kohn, 2008).

---

[86] "Derived from Greek origin, the term 'ecstasy' means to stand (*stasis*) outside (*ex*) the ordinary self or ego, whereas the term 'enstasy' ultimately denotes one's standing in (*en*) the Self – the transcendent essence or source of contingent identity, that is, the ego-personality... M. Eliade uses the Greek term 'enstasis' or 'enstasy,' which attempts to clearly demarcate the phenomena of *samadhi* from that of 'ecstasy,' a term frequently confused or conflated with 'enstasy.' R.C. Zaehner observes that enstasy 'is the exact reverse of ecstasy, which means to get outside oneself and which is often characterized by a breaking down of the barriers between the subject and the universe around him'" (Whicher, 1998: 28, 183).

> Taoist meditation takes place in an intermediary world, in a world of images 'where the spirit is embodied and the body is spiritualized,' a psychological world Mircea Eliade calls 'creative imagination' and Henri Corbin calls 'active imagination'... It is not yet the realm of the unknowable, which one can neither name nor see, the world of the void, which even when touched is yet beyond expression (Robinet, 1989: 160).

I cannot pretend to have reached this accelerated level of 'Sitting in Oblivion'. But as my meditation and *qigong* practices progress, I have accessed profound experiences in which my self seems to be dissolving into my environment; the two are no longer distinct. Psychoanalyst D.W. Winnicott describes this state as "a third space truly described neither in terms of inner psychological reality nor in terms of outer factuality... situated between the reality within and the reality without" (as cited in Robinet, 1989: 160-161). A fellow *qigong* practitioner and I ponder the message of the rooster mudra, 'looking out to look in':

September 8th is the first day of the month of the rooster. I serendipitously spend the entire day with a dear friend, hiking to the family of lakes around Willow Lake, nestled in the basin of a lofty mountain ridge. The theme of the rooster is about timing – the rooster's timing is always right. The mudra is formed by connecting the tip of the thumb with the top joint of the pinky finger, then holding both hands up as though looking over a fence: looking out to look in. I have been gradually incorporating rooster mudra into my qigong practice for a month now. 'What does it mean, looking out to look in?', my friend inquires. I reply, 'Typically I am reaching out – my tendency is to think outwardly, to direct my thoughts to the external, to try to sense my relationship with my environment by considering what is happening around me. With the rooster, though, I cycle that 'looking out' back inward, there is suddenly a process like a figure eight between me and everything else'. This figure eight guides me in transcending what has felt like the limitations of my physical self, the outermost barrier being my skin. Instead of sensing myself as a separate entity operating in this space, I feel a smooth, thick quality of connection: actually the skin that makes me distinct from the air is an illusion. I am inextricably one with an easy, calming vastness. ~September 10, 2012

I experienced the very phenomenon I attempted to explain that same day, and wrote the following account. It captures a more 'in the moment' illustration of what the above entry lays out, incorporating Cooper's previously mentioned depiction of 'finding one's true nature', where external observed nature is a kaleidoscopic manifestation of inner human nature.

I am sitting beside a majestic turquoise lake. Embedded in a golden meadow and protected by a fortress of pines, the jeweled lake is a shrine to the jagged mountain peaks beyond. I meditate with rooster mudra and softly gaze over the 'fence'. As I breathe in and let my mind rest, a message comes clearly to me. It is perceived by my whole system, its warmth spreads through every cell. This lake, this vibrant scene, is not actually outside of me. It is within me. I am not distinct from it. When I leave this place physically, I carry the sparkle of the water's surface, the integrity of the mountains, the glow of the golden grasses, the brilliant vitality of the green leaves, within me. I am the microcosm that holds the macrocosm of the universe. Looking out to look in, I detect that I am not distinct from the infinite expanse of my environment. It is all in me as much as I am in it. ~September 10, 2012

10.8 DAOIST INTERNAL ALCHEMY AND TRANSFORMING ENERGY

The school of Daoist Internal Alchemy[87] prescribes a specific process for storing, refining, and transmuting subtle body energies to attain immortality (Wong, 1997a). "The religious ideal of immortality in Daoism means that one leaves the world behind in ecstasy and survives, in an ethereal yet concrete body, in paradises and heavens among the stars" (Kohn, 2008: 186).

Wong describes transforming energy in three stages. Holistic work is required in each, as "alchemical transformations are both physical and mental, and without the changes in the skeletal structure, changes in consciousness, energy, and spirit cannot occur" (Wong, 1997a: 178). The first, or lower, stage prepares the physical body externally and internally, and cultivates stillness in the mind. Techniques such as *qigong* postures and *taiji* forms revitalize the skeletal system and cultivate external health. Internal martial arts and calisthenics gently move the spine, which strengthens

---

[87] This is not a Daoist lineage that I have personally experienced with Imanera, but it offers a clear example of energy transmutation in Daoist practice.

physical body structures and systems, massaging organs and stimulating the nervous system. Meditation and quiescence refine the mind.

The middle stage transmutes internal energy stored in the three *dan tians*: from *jing* (generative) to *qi* (vital energy) to prevent disease, and from *qi* (vital energy) to *shen* (spirit energy) to make the Immortal Fetus. This stage stores and refines energy within the *dan tians*, prevents energy leakage (which can result from sexual activity and emotional fluctuations), and regulates breath. At this stage's completion, refined *qi* can circulate throughout the body freely (Imanera 2012d; Wong, 1997a).

The final stage of alchemical work involves "emptying the mind of thoughts, dissolving the duality of subject and object, and being in a state of total emptiness" (Wong, 1997a: 182). The ultimate goal – immortality – is reached when *shen* spirit energy is emptied and the self dissolves into the greater universe (Kohn, 2008). At this time, when all three energies have been refined, purified, and merged, the seed of the Dao emerges. The original spirit has been cultivated and, with nurturing, prepared for the physical body's death; it will merge once again with the undifferentiated energy of the Dao (Wong, 1997a).

As Wong points out, the practice of internal alchemy is a lifetime commitment, and attainment of good health only a small part of its objectives. "Practicing meditation, *ch'i-kung*, or calisthenics will no doubt enhance your health, give you inner peace, and help you cope with problems in your everyday life; it is not, however, synonymous with training in internal alchemy" (*Ibid.*: 187). I have explained only the basics of Internal Alchemical training here, and agree with Wong that techniques in this tradition certainly help create inner peace, but that a very serious level of commitment is required to attain this lineage's vision of immortality.

Chapter 11: Elicitive Peacework and Daoism

Thus every aspect of internal energy work – as much as every movement of the body – creates a vibratory impact that pervades the entire living matrix and, if done in the right way and with the right intention, changes the body's system to greater subtlety and receptivity (Kohn, 2008: 186).

Elicitive conflict transformation (ECT) is a peacework model fundamental to the University of Innsbruck's Master of Arts in Peace, Development, Security, and International Conflict Transformation. It is the approach I am most interested in developing as a peaceworker in part because its innovative concepts and tools can refresh exhausted efforts in conflict and post-conflict zones, making them more effective and sustainable. ECT's assets and virtues may be cultivated through the Daoist shamanic practices I have experienced and articulated throughout this book.

The Art of War, the ancient Daoist classic by Sun Tzu, promotes understanding conflict in order to prevent and avoid violence before it begins. "This ideal strategy whereby one could win without fighting, accomplish the most by doing the least, bears the characteristic stamp of Taoism, the ancient tradition of knowledge that fostered both the healing arts and the martial arts in China" (Sun Tzu, 1988: 2). Sun Tzu's objective was not to promote warfare, but to minimize and curtail it. The text's overt subject matter – strategies and tactics for conflict – appealed to people otherwise unsympathetic to the pacifist humanism of Confucius and Mencius (*Ibid.*).[88] I conclude this chapter with several scholars' visions for increasing human consciousness in an effort to evolve our planet towards harmony and mutual respect.

11.1 AN ELICITIVE APPROACH TO PEACEWORK

To explain the elicitive approach, it is helpful to contrast it with a prescriptive one. The latter relies heavily on the peaceworker's[89] specialized knowledge, teaching specific techniques for addressing conflict which are learned and digested cognitively. A prescriptive approach is culturally neutral; its application assumes a degree of universality across various geographic, social, and political contexts (Lederach, 1995).

The <u>elicitive</u> approach "lies at the opposite end of the spectrum from the prescriptive approach" (Lederach, 1995: 55). It derives from the view that working with conflicts "is an opportunity aimed primarily at discovery, creation, and solidification of models that emerge from the resources present in a particular setting and respond to needs in that context" (*Ibid.*). Its peaceworker is more a catalyst or facilitator than an expert applying a specific model. She opens a space in which the knowledge of all involved parties is utilized as a valued resource for new possibilities and directions in the mediation process. Like the warrior in Sun Tzu's *The Art of War* (Sun Tzu, 1988), the elicitive peaceworker adapts, creatively selecting, designing, and redesigning dynamic approaches to meet the needs and conditions of a particular context (Lederach, 1995).

Lederach distinguishes this 'conflict transformation' approach from the more common strategies of 'conflict resolution' and 'conflict management':

> Conflict transformation is to envision and respond to the ebb and flow of social conflict as life-giving opportunities for creating constructive

---

[88] Cleary states that the Daoist themes in the The Art of War are not a "random cultural element", rather they are essential for a comprehensive understanding of the text (Cleary, 1988: 29).

[89] I have opted to use the term 'peaceworker', which can be used interchangeably with 'peacebuilder', 'conflict worker', or 'mediator'.

change processes that reduce violence, increase justice in direct interaction and social structures, and respond to real-life problems in human relationships (Lederach, 2003: 14).

Conflict is a normal and continuous dynamic of human relationships that holds the potential to serve as a catalyst for holistic and constructive change. Instead of an isolated or aberrant event, it is recognized within a greater pattern as an important revealer of both immediate and systematic issues. In a sense, it creates life. "... [T]hrough conflict we respond, innovate, and change. Conflict can be understood as the motor of change, that which keeps relationships and social structures honest, alive, and dynamically responsive to human needs, aspirations, and growth" (*Ibid.*: 18).

A prescriptive approach of conflict resolution or conflict management, on the other hand,

> ...implies that conflict is bad – hence something that should be ended. It also assumes that conflict is a short phenomenon that can be 'resolved' permanently through mediation or other intervention processes. 'Conflict management' correctly assumes that conflicts are long term processes that often cannot be quickly resolved, but the notion of 'management' suggests that people can be directed or controlled as though they were physical objects... [M]anagement suggests that the goal is the reduction or control of volatility more than dealing with the real source of the problem (Burgess and Burgess, 1997: n.p.).

Lederach believes that instead of striving to eliminate or control conflict, we can engage in innovative ways to work with it as a natural transformative phenomenon with great potential to change all people, places and relationships involved.

11.2 Transcending Violence: the Moral Imagination

Lederach's book, *The Moral Imagination: the Art and Soul of Building Peace*, seeks to move beyond perpetual cycles of conflict.

> Transcending violence is forged by the capacity to generate, mobilize, and build the moral imagination... Stated simply, the moral imagina-

tion requires the capacity to imagine ourselves in a web of relationships that includes our enemies; the ability to sustain a paradoxical curiosity that embraces complexity without reliance on dualistic polarity; the fundamental belief in and pursuit of the creative act; and the acceptance of the inherent risk of stepping into the mystery of the unknown that lies beyond the far too familiar landscape of violence (Lederach, 2005: 5).

To accomplish this, we must first understand the complex scenarios of protracted violence and obstacles to social change.[90] We then commit ourselves to exploring the creative process itself as a source of building peace. Lederach likens this exploration to the artist's journey into uncharted territory.

A defining characteristic of the moral imagination[91] is its capacity to give rise to something completely new that, through its very birth, changes the world and how we experience it (Lederach, 2005). Such imagination transcends narrow, dead-end inquiries to illuminate possibilities thus far unseen or inconceivable. But this illuminating moment manifests only when there is space and respect for the creative act to unfold. Lederach views creativity as a concrete human action that is simultaneously divine and mundane. In this way, it reflects the human being's unique position in the Daoist Great Triad, as an intermediary of heavens and earth.

The moral imagination constructs dynamic platforms for sustained peaceful transformation. "... [A] platform is responsive to day-to-day issues that arise in the ebb and flow of conflict while it sustains a clear vision of the longer-term change needed in the destructive relational patterns. The creation of such a platform... is one of the fundamental building blocks for supporting constructive change over time" (*Ibid.*: 47). These 'living' platforms avoid agreements and accords that tend merely to redefine the conflict, and there-

---

[90] Lederach defines social change as "The pursuit of shifting relationships from those defined by fear, mutual recrimination, and violence toward those characterized by love, mutual respect, and proactive engagement. Constructive social change seeks to move the flow of interaction in human conflict from cycles of destructive relational patterns toward cycles of relational dignity and respectful engagement" (Lederach, 2005: 181).
[91] "Moral" is not relegated here to notions of religion or religious inquiry. Nor is it about ethics, as the ethical inquiry tends to be reductionist and analytical: these qualities are contrary to those of moral imagination. "Imagination" refers to the creative act (Lederach, 2005).

fore fall short of transforming it. Instead, they employ long-term views of the multiple change processes that need to occur within a web of relationships.

11.3 ELICITIVE PEACEWORK AND DAOIST PRACTICES: MAKING THE CONNECTION

Daoist shamanic practices support elicitive peacework in two ways: 1) In the practical development of the peaceworker's skills, they encourage and access intuitive wisdom more readily. 2) Energetically, Daoist practices facilitate inner peace, a state of *being* peace that emanates outward from the peaceworker, affecting other vibrational spheres. Each of these two effects nurture and enhance the other. Lederach (2011) addresses the bridge between conflict transformation and mysticism in a recent conference lecture. Through mysticism, he says, we become more awake, seeing anew, and moving fluidly between inner and outer worlds. We bring the gifts of the mystic experience into the conflict context, nurturing love, creating new life, sustaining ourselves, and following joy.

11.3.1 Seeing the Unseen: Transcendence in the Creative Act

Lederach's (2005) recognition of intuition's role in the moral imagination reinforces the value Vaughan (1979) places on its awakening. Lederach identifies intuition as essential to creation and maintenance of previously unknown possibilities. "The moral imagination seeks to connect with the deep intuition that creates the capacity to penetrate and transcend the challenges of violent conflict. Recognizing and nurturing this capacity is the ingredient that forges and sustains authentic constructive change" (Lederach, 2005: 71). Vaughan, too, portrays intuition as a nonlinear mode of knowing that presents new options, bringing attention to otherwise overlooked solutions. This process requires playfully considering all alternatives as valid, even if the rational mind objects. "Letting all the possible and impossible alternatives into one's awareness can stimulate the creative process, which is so easily stifled by restricting awareness to a narrow range of alternatives bounded by preconceptions that perpetuate unsatisfactory patterns of behavior" (Vaughan, 1979: 43).

Sun Tzu encourages utilizing intuitive capacities to sense a conflict's inner workings directly and immediately.

> As in *The Art of War,* the range of awareness and efficiency of the Taoist adept is unnoticeable, imperceptible to others, because their critical moments take place before ordinary intelligence has mapped out a description of the situation… [W]arriors of Asia who used Taoist or Zen arts to achieve profound calmness did not do so just to prepare their minds to sustain the awareness of imminent death, but also to achieve the sensitivity needed to respond to situations without stopping to ponder (Cleary, 1988: 3-4).

The initial step, simply becoming aware of possibilities and conscious of the freedom to choose, requires development of intuitive faculties (Vaughan, 1979). As I described in Chapter 10, Daoist meditative practices help pause the mind's distractable tendencies, allowing for conscious awareness of intuitive insights. Creating space for the intuitive voice enables the peaceworker to avoid tunnel vision in conflict work. Instead, she engages peripheral vision beyond either/or dichotomies to explore multiple avenues (Lederach, 2005). "Intuitively we know that it is not a matter of either/or, but of both/and. It is always possible to think in terms of both/and, synthesizing and integrating all forms of knowledge to arrive at a deeper understanding of human destiny" (Vaughan, 1979: 179). The peaceworker must remain humble, open to unexpected outcomes, realizing that the truth – multiple truths – will unfold endlessly (Lederach, 2011).

11.3.2 Deep Listening

> "Listening is the discipline and art of capturing the complexity of history in the simplicity of deep intuition. It is attending to a sharp sense of what things mean" (Lederach, 2005: 70).

In contexts of violence and tragedy, the mediator is asked to listen to many versions of events that are often convoluted, ambiguous, or at odds. Through deep listening, she engages her intuition, attuning with the essence of what she hears. But intuitive listening is not reduction; it is synthesis, holding complexity and simplicity together (Lederach, 2005). It relies on authentic presence, the mediator becoming more true to herself, more capable of being alongside others with less judgment and anxiety. Through her attentiveness, she offers a gesture of compassion to all (*Ibid.*, 2011). This form of listening is not learned via specific techniques, but must emerge as an embodied virtue.

Daoist inner tranquility develops calm centeredness in the midst of activity and turmoil, making deep listening possible even in chaotic environments (Cleary, 1986). In the *Annals of the Hall of Blissful Development,* Huang Yuan-ch'i writes:

> People are happy when there is quiet and vexed when there is commotion. Don't they realize that since their energy has already been stirred by the clamor of people's voices and the involvements and disturbances of people and affairs, it is better to use this power to cultivate stability? ... Stay comprehensively alert in the immediate present, and suddenly an awakening will open up an experience in the midst of it all that is millions of times better than that of quiet sitting (Huang Yuan-ch'I, as cited in Cleary, 1986: 13).

The Daoist tradition supports stability in the midst of unsettling situations; its breathing techniques and subtle energy transformation can be practiced until they become second nature. These practices then enable the practitioner to reside in her stable center, and in turn engage in deep intuitive listening.

11.3.3 Letting Go

> "Zhang Yu: Adaptation means not clinging to fixed methods, but changing appropriately according to events, acting as is suitable" (Sun Tzu, 1988: 125).

Readiness to adapt to alternatives that arise through intuitive channels requires letting go of specific expectations. Awareness of expectations about how life is *supposed* to be, and of how a conflict *should* be transformed, is particularly important. "Imagining the future does not mean becoming attached to any particular object or circumstance that you want; it means creating a new context for your life... The context can be one of a balanced attitude that values both receptivity and activity" (Vaughan, 1979: 165).

In *The Moral Imagination*, Lederach (2005) recounts his own experience with letting go as a paradox he encountered during his earlier years in peacework. His description mirrors my own process of learning to facilitate transformative experiences with *Los Embajadores*: the more I attempted to produce a particular outcome or reaction in participants, the more easily disappointed I was. I had not 'succeeded' if everyone did not reach my desired outcome. As I learned to step back, let go of my expectations, and observe with a wider perspective, I grew to recognize that the experience was actually reaching participants in unique and profound ways that I could not predict or impose.

Lederach explains how these unplanned 'successes' in peacework result from "divine naiveté", the attributes of which parallel a Daoist cosmovision.

> Hence I needed the combination of divine and naiveté. Divine pointed to something transcendent, unexpected, but that led toward insight and better understanding. To see that which is not readily planned for nor apparent, however, requires a peripheral type of vision, the willingness to move sideways… in order to move forward. The ability to make that movement requires naiveté, an innocence of expectation that watches carefully for the potential of building change in good and difficult times (Lederach, 2005: 115).

Wu wei relies on making room for the serendipity of divine naiveté. The Daoist emphasis on *timing* versus *time* highlights the importance of the present moment and its dynamic forces of *yin-yang*. With these in constant flux, attempts to predict the future, recreate the past, or dictate the precise way to reach desired outcomes usually prove futile.[92] Instead, the successful peaceworker moves freely in any direction within those fluctuations, relinquishing the preconception that moving forward is the best or only option.

Daoist practices facilitate the virtues of divine naiveté. Meditation forms such as *qigong* enable recognition and embodiment of the divine nature of humanity, its predicaments, and its infinite possibilities. They exercise attunement to the present, so the practitioner may sense and respond to energetic changes and move accordingly at any given moment.

11.3.4 Non-Duality and the Web of Interconnectivity

Essential to the moral imagination is individuals' ability to imagine themselves in a web of relationships, one that reaches so far as to include even

---

[92] That being said, the *Yijing* serves as a tool and guide for observing the relative forces, discerning appropriate timing, and interpreting the need for taking action or *wu wei* non-action.

their enemies (Lederach, 2005). This implies dynamic interdependency: any change made by one will have an impact on all. Relationships are both the context in which violent patterns occur, and the locus from which transcendence of those patterns begins. Realizing one's part in the web elicits humility and self-recognition; in peacework, this may even mean seeing one's own unexpected involvement in perpetuating violence.

The moral imagination produces what Lederach calls paradoxical curiosity, which "approaches social realities with an abiding respect for complexity, a refusal to fall prey to the pressures of forced dualistic categories of truth, and an inquisitiveness about what may hold together seemingly contradictory social energies in a greater whole" (*Ibid.*: 36). Sensing one's small role within boundless interconnectivity requires transcending dualistic categories of truth. Embodying this inextricably woven human (and natural) web erases lines dividing 'us' and 'them'. Vaughan (1979) described it as dissolving the separation between knower and known by awakening intuition. Applied to elicitive peacework, we move away from 'quick fixes' based on judgments and, instead, look more deeply into the apparent contradictions and complexities of violence for their unexpected possibilities (Lederach, 2005).

Daoist shamanism's embodied energetics stimulate this non-dualistic awareness.[93] In my experience, embodied *Bagua* meditation and other mudras produce an energetic shape-shifting in which the meditator ceases to feel separate from her environment.[94] She becomes transpersonally aware, beyond the senses and beyond the mind, of her place in the greater web of relationships. *Qigong* master Ken Cohen (1997) cites experimental evidence that among the practice's many benefits is improved interpersonal sensitivity, a quality essential to one's sense of interconnectivity. For me, the embodied practices of shamanism produce some of the most powerfully transformative states of non-duality.

---

[93] In her writing about *qigong* practice in the United States, Kohn emphasizes it as a practice of embodiment, and links the Western world's need for this conceptualization to a pervasive tendency towards dualistic perspective. "Qigong is the embodied practice of universal energies for the sake of healing and/or spirituality... The fact that Western culture is in need of such a concept reveals just how systemic philosophical dualism has become. In fact, there is no activity which does not involve the body, which is not 'embodied,' and the practice of Qigong should not be anything particular or special" (Kohn, 2006: 228).
[94] As portrayed through my personal experience with 'looking out to look in' in section 10.7

11.3.5 Utilizing Intuition and Embodied Energetics

While most conflict *resolution* teaches skills that reduce or ignore intuition, many seasoned peacebuilders (including those who come from violent settings) avoid relying on technicalities and follow their senses instead (Lederach, 2005). Often, transformative moments in conflict scenarios are characterized by a sudden great insight. They appear almost artistically, not via logic or analysis. "They synthesize the complexities of experience and the challenges of addressing deep human dilemmas" (*Ibid.*: 70). Vaughan echoes the significance of these moments:

> Time after time it appears that major human achievements involve intuitive leaps of imagination. It is the intuitive, holistic, pattern-perception faculties associated with the right hemisphere of the brain that break through existing formulations of truth and expand the body of knowledge. The stabilization of intuitive insights, and their usefulness to humanity, are subsequently determined by careful, logical examination and validation, but the original vision or insight is intuitive (Vaughan, 1979: 153).

Of course, the effectiveness of intuitive versus analytical problem-solving depends on the nature of the conflict and cognitive styles of the parties involved (Lederach, 2005).Meditation again becomes a helpful tool for accessing inner wisdom that helps the mediator discern which approach is right in each context.[95] Dietrich notes shamanism's "rainbow of tools" for conflict transformation, including the medicine wheel, which offers a map for balancing opposing forces and returning to center (Dietrich, 2012b).

In the same sense, the *Bagua* is a Daoist medicine wheel, a map for reading existing energy patterns. It becomes even more relevant for conflict transformation when its elements are embodied, and energy patterns altered to center and find balance. A mediator might subtly transform the energy in a room, or parties in conflict might be invited to engage in a particular practice to bring the group energetic balance. If one party presents excessive fire energy, for example, everyone could do something as simple as rocking back

---

[95] Vaughan (1979) sees reason as a mediator guiding intuition towards the right approach at the right time.

on the heels of their feet, drawing in the cooling energy of water. This would help harmonize the room, facilitating artful and holistic peacebuilding.

Allowing this creative space for possibilities to emerge involves a willingness to take risks, another feature of Lederach's moral imagination. "To risk is to step into the unknown without any guarantee of success or even safety" (Lederach, 2005: 39). But in communities of deep-rooted conflict, peace itself is mysterious and illusive, and its alternatives unsatisfactory or even deadly.

11.3.6 Serendipity and the Dao

An entire chapter of *The Moral Imagination* is dedicated to serendipity, which Lederach refers to as "the gift of accidental sagacity". His depiction resonates with the harmonious flow of the Dao. Serendipity:

> ... is the wisdom of recognizing and then moving with the energetic flow of the unexpected... Serendipity nudges us in the direction of discovery and innovation. Accidental sagacity links the unexpected in the social environment with a capacity to observe it, see what it means, and innovate appropriate responses. Wisdom and survival are most clearly found in this capacity to recognize and adapt (Lederach, 2005: 115, 129).

In creating platforms for social change, equal attention must be paid to both the structure and to the unexpected change involved in such a process. Adaptive and dynamic, these platforms transform along with their environments, always with an eye towards maintaining their purpose. Like living in harmony with the Dao, they maintain a framework of discipline while staying open, aware, and flexible, unattached to expectations or judgments. "To live between memory and potentiality is to live permanently in a creative space, pregnant with the unexpected" (*Ibid.*: 149).

11.4 GROWING OUR PLANETARY CONSCIOUSNESS

Global visionary Ervin Laszlo notes the critical correlation between increasing consciousness and peace on our planet. "When all is said and done, the fundamental need of our time, the precondition of creating a peaceful and sustainable world, is the spread of a new and more adaptive consciousness – the planetary consciousness of oneness and belonging" (Laszlo, 2011: 268). He envisions transpersonal, planetary consciousness as the next stage in the evolution of the human mind – one that may lead to our species' salvation. With such "planetary consciousness", humans realize their oneness with nature, and therefore recognize that the way we treat it and others directly affects how we treat ourselves.

To be most effective, Vaughan adds, transformation of consciousness must further assume responsibility for social change.

> If one tries to change society without changing consciousness, one is simply rearranging the contents of experience. If one works exclusively on consciousness and abdicates social responsibility, one separates oneself from the world and again falls into the trap of identifying with a part instead of the whole. Like breathing in and breathing out, one needs both activity and receptivity (Vaughan, 1979: 184).

She names this enhanced consciousness as one of the primary, inevitable consequences of awakening intuition.

Similarly, Elgin (1993) dubs expanded states of consciousness occurring via mystical experience as the 'highest common denominator' of human experience. "This is a profoundly hopeful discovery in that, before the people of the world can cope with the problems of our global village, there must be some degree of shared agreement as to the nature of 'reality' within which we collectively exist" (*Ibid.*: 249). Relating to the global community through universal mystical experiences provides a powerful avenue to transcending cultural, political, and economic differences.

Elgin posits that the industrial revolution – which provided many with material abundance – may actually assist human societies to expand evolutionary consciousness, since it frees us from the burden of material poverty.

> Today, with simplicity, equity, and wisdom we can have both substantial freedom *from* want and freedom to evolve our consciousness as individuals in community with others... Economic necessity (which dictates either enforced or voluntarily assumed simplicity), Taoistic 'necessity' (which impels us to evolve our awareness to assume evolutionary trusteeship), and human possibility (to evolve to higher levels of awareness/consciousness) all combine to create what seems to be a gentle but increasingly insistent evolutionary imperative toward individual and societal transcendence (*Ibid.*: 250).

Somé, on the other hand, identifies materialism and technology as Western hindrances to rapid social change, suggesting that our best approach is an enlivening of spirituality through ritual.

> It is more realistic to think about the spiritual needs of family and self as a starting point for social transformation than to begin thinking we can change Hollywood... To make Self each person's own best spiritual project is to avoid the crush of the gigantic modern Machine. Ritual enables us to live a life that is much closer to what our souls aspire to (Somé, 1993: 59).

Still, Elgin and Somé both celebrate the possibility that, through a combination of individual and collective efforts, human societies are currently poised to revitalize a spiritual consciousness essential for redirecting the future of life on this planet.

Schlitz proposes changing education to integrate and attach more value to transpersonal experiences. "Whole-person education", she proposes, would focus on "worldview literacy" and call for "a new model of learning that includes global students embracing a new kind of literacy that appreciates and incorporates different worldviews and ways of knowing, including Akashic knowing" (Schlitz, 2009: 172). Her worldview literacy develops awareness of one's own unique outlook, while acknowledging the need to "recognize that our beliefs come from our particular frame of reference and to understand that others hold different and potentially equally valid worldviews out of which their assumptions, and therefore their actions, arise" (*Ibid.*). Schlitz's curriculum is grounded in cultural pluralism and "a search for the perennial across cultures... to help students move beyond simply tolerating diversity to developing a place of deep appreciation for our differences – as well as our points of connection" (*Ibid.*: 173).

Perhaps we live in an auspicious time for the introduction of such literacy, since, as Laszlo states, "the emerging cultures of peace, solidarity, and respect for nature no longer believe that all we can experience of each other and the cosmos must come to us through 'five slits in the tower' – they know that we can open the roof to the sky" (Laszlo, 2009: 7). Incorporating awareness and valuation of multiple ways of knowing into the framework of education could have tremendous impact on human evolution and planetary consciousness.

Kohn illustrates the Daoist take on transforming consciousness. She believes it is the responsibility of those who have reached harmony to guide others in that direction:

> ... by just being oneself, staying in the present moment, and doing whatever is needed without thinking, evaluating, or arguing, one can effect powerful transformation in the world... People will naturally gravitate toward harmony and peace, toward being with the flow of Dao rather than going against it. But they need to be shown the way, and that is the role of the realized one... (Kohn, 2008: 103).

This aligns with Vaughan's (1979) emphasis on uniting increased consciousness with effective social change.

The sense of unity inherent in transpersonal consciousness urges humans to come together to confront problems. It is a catalyst for people to move beyond family and community and realize our mutual vested interest in co-operating globally (Laszlo, 2011). Just as Lederach (2005) warns against the unidirectionality and tunnel vision that have historically led to extinction, Laszlo suggests that without cooperation, humans risk becoming another extinct species unable to adapt to a changing planet. Walsh reiterates the fundamental principle behind this conservation of the species: matching our advanced rational and scientific accomplishments with corresponding degrees of wisdom and spiritual development.

> The fate of our species and our planet may depend on our ability to match our intellectual and technological mastery with our emotional and moral maturity. Wise people have long recognized this kind of need, and authentic spiritual disciplines therefore offer a full complement of practices that foster maturation of many facets of personality (Walsh, 2007: 26-27).

These beliefs ring true to me, and it is my hope that this book offer one more small step towards this vision of increased planetary consciousness and peace.

CHAPTER 12: CONCLUSIONS

Comprehension in a state of quiescence, accomplishment without striving, knowing without seeing – this is the sense and response of the Transformative Tao. Comprehension in a state of quiescence can comprehend anything, accomplishment without striving can accomplish anything, knowing without seeing can know anything (from *The Book of Balance and Harmony,* as cited in Sun Tzu, 1988: 4).

Throughout this book, I have employed different faculties, rational and transrational, analytical and embodied, to weave together a response to the guiding question, 'how can Daoist shamanic practices be understood as methods for peacework?' One significant source of data has been my own experiences with Daoist shamanic techniques, which I developed and enriched with my teacher Imanera (2012a-f). I studied these direct experiences via various interpretations of intuition, the mind, and consciousness, as well as Daoist texts and philosophy. These transpersonal experiences and research were then integrated and considered within the framework of an elicitive approach to peacework. In bringing these sources together, I hope I have demonstrated how the energetic embodiment of Daoist shamanic practices allows intuitive wisdom to emerge and stimulate conflict transformation.

The response to my research question began with an overview of key concepts that place Daoism within an energetic interpretation of peace. As understood in the Great Triad, the human being is the synthesis of the infinite dual forces of the divine and the mundane, the heavens and earth, *yang-yin.* Her capacity to hold these forces in harmonious balance is an expression of peace. If inner and outer realities, psyche and universe, reflect each other and are inextricably tied together, then internal transformation stimulates external change. This change lays at the heart of the practices I have discussed throughout this book.

Mental attitudes produce patterns of energy that impact a person's vibrational frequencies and, through the magnetic activity of her nervous system, spread into the energy fields and bodies of others. These patterns may be increasing or decreasing, harmonizing or disturbing frequencies. The transpersonal experiences I access through *qigong* and other meditative forms increase conscious awareness of one's place in a web of relationships, as well as the fundamental oneness of that web. They also offer methods for adapting and adjusting *qi* flow to resonate harmoniously with the cosmic breath of the Dao. Even one person vibrating in such resonance becomes a seed of peace.

Like Daoist practice, elicitive peacework is not just about what you do or what you know; it is so nuanced and holistically engaging that it also matters *who* and *how* youare. The elicitive method goes beyond acquiring skills and applying them to require embodiment itself. This approach takes into account humans' and conflicts' utter uniqueness to each moment and place in the world. As a species, we constantly adapt our needs and desires according to corresponding changes in our communities and our planet. Peaceworkers must be aware of their role in this ever-changing interplay of external forces, and the ways these forces manifest within us. Adaptivity hinges on developing a highly intuitive understanding of time, context, and change. This can be achieved by living *wu wei,* listening deeply, observing energetic patterns, and maintaining a non-dualistic perspective.

With practice, Kirschner (2012) teaches, we can access 'holy silence' at any moment. The virtues of Daoist meditation I have described extend beyond quiet, centered, sitting to emerge as natural qualities while managing ordinary, everyday routines. In high-pressure conflict scenarios, prior training in regaining equilibrium is essential for the peaceworker. A regular practice of body awareness meditation such as *qigong* can make the difference between succumbing to chaos and despair or maintaining clear thought and access to intuitive guidance.

Daoist shamanic practices are best understood and practiced through direct experience. They provide the peaceworker useful abilities for reading, embodying, and transforming energy, enabling her to take care of herself holistically. The importance of physical wellness cannot be overlooked; cohesion of mind and body is imperative in urgent and overwhelming situations. Moreover, the peaceworker can replenish and stimulate her divine creative potential in any environment by gathering *qi* and meditating with mudras.

I would like to share some conclusive personal reflections before I finish with a personal *Yi Jing* divination. At the end of an interview with Imanera (2012f), we reversed roles. She asked me a series of questions, including, "How have you changed recently?" While much of my growth has been expressed here via my research journal narratives, I am aware that these lessons and revelations are flexible and alive, informing my awareness in different ways every day. The combination of embodied writing with rational interpretation of energetic experiences has also helped me observe how my analytical capacities operate, and sometimes interfere. This leads to provocative, and at times unsettling, self-realizations. But in my Daoist training I have acquired techniques, some as simple as forming a mudra with my fingertips, for integrating such discoveries.

Other personal changes occurred because I have been given highly effective tools for managing the challenges inherent in being human. I have adjusted, for example, how I address acquired emotions such as anxiety and grief. These tools are powerful because they involve embodiment, which incorporates transformation of body, senses and spirit. Finding this clarity has allowed me to trust my inner wisdom and more spontaneously act – or *wu wei* not act.

The importance of letting go is an important topic addressed throughout. This book itself took on a life of its own, and I followed its flow. At times, I met turns in the path with resistance. But as I learned the value of not forcing circumstances to conform to my personal attachments and expectations, I was able to embrace the journey and its unexpected gifts more fully. Trusting intuition required a willingness to take risks and face the unknown, a lesson I first learned traveling around the world that is now central to my decision-making. Facing the unknown soon translated into journeying across a perplexing realm of transpersonal spheres. These journeys forced me to recognize myself as the intermediary where divine and mundane energies meet. Moving into this awareness has been quite profound, and I am grateful that as I have developed, I have been able to nurture my perceptive abilities' emergence gradually and adapt to this transformed consciousness fairly smoothly.

I acknowledge that my research journal contains narratives written from a safe, supportive place, where I have not been exposed to the instability of violent conflict. I have included accounts of anxiety and grief, acquired emotions that hold the power to throw me off center, and would arise with greater intensity in high-pressure scenarios. I practice addressing my own well-being with new tools in my current environment so that, ideally, I am prepared to most effectively help others in any setting. Imanera (2012d) describes uniting one's own physical, energetic, and spirit bodies as conflict transformation within the self. In this sense, I engage in a powerful form of conflict transformation every day.

Still, I would never imply that I have it all figured out. As a peaceworker, I see all too clearly my own humanness, and I continue challenging myself to keep my perspective open, accepting the shadows while embracing the light. Of utmost importance to me now is to exist like the willow tree: free to sway in the world's wind, personal roots grounded, coming to rest at center. I search for the presence and absence of sunlight on mountains, which remind me to remain aware of the playful *yin-yang* of life.

Though this chapter concludes the text, from a broader perspective, this moment is about beginnings. This book has been a genuine adventure of discovery and transformation, serendipitously pointing me in another new direction along a nonlinear path that has only just begun. I close for now with a shamanic casting of the *Yi Jing,* one final embodied experience to bring some perspective to this particular endeavor. In my last meeting with Imanera to discuss my progress, she suggested I perform my first embodied casting. This is fitting, since, as a divination tool, the *Yi Jing* reads the present as a guide for the future, a conclusion that is also very much a beginning.[96] Closing with this guiding text's divination also reflects the joyful nature of the Dao.

I performed this *Yi Jing* reading through an energetic casting of the mudras of the *Bagua.* The resulting hexagram was "lake over mountain", number thirty-one in thetext. Karcher's edition (2009: 254) edition[97] names this reading 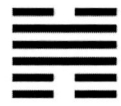 "Conjoining/Uniting in Spirit". Conjoining brings together what belongs together: welcoming spirit into the heart, spirit transforms the heart. "This is the attraction and union of contraries, man and woman, human and spirit" (*Ibid.*). A central teaching of this reading embraces *yin* energy, and allows inner force to submit to outer stimulation, "drawing down the spirit to the sacred place" (*Ibid.*: 257). Applying "conjoining" to the present situation

---

[96] Because I cannot in this moment produce a *Yijing* divination for the reader, I invite you instead to continue your engagement with the topic through your harmonious participation in "World Tai Chi & Qigong Day". More information is available at: www.worldtaichiday.com.

[97] Imanera and I decided to use Karcher's translation because he acknowledges the shamanic quality of the *Yijing*, and includes a section for each hexagram titled "The Shaman Speaks" (Karcher, 2009).

entails uniting with an influence that excites me and inspires me into action. On that note, my Daoist shamanic journey continues, with plenty of room in my heart for love and spirit.

List of References

AN, LIU (2012): *The Essential Huainanzi*, Translation. Trans. & Eds. John S. Major, Sarah A. Queen, Andrew Seth Meyer, Harold D. Roth, Columbia University Press, New York.

ANDERSEN, POUL (1990): "Bugang", *The Encyclopedia of Taoism,* Routledge, Oxon, Vol. I. Print.

ANDERSON, ROSEMARIE (2001): "Embodied Writing and Reflections on Embodiment", *Journal of Transpersonal Psychology,* 33 (2), 83-98. Pre-publication manuscript copy.

ANDERSON, ROSEMARIE & WILLIAM BRAUD (2011): *Transforming Self and Others Through Research: Transpersonal Research Methods and Skills for the Human Sciences and Humanities,* SUNY Press, Albany.

AUSTIN, JAMES (2006): *Zen-Brain Reflections: Reviewing Recent Developments in Meditation and States of Consciousness,* MIT Press, Massachusetts.

BALDRIAN-HUSSEIN, FARZEEN (1990): "Neidan", *The Encyclopedia of Taoism,* Routledge, Oxon, Vol. II. Print.

BARRETT, T.H. (1990): "Taoism and Chinese Buddhism", *The Encyclopedia of Taoism,* Routledge, Oxon, Vol. I. Print.

BLOFELD, JOHN (1965): *I Ching: The Book of Change,* Trans. John Blofeld, Penguin Putnam Inc, New York.

BOCK-MÖBIUS, IMKE (2012): *Qigong Meets Quantum Physics: Experiencing Cosmic Oneness,* Three Pines Press, Florida.

BURGESS, GUY & HEIDI (1997): "Conflict Transformation", http://www.colorado.edu/conflict/transform/jplall.htm, accessed October 1, 2012.

CHAN, WING-TSIT (1963): *A Source Book in Chinese Philosophy,* Trans. Wing-Tsit Chan, Princeton University Press, New Jersey.

CHIA, MANTAK & DIVA NORTH (2010): *Taoist Shaman: Practices from the Wheel of Life,* Destiny Books, Vermont.

"CHINESE RELIGION" (1996): *The Harper Collins Dictionary of Religion,* Harper Collins, London, Print.

CHUANG-TZU (1964): *Chuang Tzu: Basic Writings*, Translation. Trans. Burton Watson, Columbia University Press, New York.

CLEARY, THOMAS (1996): *The Taoist Classics, Volume II,* Shambhala Publications, Massachusetts.

------------------ (1991): *The Essential Tao: An Initiation into the Heart of Taoism through the Authentic Tao Te Ching and the Inner Teachings of Chuang-Tzu,* Harper Collins, San Francisco.

------------------ (1986): *The Taoist I Ching*, Trans. Thomas Cleary, Shambhala Publications, Massachusetts.

COHEN, KEn (1998): *Taoism: Essential Teachings of the Way and its Power,* Sounds True. CD.

------------------ (1997): *The Way of Qigong: The Art and Science of Chinese Energy Healing,* Ballantine Books, New York.

COOPER, J.C. (1972): *Taoism: The Way of the Mystic,* Samuel Weiser Inc., New York.

DIETRICH, WOLFGANG (2012a): *Interpretations of Peace in History and Culture,* Palgrave Macmillan, London.

------------------ (2012b): Interview via Skype, October 4, 2012.

------------------ and others, Eds. (2011): *The Palgrave International Handbook of Peace Studies,* Palgrave Macmillan, London.

------------------ (2010a): "Elicitive Conflict Transformation About the Methods of Transrational Peaces", MA Program for Peace, Development, Security and International Conflict Transformation, University of Innsbruck, Innsbruck. July 9 & 12, 2010. Lecture.

------------------ (2010b): "Why Peace Studies Go Native", MA Program for Peace, Development, Security and International Conflict Transformation, University of Innsbruck, Innsbruck. August 14, 2010. Lecture.

------------------ (2006): "A Call for Trans-Rational Peaces" http://www.uibk.ac.at/peacestudies/downloads/peacelibrary/transrational.pdf, accessed March 12, 2012.

ELGIN, DUANE (1993): "The Tao of Personal and Social Transformation". *Paths Beyond Ego: The Transpersonal Vision.* Eds. Frances Vaughan and Roger Walsh, Tarcher/Putnam, New York.

ELIADE, MIRCEA (1964): *Shamanism: Archaic Techniques of Ecstasy*, Princeton University Press, New Jersey.

EPSTEIN, MARK (1993): "The Varieties of Egolessness". *Paths Beyond Ego: The Transpersonal Vision.*Eds. Frances Vaughan and Roger Walsh, Tarcher/Putnam, New York.

FREUD, SIGMUND (1960): *The Ego and the Id*, trans. Joan Riviere, W.H. Norton & Company, Inc., New York.

GAWLER, IAN & PAUL BEDSON (2010): *Meditation: An In-Depth Guide*, Tarcher/Penguin, New York.

GOENKE, S.N.(1980): "The Art of Living: Vipassana Meditation". Printed material distributed at Vipassana meditation retreat.

GROF, STANISLAV (2009): "Evidence for the Akashic Field from Modern Consciousness Research".*The Akashic Experience: Science and the Cosmic Memory Field*,Ed. Ervin Laszlo, Inner Traditions, Vermont.

------------------ AND CHRISTINA GROF (1993): "Addiction as Spiritual Emergency".*Paths Beyond Ego: The Transpersonal Vision.* Eds. Frances Vaughan and Roger Walsh, Tarcher/Putnam, New

------------------ AND CHRISTINA GROF (1993): "Spiritual Emergency: The Understanding and Treatment of Transpersonal Crises".*Paths Beyond Ego: The Transpersonal Vision.* Eds. Frances Vaughan and Roger Walsh, Tarcher/Putnam, New York.

------------------ AND CHRISTINA GROF (1990): *The Stormy Search for the Self*, Penguin Group Inc., New York.

------------------ (n.d.): *A Brief History of Transpersonal Psychology,* http://www.stanislavgrof.com/pdf/A%20Brief%20History%20of%20Transpersonal%20Psychology-Grof.pdf, accessed September 26, 2012.

HALIFAX, JOAN (1982):*Shaman: The Wounded Healer,* Crossroad Publishing Co., New York.

HARNER, MICHAEL (1990): *The Way of the Shaman,* Harper & Row, New York.

HUXLEY, ALDOUS (1945): *The Perennial Philosophy*, Harper, New York.

IMANERA (2012a): "One is Fun: Introduction to Daoism", Lazuli Dipper School of Daoist Arts. May 16, 2012. Lecture.

------------------ (2012b): "Abiding in Non-Dual Presence", Lazuli Dipper School of Daoist Arts. June 20, 2012. Lecture.

------------------ (2012c): "TaijiRuler & Seasons of Change", Lazuli Dipper School of Daoist Arts. August 15, 2012. Lecture.

------------------ (2012d): "Practicing Immortality", Lazuli Dipper School of Daoist Arts. September 22, 2012. Lecture.

------------------ (2012e): "Eight Piece Brocade", Lazuli Dipper School of Daoist Arts. October 3, 2012. Lecture.

------------------ (2012f): Personal Interview. September 27, 2012.

INGERMAN, SANDRA (2008): *Shamanic Journeying: A Beginner's Guide,* Sounds True Inc., Boulder, Colorado.

IXEEYA(2012a): "Earth Connection & Sacred Tools", The Rattle and the Brush. May 17, 2012. Lecture.

------------------ (2012b): "Embodying Fire & Water: Splat & Smear", The

Rattle and the Brush. May 24, 2012. Lecture.

------------------ (2012c): Personal Interview. October 16, 2012.

JAKOBSEN, MERETE DEMANT (1999): *Shamanism: Traditional and Contemporary Approaches to the Mastery of Spirits and Healing*, Berghahn Books, New York.

JUNG, CARL GUSTAV (1969): *The Collected Works of C.G. Jung*, (Vol. 9, Part 1), Princeton University Press, New Jersey.

------------------ (1959): *The Basic Writings of C.G. Jung*, Ed. Violet Staub de Laszlo, Random House, Inc., New York.

------------------ (1949): Foreword. *The I Ching*. By Richard Wilhelm, Bollingen Series, Princeton University Press, New Jersey.

KAPTCHUK, TED J. (1983): *The Web That Has No Weaver: Understanding Chinese Medicine*, Congdon & Weed, Inc., Illinois.

KARCHER, STEPHEN (2009): *Total I Ching: Myths for Change*, Trans. Stephen Karcher, Piatkus, London.

KEIKO, MITAMURA (2002): "Daoist Hand Signs and Buddhist Mudras" *Daoist Identity: History, Lineage, and Ritual*, Eds. L Kohn, HD Roth, University of Hawaii Press, pp. 235-255.

KIRSCHNER, PETER & HANNA RAAB (2012): Personal Interview. July 15, 2012.

KOHN, LIVIA (2011): Chuang Tzu: The tao of Perfect Happiness, Selections Annotated & Explained. Trans. Livia Kohn, SkyLight Paths Publishing, Vermont.

------------------ (2010): *Sitting in Oblivion: The Heart of Daoist Meditation*, Three Pines Press, New Mexico.

------------------ (2009): *Introducing Daoism*, Routledge, New York.

------------------ (2008): *Meditation Works,* Three Pines Press, New Mexico.

------------------ (2006): *Daoist Body Cultivation,* Three Pines Press, New Mexico.

------------------ (2000): "Wuwei", *The Encyclopedia of Taoism,* Routledge, Oxon, Vol. II. Print.

KOPPENSTEINER, NORBERT (2011): "Energetic Concepts of Peace", MA Program for Peace, Development, Security and International Conflict Transformation, University of Innsbruck, Austria. January 3-14, 2011. Lecture.

KUMAR, SATISH & FREDDIE WHITEFIELD, EDS. (2006): *Visionaries: The 20th Century's 100 Most Important Inspirational Leaders*, Chelsea Green Publishing, Vermont.

KUNIO, MIURA (1990): "Zhenren", *The Encyclopedia of Taoism,* Routledge, Oxon, Vol. II. Print.

LASZLO, ERVIN (2011): *Simply Genius! And Other Tales from My Life*, Hay House Inc., California.

------------------ (2009): "Introduction: The Akashic Experience: What It Is and What It Means". *The Akashic Experience: Science and the Cosmic Memory Field*,Ed. Ervin Laszlo, Inner Traditions, Vermont.

LAO-TZU (1993): *Tao Te Ching*, Translation. Trans. Stephen Addis and Stanley Lombardo, Hackett Publishing Company, Inc., Indiana.

LEDERACH, JOHN PAUL (2011): "Conflict Transformation and Mysticism", 5th International Congress in the Series *Fields of Conflict—Fields of Wisdom*, Wuerzburg, Germany. April 29 - May 1, 2011. Lecture.

------------------ (2005): *The Moral Imagination*, Oxford University Press, Oxford.

------------------ (2003) *The Little Book of Conflict Transformation,* Good Books, Oregon.

------------------ (1995): *Preparing for Peace: Conflict Transformation Across Cultures*, Syracuse University Press, New York.

LITTLEJOHN, RONNIE L. (2009): *Daoism: An Introduction,* I.B. Tauris & Co. Ltd., New York.

LIU HE (2009): *Jade Woman Qigong: The Healing Power of Taoist Medicine for Every Woman,* Trafford Publishing, Indiana.

LU JI (1996): *The Art of Writing*, Translation. Trans. Tony Barnstone and Chou Ping, Shambhala Publications, Inc., Boston.

MAJOR, JOHN, ANDREW SETH MEYER, SARAH A. QUEEN, HAROLD D. ROTH, Eds. (2012): Introduction. *The Essential Huainanzi*, Columbia University Press, New York.

MASLOW, ABRAHAM (1971): *The Farther Reaches of Human Nature,* Viking Press, New York.

------------------ (1970): *Religions, Values, and Peak-Experiences,* Penguin Compass, New York.

MASPERO, HENRI (1978): *China in Antiquity,* Trans. Frank A. Kierman Jr., The University of Massachusetts Press, Massachusetts.

MILLER, JAMES (2008): *Daoism: A Beginner's Guide,* Oxford, London. Introduction-excerpt at http://www.daoiststudies.org/dao/book/export/html/681, accessed September 26, 2012.

MIPHAM, SAKYONG (2003): *Turning the Mind Into An Ally*, Riverhead Books, New York.

NI, HUA-CHING (1997): *Entering the Tao: Master Ni's Guidance for Self-Cultivation,* Shambhala Publications, Inc., Massachusetts.

NICKERSON, PETER (1987): "Taoism and Popular Religion", *The*

Encyclopedia of Taoism, Routledge, Oxon, Vol. I. Print.

NOBLE, VICKI (1991): *Feeling Our Fire, Healing Our World- The New Female Shamanism*, Harper San Francisco, California.

OSCHMAN, JAMES (2003): *Energy Medicine in Therapeutics and Human Performance*, Butterworth-Heinemann, Edinburgh.

OSPINA, MARIA B., et al. (2007): *Meditation Practice for Health: State of the Research,* AHRQ Publication No. 07-E010, Agency for Healthcare Research and Quality, Rockville, MD.

PALMER, WENDY (1999): *The Intuitive Body: Aikido as a Clairsentient Practice*, North Atlantic Books, California.

ROBINET, ISABELLE (1989): "Visualization and Ecstatic Flight in Shangqing Taoism".*Taoist Meditation and Longevity Techniques.* Ed. Livia Kohn, Center for Chinese Studies of the University of Michigan, Michigan.

ROMANYSHYN, ROBERT (2007): *The Wounded Researcher: Research with Soul in Mind,* Spring Journal, Inc., New Orleans.

ROSENBERG, LARRY (1999): *Breath by Breath: The Liberating Practice of Insight Meditation,* Shambhala, Boston.

SAIONJI, MASAMI (2009): "Shaping Creative Fields: Lessons from My Akashic Experiences".*The Akashic Experience: Science and the Cosmic Memory Field*,Ed. Ervin Laszlo, Inner Traditions, Vermont.

SCHIPPER, KRISTOFER (1993): *The Taoist Body,* Trans. Karen C. Duval, The University of California Press, California.

SCHLITZ, MARILYN MANDALA (2009): "Exploring the Akashic Experience: Bridging Subjective and Objective Ways of Knowing".*The Akashic Experience: Science and the Cosmic Memory Field*,Ed. Ervin Laszlo, Inner Traditions, Vermont.

SCHULZ, MONA LISA (1998): *Awakening Intuition: Using Your Mind-Body Network for Insight and Healing*, Harmony Books, New York.

SOMÉ, MALIDOMA PATRICE (1993): *Ritual: Power, Healing, and Community*, Penguin Putnam, New York.

SUN TZU (1988): *The Art of War*, Translation. Trans. Thomas Cleary, Shambhala Publications, Inc., Boston.

VAUGHAN, FRANCES E. (1979): *Awakening Intuition,* Anchor Books, New York.

VAUGHAN, FRANCES & ROGER WALSH, Eds. (1983): *Accept this Gift: Selections from A Course in Miracles,* Penguin Group, New York.

WALSH, ROGER (2007): *The World of Shamanism: New Views of an Ancient Tradition,* Llewellyn Publishing, Woodbury, Minnesota.

------------------ (1993): "Meditation Research: The State of the Art". *Paths Beyond Ego: The Transpersonal Vision.* Eds. Frances Vaughan and Roger

Walsh, Tarcher/Putnam, New York.

WHICHER, IAN (1998): *The Integrity of Yoga Darsana: A Reconsideration of Classical Yoga,* State University of New York Press, New York.

WICKERI, PHILIP L. & YIK-FAI TAM (2011): "The Religious Life of Ethnic Minority Communities", *Chinese Religious Life.* Eds. David A. Palmer, Glenn Shive, & Philip L. Wickeri, Oxford University Press, New York.

WONG, EVA (1997a): *The Shambhala Guide to Taoism,* Shambhala Publications Inc., Massachusetts.

------------------ (1997b): *Teachings of the Tao*, Shambhala Publications, Inc., Boston.

YANG, FENGGANG (2012): *Religion in China: Survival & Revival Under Communist Rule*, Oxford University Press, New York.

YANG, JWING-MING (1997): *The Root of Chinese Qigong: Secrets for Health, Longevity, & Enlightenment,* YMAA Publication Center, Massachusetts.

Appendix A

"Self-Analysis of Chakras"
(Imanera, 2012b)

Please read the instructions before turning the page.

Part 1:

First, sit comfortably and take some deep breaths until you are feeling calm and quiescent.

Next, you are going to close your eyes and visualize the whole vertical axis of your body, from the crown of your head to the base of your pelvis. Note any light that you see and what colors appear.

(Now close your eyes and turn your vision inward.)

When you are done, open your eyes and continue.

Part 2:

The following page has seven open-ended prompts. Respond to each prompt as quickly as possible, i.e. devote only a few seconds to each prompt if you can.

Answering in this way allows you to enter your subconscious, the faster the better!

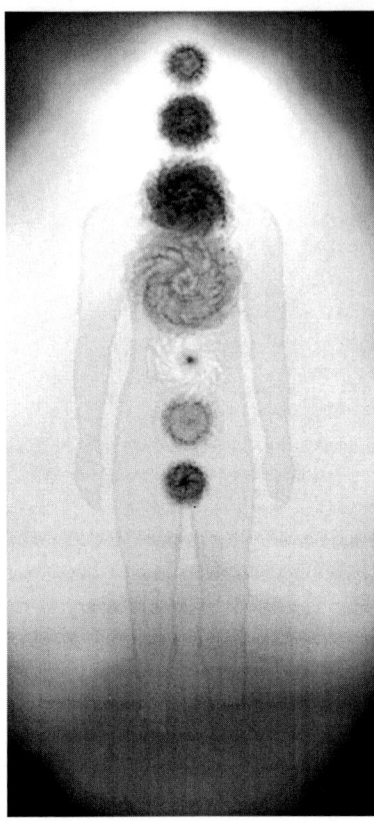

I know

I see

I communicate

I love

I do

I feel

I am

This analysis is an embodied way to get in touch with your energetic vortexes, or chakras. When you answered the prompts quickly, it was an example of immediacy meditation. Then, when you go to read through your responses again, this becomes a contemplative meditation. You may be able to learn from your responses where you are holding psychic knots or where energy is blocked.

Imaging of galvanic response recorded by Imanera in 2010. Reprinted with permission from Imanera, 2012.

Further Reading

BAPTANDIER, BRIGITTE (2008): *The Lady of Linshui: A Chinese Female Cult,* Stanford University Press, California.

DIETRICH, WOLFGANG (2013): *Elicitive Conflict Transformation and the Transrational Shift in Peace Politics,* Palgrave Macmillan, New York.

SHAHAR, MEIR & ROBERT P. WELLER, EDS. (1996): *Unruly Gods: Divinity and Society in China,* University of Hawaii Press, Honolulu.

TEISER, STEPHEN F. (1988): *The Ghost Festival in Medieval China,* Princeton University Press, New Jersey.

http://www.daoiststudies.org

http://www.daousa.org

Thank You

To the absence and presence of sunlight on the mountains, for welcoming me to the Dao.

Norbert Koppensteiner, who gently challenged me to forgo the expected path and encouraged me to be in a space where intuition is allowed to emerge and inform. If not for your insightful comments and candid advice, delivered ever so lightly in an Austrian Army mess hall in the recesses of the Alps, I would not have embarked on this transformative endeavor. I am so grateful for your inspirited guidance.

Imanera and Bongo: "True practice is total sincerity. It is not a matter of avoiding the world or leaving society. And neither does it depend entirely on deliberate sitting and reciting scriptures. The essential thing is to refine away the false within the true to filter out the true from the false. Only then do you attain the true reality of perfect sincerity".[98] Thank you for your practice.

Wolfgang Dietrich, for founding the Innsbruck Peace Studies program and sharing your perspective of peace(s) with the world. Your ideas are the wellsprings of experiences that changes people's lives.

Mom and Dad, who never cease to amaze me with your unconditional love and trust throughout all the unexpected intuitive decisions I have made. Patrick, for

---

[98] From Thomas Cleary's translation of the "Secret Records of Understanding the Way".

generously opening your home and being present with me through this chapter of my life. Mike, for reminding me to breathe and believe. My nephew Jaden and my niece Lil K, two of the greatest sources of my joy and inspiration.

Friends around the world, for making life so wonderful and dancing with me and my funny heart. Dan Yolles and Nikki Severson, for infusing this project with music and love. Joe Blaney and Vanessa Lichon, for being there for me, always.

Jesse Elliott, for helping me refine the message I wish to share with the world. Chris Huang and Aaron Stueck, for your artistic touch.

Kathleen McGoey lives in Boulder, Colorado.
www.kathleenmcgoey.net

Artwork reprinted with Chris Huang's permission, 2013.

Masters of Peace
edited by Prof. Dr. Wolfgang Dietrich (UNESCO Chair for Peace Studies)

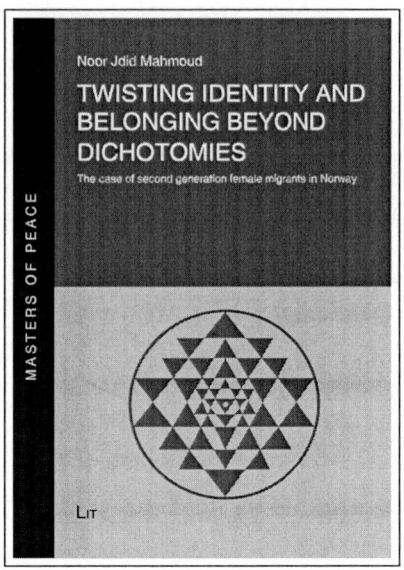

Catalina Vallejo
Plurality of Peaces in Legal Action
Analyzing Constitutional Objections to Military Service in Colombia
This book offers an application of the transrational model of interpretation of peace onto the area of legal studies. By building on the idea that there are various and many times contradictory interpretations of peace in history and culture, this book examines how these many forms of peace interplay in legal spheres, shaping legal discourses and practices, concretely those concerning the exercise of rights. By arguing that different perspectives on peace influence different argumentations of rights, the author challenges some of the political and legal discourses framed within the "war against terror" since 2001 and the resulting militarization of the Colombian society and its rights discourses.
Bd. 7, 2012, 160 S., 19,90 €, br., ISBN 978-3-643-90282-5

Noor Jdid Mahmoud
Twisting Identity and Belonging beyond Dichotomies
The case of second generation female migrants in Norway
This book brings together personal stories and theoretical concepts in the exploration of how second generation female migrants (SGFMs) in Norway negotiate their identities and give new form and content to their own notions of peace and belonging beyond a double life. By applying postmodern and feminist scholarship, the author challenges static ideas of cultural identity in discourses about the national and the family contexts. Mahmoud takes the reader on a journey through the transformations of conflicts on sexuality, identity and belonging by the SGFMs themselves. This is an important book for feminist and migration researchers and those concerned with minority issues.
Bd. 8, 2013, 168 S., 19,90 €, br., ISBN 978-3-643-90356-3

LIT Verlag Berlin – Münster – Wien – Zürich – London
Auslieferung Deutschland / Österreich / Schweiz: siehe Impressumsseite